MAKING CHANGE
▼

MAKING CHANGE

▼

Three Educators Join the Battle for Better Schools

HOLLY HOLLAND

HEINEMANN
Portsmouth, NH

Heinemann
A division of Reed Elsevier Inc.
361 Hanover Street
Portsmouth, NH 03801-3912

Offices and agents throughout the world

Copyright © 1998 by Maureen O'Meara Holland
All rights reserved. No part of this book may be reproduced in any form or by any electronic or mechanical means, including information storage and retrieval systems, without permission in writing from the publisher, except by a reviewer, who may quote brief passages in a review.

The author and publisher wish to thank those who have generously given permission to reprint borrowed material:

A portion of chapter one originally appeared as "A Passion To Teach," an article the author wrote for the December 4, 1994 issue of *The Courier-Journal*.

A portion of chapter three originally appeared as "Change Comes to Bluegrass Country," an article the author wrote for the April 1995 issue of *The American School Board Journal*.

Portions of chapters four and eleven originally appeared in "Focus on Kentucky's Education Reforms," a February 1996 research summary the author wrote for the Kentucky Institute for Education Research.

Library of Congress Cataloging-in-Publication Data
Holland, Holly
 Making change: three educators join the battle for better schools / Holly Holland.
  p. cm.
 Includes bibliographical references (p.).
 ISBN 0-435-08152-7
  1. Educational change—Kentucky—Henderson County—Case studies.
 2. Education—Kentucky—Administration—Case studies.   3. Education—Kentucky—Curricula—Case studies.   4. Education—Kentucky—Finance—Case studies.   5. Education and state—Kentucky—Case studies.   I. Title.
 LA293.H4H65 1998   97-31509
 371.2'009769—DC21   CIP

Editors: *Cheryl Kimball* and *Amy Cohn*
Cover design: *Barbara Werden*
Manufacturing: *Louise Richardson*

Printed in the United States of America on acid-free paper
01 00 99 98 EB 1 2 3 4 5 6 7

*To my wonderful son, Dylan Patrick Holland,
and to all of the other children
in Kentucky's public schools.*

Contents

Preface
ix

Acknowledgments
xiii

Introduction
xv

Chapter One
A Passion to Teach
1

Chapter Two
A Second Chance
21

Chapter Three
A New School Year, the Same Old Excuses
39

Chapter Four
The Challenges of Change
63

Chapter Five
Jackpot
85

Chapter Six
Democracy Is a Messy Business
105

Chapter Seven
How I Spent My Summer Vacation
129

Chapter Eight
Letting Go
143

Chapter Nine
The Long Goodbye
160

Chapter Ten
Reconsidering the Revolution
173

Chapter Eleven
Endings and Beginnings
183

Bibliography
205

Preface

Jimmy and Earl were in their late 60s when my husband, John, discovered them in a Louisville, Kentucky, nursing home during the summer of 1977. Home from college between his sophomore and junior years, John worked the night shift as an orderly, viewing the job as training for his vague ambition to be a doctor.

Jimmy was two years older than Earl, and a shorter, stouter version of his big brother. Both men wore their graying hair in unfashionable crew cuts. Their rounded bellies swelled over their boxer shorts as they sat for hours at a stretch reading paperback spy novels or, occasionally, heftier crime fiction like *The Godfather*. They lived together in a cozy double room with matching rocking chairs, a large television set, and photographs of loved ones arranged on the dresser.

John didn't have a lot of contact with Jimmy and Earl that summer. They were pleasant fellows, mostly self-sufficient, unlike the more demanding residents afflicted with strokes, Alzheimer's disease, and assorted mental disorders. But after several weeks on the job, John became curious. What were these two relatively youthful, able-bodied men doing in a nursing home? What was their impairment?

None of the other night-shift employees had an answer to these questions, so John looked to the medical records for an explanation. What he found there stunned him.

Jimmy and Earl lived in a nursing home because they were stupid.

At least that's what they had been told. The reason for their confinement might have been more complicated than that. But in truth, the records clearly stated that their limited options in life had everything to do with a brief assessment of their intelligence nearly six decades before.

According to the records, Jimmy and Earl went to school for the first time when they were eight and six years old, respectively. Their destination was a one-room schoolhouse in Kentucky. They lasted exactly one day. When they returned home from class that afternoon, the two brothers carried a note from the teacher. "Jimmy and Earl aren't smart enough for school," the teacher wrote to their parents. "No need to send them back."

The records did not say what happened to Jimmy and Earl afterward, only that they had never received a formal education. At some point in their lives, they taught themselves to read, and they took great pleasure in their books. Yet the education system had stamped them incapable of learning.

Perhaps Jimmy and Earl had worked a series of menial jobs over the years. Perhaps they had depended on family members for support or on other people's charity. Perhaps they were content with what they had. It was difficult to know.

As for John, he quit the nursing home that summer and abandoned his intended medical career. Instead, he became a teacher.

The story of Jimmy's and Earl's missed opportunities is just one example of the sad legacy of public education in Kentucky. It is a saga about generations of children who were cheated out of the chances this state—indeed, the nation—has to offer.

At least partly as a result of its weak support for education over the years, Kentucky has been the target of searing stereotypes—hicks and hillbillies, barefoot and pregnant, family feuds, political corruption, and greedy profiteering. Unfortunately, many of the stereotypes have endured because they are substantially true. A physically beautiful state with a wealth of natural resources, Kentucky historically squandered its good fortune through a series of bad decisions and short-sighted goals.

In 1990, however, the outlook suddenly changed. As one of several states stung by lawsuits challenging the way tax dollars were dispersed to local school districts, Kentucky took the unprecedented step of throwing out its entire educational system. Not only did the state's highest court agree that Kentucky's school finance plan was unfair, it said the poor quality of the state's classrooms violated the constitutional requirement for an adequate and equal education for all children. The court told the state legislature to wipe the slate clean.

In rebuilding Kentucky's public school system, state leaders dared to dream. Using outside consultants, they fashioned a model of education reform that many experts considered the best in the United States. Instead of being held up for ridicule, Kentucky finally produced something that was hailed as a revolution. The Kentucky Education Reform Act (KERA) became a beacon of hope for a nation struggling to energize its classrooms.

As a native of Kentucky, I have a vested interest in the outcome of these reforms. I also have a front-row seat at the drama. I have covered KERA from its inception, first as a reporter for *The Courier-Journal*, Kentucky's largest daily newspaper, and later as a freelance writer specializing in education issues. In addition to writing about the policies and the people who put them into practice, I observed the impact of these changes on a personal level as my child went off to public school in the middle of the state's great experiment.

Over time, I understood that the real story of school reform lies in the experience of ordinary Kentuckians—their ambitions and their accommodations. As I began writing this book, three major questions intrigued me: How far would the state go to redress past mistakes? Was it possible for all students to meet substantially higher standards? And what conflicts awaited the people most involved in school change?

Finding the answers proved more difficult—and disappointing—than I imagined.

I decided to follow three people—a superintendent, a principal and a teacher—because I wanted to view the transformation of Kentucky's public schools from different levels. My subjects worked for the Henderson County Public Schools, a district in western Kentucky. Two of the educators are natives of the state; the other educator grew up in Cincinnati, Ohio, about 250 miles northeast of Henderson. One of them has more enemies than a pirate. Another inspires people to think of synonyms for saint. Two of them have won major awards for excellence in their fields. All three would rather work in education than do anything else on earth.

I chose these people because they were idealists. They believed in education reform and worked diligently to help the state's plan succeed. I figured (correctly, as it turned out) that because they were in front of the pack they would discover the problems and the potential of Kentucky's school reforms more quickly than resisters. As I observed and interviewed them, I wondered about the lessons they would discover. What sacrifices would they make? Could they persuade others to join their cause?

Their adventures are testaments to one of the most sobering lessons of education reform: Even when people believe in the mission and rise to the challenge, achieving broad-based change is nearly an impossible task.

Henderson County's school leaders reached a point of deep tension earlier than most educators in Kentucky because they worked harder and faster, although the commitment to change was by no means universal. Led by a superintendent who was almost obsessed with the need for continual self-evaluation, the Henderson community engaged in several years of scrutiny of its schools. Like any self-help program, this one brought out the best and the worst in people. Some denied their problems. Some continued feeding their addictions to power and control. Some collapsed under the pressure, choosing to quit instead of convert. And some performed amazing acts of heroism in the quest for better schools.

This book is an attempt to give readers a framework for understanding the painful transitions and personal reflections that accompany significant change to one of society's most fundamental institutions. I followed these three educators from 1994 through 1996, concentrating on the 1994-95 school year. I spent hundreds of hours observing and interviewing them. I also consulted dozens of their colleagues, family members, and friends. I interviewed parents, students, and other residents of the Henderson County community. The events described in this book are based on my observations or recreated with help from the participants.

Henderson County lies just south of the Ohio River along western Kentucky's border with Indiana. This mostly conservative community of about 43,000 people supports three times as many churches as schools. Agriculture, coal mining, and river trade sustained the county's economy for decades, but light industry and retail services have provided most of the jobs in recent years. The public school district is the county's largest employer. It serves about 7,500 students, making it the seventh largest in the state.

Henderson County does not represent all the issues that surfaced with the Kentucky Education Reform Act. It is not necessarily average. It simply offers a lens for observing the human cost of change.

This book follows Gayle Ecton (superintendent), Johnny Duckworth (principal), and Irmgard Williams (teacher), during a critical period in Kentucky's battle for better schools because it marks the beginning of deep doubts among supporters that they would ever meet the state's goals. When so many people continued to resist the changes, the early optimism of these maverick educators started giving way to despair. Their concerns suggested that the long-term outlook for school reform in Kentucky might be bleak indeed.

If the pioneers lose hope, who will continue fighting for better schools?

Acknowledgments

I want to thank the main subjects of this book, Irmgard Williams, Johnny Duckworth, and Gayle Ecton, for graciously permitting me to peer into their personal and professional lives over several years so others might learn from their experiences with school reform. Their willingness to reveal their lives, to reflect on their everyday actions, and to recall important details from the past enabled me to infuse this book with a strong sense of humanity. I am grateful for their candor and their friendship. They are talented, courageous educators, and Kentucky is very lucky to have met them.

The Education Writers Association planted the seed for this book through a fellowship that enabled me to start researching in depth the Kentucky Education Reform Act. As a recipient of the National Fellowship in Education Reporting, I was fortunate to have met project editor Bill Salganik, of *The Sun* in Baltimore, Maryland. Bill helped give shape to the stories that inspired this book and later volunteered to read and edit several drafts. His guidance was invaluable.

Cheryl Kimball, former trade division publisher at Heinemann, heard me speak about my fellowship at a national education conference and encouraged me to write this book. I am very grateful for her support. I also want to thank Amy Cohn, my wonderful, tenacious editor at Heinemann, whose enthusiasm for this book inspired me to continue making significant improvements until the end.

My good friend, Kit Lively, senior editor for special projects at *The Chronicle of Higher Education* and a former colleague at *The Courier-Journal*, provided important editing advice from the early stages of the book through the end. I also give special thanks to Mary O'Doherty, city editor of the *Lexington Herald-Leader*, who offered feedback and emotional support throughout the long months of this project. I received excellent advice from other friends, including Ralph Dunlop, special projects reporter and former metro editor of *The Courier-Journal*, and Jessica Siegel, a teacher and former managing editor of *Electronic Learning* magazine. I thank all of these people for their unyielding faith in me.

Sharon Wright, education writer at *The Gleaner* in Henderson, was kind enough to steer me to local sources and background material. Researchers at the Louisville Free Public Library, the University of Louisville's Ekstrom Library, and the Kentucky Department for Libraries and Archives in Frankfort answered dozens of obscure questions about Kentucky history and education. I also want to thank Jim Parks, press secretary of the Kentucky Department of Education, for his patient assistance in filling numerous information requests.

Marty Szymansky earned my everlasting gratitude for teaching my son, Dylan, from kindergarten through third grade at Martin Luther King Elementary School in Louisville. Although she didn't play a direct role in the book, Marty's magnificence in the classroom showed me on a personal level the power of Kentucky's education reforms.

The final words of thanks I reserve for my husband, John Herzfeld, an inspiring teacher, loving father, and patient partner. I know it was difficult living with me while I wrote this book, but John never wavered in his support or let my self-doubts go unchallenged. Every writer, every woman, should be so lucky.

Introduction

Kentucky was an unlikely place for the birth of a national model of school reform. For more than 150 years, the state stood at the bottom of nearly every measure of educational and economic success. Whenever some national comparison of school performance was released to the public, the best the state's citizens could say about the results was, "Thank God for Mississippi."

Before KERA, Kentucky produced some dismal statistics: fiftieth in the nation in the percentage of adults with high school diplomas; forty-ninth in the percentage of college graduates; fiftieth in the number of engineers and Ph.D. scientists in the work force; forty-sixth in spending per-pupil for education; forty-seventh in high school dropouts; first in adult illiteracy; and first in teenage pregnancy.

Although American schools routinely neglected children in the first part of this century, as the top students went to college and the rest went to work, Kentucky was slow to catch up to the changing mission of public education. From 1940 to 1970, for example, the number of Kentuckians with a high school education rose from 30 percent to 60 percent, but the median number of years of school completed by adults was still only 9.9 years. That meant that half of Kentucky's citizens age twenty-five and older had completed less than 9.9 years of school. While Kentucky was just two-tenths of a year behind the national median in 1940, it was 2.3 years behind the rest of the country by 1970—last among the fifty states.

A certain percentage of the population received a solid education in Kentucky—by enrolling in private schools or by attending the public school's accelerated classes, filled mostly with white students from middle- and upper-income families. But, particularly in the most rural areas of the state, students often languished in classrooms led by uninspiring and undereducated teachers who had few resources and little motivation to do a good job. Some of these students struggled to get to college where they discovered they would have to play catch-up for years—or quit. Over time, a growing number of the state's top students left Kentucky to attend college and pursue careers. This brain drain was a sore point for state leaders who started pumping money into scholarship programs for Kentucky's best students so they would attend state-supported colleges and universities. Leaders did little, however, to improve education for all students in the K through 12 public schools.

Kentucky has a history of selective compassion for its children. In 1837, for example, the state founded its public school system and received $1.4 million from the federal government to help pay for it. But state leaders immediately robbed the fund for other purposes. Only one million dollars of the initial appropriation was set aside for education, and the legislature promptly reduced that amount to $850,000, thus "plundering the school fund . . . at the very beginning of its existence" (Hamlett 1914). Until 1912, Kentucky distributed education funds to counties based on the number of children living there, whether or not they attended school. There was no incentive to teach them.

In 1961, state leaders established a curriculum study committee to assess the condition of Kentucky's public schools. After a three month review process, the researchers concluded that based on the weak preparation and low pay the state's teachers received, "It is remarkable, not that we have as many poor teachers as we have, but that we have any good ones at all" (Tomizawa 1961b).

During a visit to Fredonia High School in eastern Kentucky, the researchers found a home economics major who taught history and English, an agriculture major who taught science and mathematics, and no one teaching foreign languages.

Thomas Tomizawa, a reporter with *The Courier Journal* in Louisville, described a visit to a basement classroom that pulsated from a basketball game being played overhead in the gym. There the researchers met thirty-year-old Robert Metcalfe who was teaching an economics lesson that consisted of a student reading aloud from a textbook for nearly an hour. Throughout the period, other students paraded through the classroom to get to an adjoining room that did not have a separate exit.

Metcalfe told the students that, "Farmers want crop-price supports and that is why the government 'has took the step' to give subsidies."

"A student, in a rare move, undertook to break into the reading to ask a question about the legality of a person going on strike, presenting an opening for a discussion period. The teacher only answered, 'I don't know.'"

"Another student offered, 'Isn't there a minimum-wage law?' And the teacher, after hesitating, replied, 'I believe so.'" Then the reading continued (Tomizawa 1961a).

In 1970, representatives of the National Education Association (NEA) toured Kentucky schools at the request of the state affiliate, which was pressuring state leaders to consider comprehensive education reforms. The NEA researchers found that only one in seven Kentucky children who needed special education services received them and only 7 percent of the state's five-year-olds attended public kindergartens. In some regions of the state, students didn't have desks or tables. In other regions, the researchers found one state-furnished textbook for every three students, no water in bathrooms, and rats whose attendance rates rivaled those of the students. At some public high schools around the state, they discovered that students were being charged for basic courses and missing out if they couldn't afford the fees.

The disparities were greatest in eastern Kentucky, the Appalachian region that includes some of the poorest and most isolated counties in the nation. For example, schools in Elliott County regularly received truckloads of outdated supplies that had been thrown out by schools around the country. Claudette Green, principal of Sandy Hook Elementary School, attended the county's public schools and later taught in them. She recalled having to make do with desks, maps, and other resources that were often thirty years old.

"It was like other people's trash, that's what we had," she said (Holland 1995c).

By the late 1980s, learning conditions were still appalling in many Kentucky schools. In an elementary school in eastern Kentucky, classrooms were so overheated and roach-infested that children cried when they had to go to school. In some high schools, the science laboratory consisted of a table and a sink. Students routinely left school early for hairstyling appointments and hunting trips.

Politics played a large part in the problems that plagued Kentucky's public schools. The thirty-seventh largest state in the country, Kentucky has 120 counties—the third largest in the country behind Texas and Georgia—and 176 public school districts, ranging from 232 students in the West Point Independent schools in Hardin County to 95,000 students in Jefferson County, which includes Louisville. In most Kentucky counties, weak legislative controls enabled powerful political machines to grab hold of local governments. The influence peddling was particularly strong in school districts, the largest employers in most counties. In areas of eastern Kentucky where half the adults were unemployed and two-thirds hadn't graduated from high school, the abuses accumulated faster than favors from the political machine.

A special state legislative committee noted in 1960 that this "octopus-like political web (was) so well-financed, so broadly based and has for its perpetuation such powerful and entrenched political interests that its defeat at the polls becomes all but impossible in many instances."

The same school board members tended to be elected year after year—many of them related to people who held other political offices in the county. Until 1990, citizens could serve as school board members in Kentucky even if they had dropped out of school in the eighth grade. The major criterion for election was a candidate's political connections, not his or her platform for educational excellence.

The subservience of education to politics proved disastrous in many Kentucky schools. For example, at the same time that teachers and students lacked basic supplies and comforts, county tax collectors routinely exempted favored individuals and industries from paying their share of local taxes. In an award-winning, twelve-part series published in 1989, the *Lexington Herald-Leader* documented case after case of property owners, including the sitting governor and many school board members, who paid little or no local taxes while schoolchildren went door-to-door to raise money for pencils and trash bags. During the 1986–1987 school year, students in Floyd County raised $1.7 million from fundraisers and vending-machine sales—$200,000 more than adults paid in school property taxes (Brammer and Wagar 1989).

To demonstrate the depth of the funding problem, a *Lexington Herald-Leader* photographer displayed a computer list of the names of Pike County landowners who did not pay their property tax bills in 1988 and unfurled it on the steps of the state Capitol. The list extended 525 feet and contained 9,370 names—one-third of all property owners in the largest and most tax-delinquent county in the state.

School administrators in many counties boosted payrolls with patronage positions; school jobs were considered political plums. A man could drive a bus or sweep floors and so obtain health insurance for his family, as long as he supported the right candidate for school board. Conversely, supporting the wrong candidate could cost him his job.

Teachers and students often paid the price of politics. During the NEA investigation in 1970, antipoverty workers in eastern Kentucky reported that school administrators withheld free school lunches from poor children "if their parents did not 'vote right' at election time." In a 1989 statewide poll conducted for the *Lexington Herald-Leader*, 57 percent of Kentuckians said teachers and parents were afraid to speak out against their school boards.

Small wonder. Pamela Williams was a third-year kindergarten and remedial teacher in the Barbourville Independent school system when she suggested the district change its kindergarten schedule to better meet the needs of students. Butt out, said the principal and superintendent. When Williams complained about the school's dirty bathrooms, the principal suggested she clean them herself. Later, Williams read in a local newspaper that she would not be rehired. School officials cited budget cuts as the reason for her dismissal, but they later hired Williams's former aide to teach kindergarten and created an additional position for a teacher just out of college (Estep and Brammer 1989).

One result of this abuse of power was a substandard education for many Kentucky children. The year before KERA was implemented, only 67 percent of students who entered ninth grade together reached twelfth grade and graduated. Only 58 percent of ninth-graders stayed through their senior year, even in Jefferson County—the Louisville-based school district that won national accolades in the 1980s for education innovations such as forming committees of teachers and principals to run local schools. That ranking placed Jefferson County in 164th place among the 178 Kentucky school districts in 1989–1990.

Such details were lost on the many people in Kentucky who valued practical skills over academic achievement. Outside some social circles, there wasn't much stigma if a teenager quit school in the eighth or ninth grade to help out on the family farm or start a factory job at General Electric, Ford, or one of the smaller manufacturers that dotted the state. In days past, most people could support a family decently with a limited education, even afford to buy a boat, a camper, or other middle-class status symbols by the time grandchildren were born.

But then those low-skill factory jobs started drying up. And the few new industrial positions, such as those offered in the highly-automated Toyota plant that opened in Georgetown, Kentucky, in

1988, required at least a high school education and often some college. Many people in Kentucky were unprepared for this changing economic climate.

Over the years, various groups tried to make Kentucky's schools better. However, the important players never seemed to be in line at the same time, as Ronald G. Dove Jr., pointed out in "Acorns in a Mountain Pool," a 1991 study of the legal history of school reform in Kentucky. In 1930, for example, the state legislature created a special fund to help equalize spending among poor and more affluent school districts, but the Kentucky Supreme Court struck it down. Lawmakers decided in 1954 to distribute state money on the basis of need to school districts that set a minimum tax rate, but the effort was weakened by the routine practice of assessing property below market value. A citizens' group successfully challenged that practice in state court in 1965, but the legislature countered on two different occasions by reducing property tax rates to nullify any gains achieved through higher assessments.

Kentucky's massive education problems could not be solved simply by boosting the amount of money contributed by the state, but any serious attempt at change had to start there. By 1987, Kentucky's $3,355 expenditure per-pupil was still far below the national average of $4,216. Reformers estimated that the state needed to invest an additional $500 million a year just to match the national average. After decades of dealing with widespread apathy and corruption, however, many people who cared about public education began to wonder if progress was worth the effort.

In the mid-1980s, the climate started to change. The sorry condition of public education was making it difficult to attract new business to the state. This development caught the attention of corporate and political leaders. And in a period of anti-tax sentiment, leaders knew they either had to generate new jobs or risk raising the levies on the companies that already provided work. Meanwhile, ordinary citizens were speaking up about embarrassing high school dropout rates and fast-food workers who could not make correct change.

The simultaneous growth of citizen, business, and political leadership in Kentucky over the next few years was unprecedented in the state's history. The convergence of similar agendas for repairing Kentucky's public schools emboldened people to take their first courageous steps out of the educational cellar. Their efforts caught the nation—and plenty of Kentuckians—by surprise.

Some of the early leaders of school reform were members of the Prichard Committee for Academic Excellence, a Lexington-based citizens' group, that had been building grassroots support for reform over several years. The organization was founded in 1983 and headed by the late Edward F. Prichard, Jr., a lawyer and a chief economic adviser to President Franklin Roosevelt during the development of New Deal legislation. Prichard led a thirty-member citizens' panel that made sweeping recommendations for improving the state's higher education system in 1981. Although he died in 1984, Prichard's legacy of citizen activism lived on in the organization that took his name. On a single night in November 1984, the Prichard Committee arranged for meetings in all 176 school districts at the time, events that prompted more than 20,000 people to make suggestions for improving public education in Kentucky.

The court challenge started in 1985 when leaders of sixty-six Kentucky school districts formed a non-profit corporation, the Council for Better Education, and sued the state for failing to provide an "efficient" education for all students. Most of these districts had meager amounts of real estate to tax for public education or political leaders who refused to fully tax the property they did have. In 1988, in *Council for Better Education v. Collins (No. 85-CL-1759, Sup op. 10)*, the plaintiffs argued in their petition to Franklin Circuit Court that there was a direct link between the amount of money a school district spent on each student and how well those students performed.

On June 8, 1989, responding to the state's appeal from a lower court ruling in favor of the Council for Better Education's petition, the Kentucky Supreme Court declared the state school system inadequate, unconstitutional, and discriminatory to children in the poorest districts. The court gave the state legislature only one year to come up with a new plan.

More than anything else, that deadline produced the broad changes that are now known as the Kentucky Education Reform Act. There's nothing like a hammer held over your head to produce instant statesmanship. Meeting during its regular biennial, sixty-day legislative session in 1990, the Kentucky General Assembly produced a 270-page reform document. Harassed by the court's urgency and the demands of the legislative leadership, some lawmakers said they did not have a chance to study the law before approving it.

To help them write the plan, state legislative leaders brought in national education experts who shaped a new school system around three major areas: administration, curriculum, and finance. Lawmakers also heeded many of the recommendations that a Kentucky education coalition produced in 1989. The coalition's members—including groups representing teachers, superintendents, school boards, and businesses—usually had been at odds over the years. Their agreement on a joint agenda inspired confidence that school reform in Kentucky might be possible after all.

On the administrative side, Kentucky's reform law required each school to elect a council—made up of a principal, three teachers, and two parents. The council would have the power to control the budget, hire staff, and choose curriculum. The law weakened the authority of local school boards and gave them responsibility only for the more limited areas of setting district goals and hiring superintendents. School board members and superintendents could no longer hire their relatives. Legislators abolished every job in the Kentucky Department of Education and gave the newly appointed Commissioner of Education the power to establish positions. Legislators also set up an independent Office of Educational Accountability to sniff out fraud and waste.

The instructional changes flowed from the Kentucky Supreme Court's admonition that all students can and must do better. The legislature established six broad objectives, stating that students must develop the ability to:

- achieve at high levels;
- use basic communication and math skills;
- apply principles from math, sciences, arts, humanities, social studies, and practical living skills to situations they will encounter throughout their lives;
- become self-sufficient;
- become responsible members of a family, work group, or community; and
- think and solve problems, connect and integrate experiences, and learn how to research.

The state Council on School Performance Standards later expanded on those objectives by defining seventy-five learning goals, or "valued outcomes." One of the goals for mathematics was understanding and appropriately using statistics and probability. The goals were not meant to serve as state-mandated curriculum; local school districts would determine the details.

Lawmakers were much more specific about the structural changes they expected to see in Kentucky's classrooms, especially a reorganization of the lower elementary grades. Gone were the traditional first- and second-grade classrooms. Instead of sorting children ages five through ten chronologically by age, schools had to include students of different ages in the same classrooms. Most teachers chose to group students across two grade levels, but some elected to teach the whole complement of students in kindergarten through third grade.

One of the major goals of the primary program was to eliminate early failures by recognizing that children who are labeled "slow," typically poor and minority children, might just need more time to catch up with their more advantaged peers. The concept was hardly new. Back in the late 1950s and early 1960s, seven Kentucky counties had instituted multi-age primary classes to great success. In Hustonville, which had the first elementary school in the state to try these ungraded primary classes, a comparison of test scores over several years showed that students who had classmates of different ages learned more than those in traditional classes.

Under the new education reform law, the state also mandated free preschool for children who were poor or disabled to make sure they arrived in kindergarten with the necessary skills. In addition, the law provided for extended school services such as after-hours tutoring for students who needed extra academic help. Schools serving high percentages of poor families had available to them money to set up on-site Family Resource and Youth Service centers to provide counseling, financial assistance, tutoring, and other services. With these centers, reformers hoped to reduce those barriers to learning that often fall outside a school's control.

To monitor the impact of these changes on student learning, the state set up a controversial system that included financial rewards for schools demonstrating the most improvement on test scores and sanctions for those showing the least. It was no longer good enough for schools to report high average test scores and ignore the fact that some children had failed to learn.

The high-stakes system included a test with several parts. It shunned multiple-choice questions and, instead, evaluated collections of students' written work and assignments they completed individually and in groups. Although students took the test in selected grades, the state expected teachers at all levels to change their instruction to prepare students. State education leaders urged teachers to use more active problem-solving exercises instead of straight lectures and to require students to complete original research instead of passively following along in the textbook.

To measure student learning, the state devised a baseline score for each school that included test scores and factors that can affect academic performance such as dropout rates and family poverty. Using a one hundred-point scale, Kentucky gave each school a new threshold, or score, to meet over two years, roughly equivalent to a 10 percent gain each biennium. Schools that exceeded their goals in the two years were to receive cash rewards. Schools that fell short by small margins were to write improvement plans and receive help from an appointed "distinguished educator." Schools that posted declines of five points or more would work with a distinguished educator who had the authority to keep, fire, or reassign staff members.

To pay for the school reform plan, Kentucky legislators approved a $1.3 billion spending package that included a one-cent increase in the state's sales tax. Business support for the tax hike proved critically important; executives of many top corporations publicly endorsed the reforms. The state also set a guaranteed minimal level of funding per student and forced local districts to assess property at its full market value to raise more money for schools. However, in an effort to equalize funding between high- and low-end school districts, the state effectively froze for several years the amount of money it gave to the top-tier districts so the other districts could catch up. School districts that had played by the rules and assessed property at its full value were penalized while the state tried to level the playing field for students in other districts.

National opinion-makers salivated over Kentucky's education reform law, with its ambitious agenda and lofty promises. *Education Week,* the national newspaper devoted to education coverage, called Kentucky's reform plan "one of the most comprehensive restructuring efforts ever undertaken by a state legislature." *The New York Times* labeled it "the most sweeping education package ever conceived by a state legislature."

The late Bert T. Combs, a former Kentucky governor and federal judge who was the lead attorney for the sixty-six school districts that filed the original lawsuit, had attended schools in eastern Kentucky "that had no library, or well-conceived curriculum." In 1991, Combs wrote in *The Harvard Journal on Legislation* that "the extensive publicity" generated by Kentucky's new education plan "seemed to be partially based on the surprise of the news media that a bold, revolutionary reform movement in education would be born in Kentucky. Excellence in education had never been a hallmark of the state."

It was heady stuff to finally have outsiders take notice of what the state did well besides sponsor the Kentucky Derby, win national collegiate basketball championships, and produce world-class whiskey. The state's reform leaders knew they had a lot to prove. If a state with such a long history of educational failure could transform itself into a national academic leader, then no other place in the country would have an excuse for not trying.

Kentucky offers the best example of what can happen when a court and a legislature aggressively deal with the issue of an adequate education for all students. It is a local event with a national message. But it is certainly not the only example of far-reaching school reform in the nation. Chris Pipho, of the Education Commission of the States in Denver, Colorado, noted in an interview that since 1983 "at least fifteen states have implemented mega-reforms." He said many state initiatives started from lawsuits over financial inequities between poor and affluent school districts, although no other state has gone as far as Kentucky in trying to address past problems. Almost all of the state responses have focused on two major areas, Pipho said—producing a higher-quality teaching force and raising academic standards, including tougher high school graduation requirements and innovative ways to test students.

By 1994, however, the pendulum began to swing back nationally, and Kentucky got caught in the shift. When the first few years of their school reforms did not show significant improvements in the traditional barometers of educational success—national standardized tests—some states and local school districts began favoring more free-market approaches such as charter schools and public schools managed by private corporations. Politicians were not much help sorting out the issues. They changed directions faster than a weather vane caught in a hurricane. Buoyed by the results of the 1994 conservative revolution in Congress, opponents of school reform seemed to gain clout with their cries of "back to basics." It did not seem to matter that few people could agree on what a basic education should include.

Meanwhile, leaders of state and national school reforms were wringing their hands. While they believed they had figured out the solutions to improving education, they had failed to show that the changes would work in public schools beyond the pilot stage. The dissension stymied many educators. Although they were afraid to break from tradition, they also didn't want to be left behind.

In Kentucky, opponents of school reform made headway in 1994, persuading the state legislature to refine and reduce the number of learning goals, eliminating the requirements that students become "self-sufficient individuals" and "responsible members of a family, work group, or community." These critics chiefly objected to what they called "liberal values," such as the expectation that "students demonstrate an open mind to alternative perspectives." Although they did not succeed in changing the focus of the reform law, the critics continued challenging the state's goal to help all students achieve at high levels, arguing that such efforts would weaken the curriculum.

By mid-1995, a statewide poll conducted by *The Courier-Journal* in Louisville revealed that only 41 percent of Kentuckians approved of the education reform plan, down from 57 percent two years before. Worse, half of the people in the state confessed to never having heard of it.

While Kentucky's education reform law became the darling of the education establishment nationwide, it didn't inspire great enthusiasm at home. Some Kentuckians were excited about the possibilities and quickly signed on in support. But the majority of people, including most of the state's educators, thought the schools were already doing enough. In Frankfort, the state capital, legislators, education consultants, and business leaders agreed on the big ideas that would govern school reform in Kentucky. But skeptics wondered how the plans would play out in the state's classrooms. It would take more than good intentions to fix all that ailed Kentucky's schools.

In trying to repair a corroded system of public education, Kentucky's reform leaders assumed that citizens would respond like trained athletes—a few high-speed workouts and they would be ready and eager to enter the big race. Instead, most have been unwilling, sometimes unable, to get into shape. At any given moment, they are prone to fall back on the couch.

Although change rarely happens neatly, people who have grown up with fast cars and fast food expect almost instantaneous results. Most people want change to taste good, to feel good, and to require no additional time or energy. People cling to the familiar, even when they know it is ineffective or harmful, because the alternatives are simply too frightening to imagine.

Fear of change is one of the reasons American education is such a bastion of tradition. The past decade has included a flurry of education reform initiatives from public and private groups nationwide. But while each has promised some degree of school renewal, broad change has not happened. Policy has not become practice.

Americans can draw many lessons from the Kentucky Education Reform Act. Here's the most important: Nothing changes in the classroom unless people want it. To achieve change on the grand scale of Kentucky's school reforms, thousands of individuals—each with his or her own excuses, resentments, and doubts—must be persuaded that they can collectively create something better. Then they must practice until they get it right. Not just some of them, but all of them.

Many in Kentucky did not receive a good education in the state, so they never demanded better for their children. Those who did succeed in school tended to support a system that perennially sorted out winners and losers. The old methods of instruction never worked for all children. Some students inevitably fell through the cracks. But many people, then and now, would rather keep their children at the top of a mediocre system than support reforms that could lead to universal achievement in a better one.

Educational change is still under siege in Kentucky, and it isn't clear whether reform will last. The biggest impediment might be ignorance, but the loudest is fear. If the first few years of KERA have demonstrated anything, they have exposed the vulnerability of mandated reform. Anxiety can cause people to beat a hasty retreat from any situation, most especially when their children are at stake.

The Kentucky law originally provided six years for full implementation, but budget problems moved the target date back to 1998. Although it will take several more years to evaluate the full impact of reform, now is the time to walk with some of the witnesses to change.

Chapter One

A Passion to Teach

Irmgard Williams drove east along Interstate 64 in Kentucky; her dented, white Ford LTD rattled like coins sorting through a pop machine. She hoped the old car wouldn't conk out on the long drive between Henderson and Frankfort. To be sure, she had left home at 5:45 A.M. so she could arrive in time for her interview at 1 P.M. Frankfort's clocks were set an hour ahead of those in Henderson, which was on central standard time. She always stayed within the speed limit, and with the possibility of car trouble, well, she wanted to be prepared.

So little time, always so little time. After thirty-two years of teaching elementary school, Williams was accustomed to pressure. But during the past four years, with the barrage of changes created by the Kentucky Education Reform Act, Williams had begun to feel like a goalie dodging pucks.

She loved the new teaching strategies; she loved the way the reforms set her free "like a bird out of a cage" to give children hands-on activities to help them make connections across subjects, instead of requiring them to memorize isolated facts. But teachers had been so busy implementing new programs, attending workshops, and filling out paperwork that they had had little time to take stock of what had been accomplished.

Williams was starving for affirmation. She wanted someone to understand just how hard it had been. Maybe she would get some feedback today.

It was October 1994, and Williams was to be interviewed by a panel that would select Kentucky's Teacher of the Year. Her application and letters of recommendation had earned her a semifinalist's spot. She was one of nine teachers, three at each grade level, who had been winnowed from the field of district winners from around the state.

Williams was proud to have been chosen but also felt some pangs of guilt. She had always cast herself in a giving role, not as the receiver: the minister's wife who had helped build her husband's career in the Church of the Nazarene; the mother who had raised her own three children, along with three foster children from Haiti and South Africa; and the teacher who had taken class after class of children who were poor and disabled and helped them love to learn.

Was it finally her turn to be recognized?

She pulled off the highway, darted into a convenience store restroom, and changed into a pink and black suit with black stockings and black high heels. She hadn't wanted to get the outfit wrinkled during the nearly four-hour drive.

Once inside the state office building, she felt uneasy. Williams is a gentle, chatty person; she likes to please people. The panel evaluating her consisted of three judges—a former State Teacher of the Year, a former State Principal of the Year, and a University of Kentucky education professor. Williams sensed a kindred spirit in the teacher but didn't know how to act or what to say to the other judges who were more formal and stiff.

The interview ended, and everyone shook hands. Nobody said much, just "Thank you" and "Goodbye." Afterwards Williams leaned over a water fountain in the hallway and sipped slowly, trying to calm her nerves. Did she remember to tell the judges about her missionary work abroad? Had she mentioned that she was teaching English to the Chinese-born mother of one of her students? Did she describe the progress her special needs students had made in only the first two months of school?

Well, no matter. It was over now. She stopped at a Taco Bell for lunch then got back on the highway. All she could do now was wait.

Teaching is one of life's most isolating jobs. Usually, conversations with adults are reduced to sound bites during twenty-minute lunches in noisy cafeterias. The wonderful moments good teachers share with their students in the classroom rarely are witnessed by anyone.

For a long time in Kentucky, teachers believed they couldn't do anything to change the system. Close the door to the outside world, supervisors ordered. Bury students in textbooks and worksheets. Keep them under control. Don't stop. Don't think. Don't worry.

Then along came the Kentucky Education Reform Act, the sweeping state mandate that promised to raise the educational standards for the state's children and boost the pay and prestige of teachers who helped students soar. A court required it, legislators created it, and state bureaucrats regulated it. But it is the individual teacher who is responsible for making reform work.

It is a profound power. And yet it presents teachers with a new set of challenges that many still struggle to understand. Education reform means teachers must do more than raise the achievement level of students. They also must improve their own practice. Instead of following the curriculum choices determined by the selection of the state's textbooks, teachers now must make decisions on an hourly and daily basis about what and how to teach.

"The whole challenge of a reform like this is to change the way people work," said Robert Sexton, executive director of the Prichard Committee for Academic Excellence in Lexington, Kentucky, a reform advocacy group. "It wasn't presented to the profession or to the public as something that would happen quickly."

State and local districts provided extra days so teachers could learn new instructional techniques and study Kentucky's new academic standards, but the additional time was mostly inadequate to the task. Legislators increased the number of paid days available for staff training from four to nine and initially allowed school districts to absorb some of the extra days by replacing up to five of the required 175 instructional days with paid staff training. Legislators also boosted spending on staff training from one dollar per student per year to twenty-three dollars per student per year—a cumulative total of twenty-six million dollars from 1990–1994. But the state funds were earmarked exclusively for training. The funds did not help districts pay the larger cost of salaries for teachers and administrators who would be expected to work extra days. In addition, the state did little to ensure that the money was spent on quality training.

Kentucky discouraged districts from the old practice of training teachers and administrators in large assemblies where they listened to generic education topics. Instead, districts started targeting the specific skills teachers needed in the classroom. But most districts still limited training to approved group settings, such as workshops. The hours and hours teachers needed to plan new lessons, consult with experts, observe excellent instructors, read, and practice could not be found during paid time. Teachers also had limited time to work together. By 1995, only 20 percent of the state's primary school teachers—grades K through 3—had regularly scheduled individual and group planning time on the clock (Bridge 1995, xiv).

"We still have this mindset that teachers are only working when they're in the classroom with children," Sexton said. "Almost no other profession is like that. In any other profession we assume that learning something new takes time."

Studies have shown that teachers forget about 90 percent of what they learn in one-shot workshops. It takes about twenty follow-up sessions to ensure that teachers can apply new lessons in the classroom—if they have the desire to change. With rare exceptions, the kind of retraining teachers needed to make permanent and skilled adjustments did not occur in Kentucky schools during the early years of education reform.

Consider what happened in the Oldham County Public Schools, northeast of Louisville. The school district had one of the best records in the state on KERA's new testing program. During the 1994–1995 school year, eight of the district's ten schools earned financial rewards for exceeding their performance goals. Teachers, principals, and Superintendent Blake Haselton claimed that the extra training had been crucial to the district's success. But in early 1995, the Oldham County Board of Education eliminated the optional training days and increased the number of instructional days from 170 to 175, requiring teachers to spend those five days in the classroom with students.

"I do not see an overwhelming need for additional training compared to what can be accomplished by spending extra time with the kids," said Tim Feeley, the board member who led the effort to change the district's calendar.

Unwilling to spend more money to accomplish both objectives—provide extra instruction *and* extra staff training—Oldham County's school board members took the easy way out and deprived the teachers.

"What they don't realize is that the days we have in staff development we learn ten-fold what we can take back into the classroom," said Julie Berry, a fourth-grade teacher at La Grange Elementary School. "The child benefits from it" (Ellis 1995).

Yet, at the same time that many individual school districts begrudged teachers the time and money to learn new skills, the state was holding teachers accountable for making education reform succeed. Teachers and principals could be sanctioned and ultimately lose their jobs if students didn't reach goals set by the state. The measure of success was a series of state tests given to a different group of students in selected grades each year. The test results used a broad brush to paint a school's reputation but did little to help teachers understand what worked and what didn't. Through 1995, the state sent the test results back to schools up to a year after students had answered the questions. By then, it was too late to help students who had taken the test the previous year, and too late to make substantial adjustments in instruction during the current year.

While teachers were trying to learn how to do their jobs differently, they also had to field questions from parents, listen to grousing from colleagues, and deflect criticism from observers who claimed they weren't working hard enough, smart enough, or fast enough.

For many of Kentucky's thirty-eight thousand certified public school teachers, the cost of change was too high. They found themselves caught between the desire to do a better job and the impulse to stick with what they knew. Because they lacked the confidence and training to teach differently, many teachers continued planning narrow lessons, passing out worksheets, and wrapping their classrooms in cocoons of isolation.

In the primary grades—the elementary level that saw the most changes in the early years of KERA—researchers at the University of Kentucky's Institute on Education Reform found that the nature and quality of instruction varied greatly from teacher to teacher and from school to school. Treating each child the same was the old habit. Developing lessons geared to each child's needs was the new standard—but few teachers were meeting it.

For Irmgard Williams, however, the choice was clear. At age fifty-seven, with the twenty-seven years of experience needed to qualify for full teacher retirement benefits in Kentucky, Williams could have left South Heights Elementary School in Henderson County with a satchel full of memories and a disinterested wave goodbye to that stranger called education reform. Instead, she plunged in like a swimmer on Memorial Day, eager to be among the first to try the new strokes.

"In Kentucky we had to have reform," she said. "It's KERA or die."

Williams had been smothered by the old system of education in Kentucky, and it didn't take much to persuade her to change her habits. Most of the time she had felt like an assembly line worker instead of a professional educator. Open the textbook and turn the page. Pass out one worksheet and collect another. Watch the clock and switch to the next subject. On and on and on. A robot could do the job.

Every day was rigidly prescribed, as demonstrated by Williams's "Overview and Schedule of First Grade Curriculum," a calendar of daily student activities that she prepared for parents in 1986: music, five minutes; reading, sixty minutes; writing, thirty minutes; spelling, thirty minutes; language, thirty minutes; lunch (includes five minutes to and from cafeteria), thirty minutes; physical education (organized play), fifteen minutes; math, sixty minutes; science, forty minutes; and social studies, twenty-five minutes. Once a week, students also had music for forty-five minutes and art for fifty minutes. They visited the library for forty-five minutes a week and spent ten minutes a week swishing a fluoride rinse in their mouths.

The state's emphasis on meeting these timed objectives meant that students covered the material. But when teachers were required to follow the schedule and use only the approved textbooks, they had few opportunities to provide individualized or imaginative instruction. Williams knew that children didn't necessarily learn something just because the schedule said they should. Motivated students generally stayed on track. But many others never saw the point. Year after year, Williams watched the lights flicker, then dim in their eyes.

When Williams suggested some changes in the prescribed curriculum, such as using Friday afternoons for enrichment activities (which were similar to the primary school learning centers that later would be recommended by the state's reform law), former principals looked at her, as Williams noted, "like I had come from Mars." She remembered being reprimanded by a principal for teaching her students a song about colonial America because it wasn't in the approved textbook. Another time she was criticized by a principal for moving her students ahead in the textbook after their next teacher complained that she wouldn't have enough material to fill her schedule for the following year. Principals forbade her to take students on field trips or to display their work in the halls. One principal refused to let the school form a PTA.

"I almost lost my identity as a teacher," Williams said. "I went out the back door crying."

Although some teachers flouted authority and did what they wanted behind closed doors, Williams never could bring herself to disobey. Instead, she struggled to reconcile the moral conflict between meeting the requirements of her job and serving the needs of her students. She was a good teacher under the old system, but she knew she could be so much better without all the constraints.

She fondly recalled a time when she had loved, not just tolerated, the expectations of her job. Williams's first teaching positions were in small schools in the Appalachian region of east Tennessee, a poor, mountainous area similar to many parts of Kentucky. In 1959, her first year on the job, Williams taught grades one through three in a single classroom at Hensley's Chapel School, located on the boundary between Smith and White Counties in Tennessee. The next year, she moved to the two-room Peeled Chestnut School on Gum Spring Mountain in Sparta, Tennessee, where she taught grades five through eight and served as principal. Working in the isolated region was an abrupt change from urban life in her native Cincinnati. But Williams learned to love the mountains and her students—some of them shoeless, some of them slow, most of them hungry. Like the teacher in the book and television series, *Christy*, Williams arrived early each morning to build a fire in a black pot-bellied stove set in the middle of the classroom—a skill she mastered only after mischievous students supposedly showed her how. That first time, the room filled with black smoke, which forced her to dismiss class early. At 8 A.M. weekdays, Williams rang an iron bell attached to a pole in the schoolyard. For lunch she fixed cheese and peanut butter on crackers, rations that the Save the Children Foundation provided, and the children who had not brought their own lunch in tied cloth sacks gobbled their biggest meal of the day.

In the classroom, Williams struggled to help her students overcome the penurious legacy of low expectations. Her students often didn't make it to school because of bad weather—the bus couldn't ascend the steep, gravel road when it was icy. Good weather also kept them out of school—mountain parents allowed their children to cut school to pick strawberries or plant crops. But when they came to school, the children learned. And they were happy; Williams could see that.

Partly by instinct, mostly by necessity, Williams used many of the same strategies that education reform later brought to Kentucky's schools. Children moved ahead at their own pace, on a schedule that had more to do with their individual development than their chronological ages. Younger students learned from older students, and older students gained proficiency by explaining their lessons to someone else. Williams grouped and regrouped students according to their needs. It was incredibly hard work for a teacher to keep all the children challenged. In the first two years, as she put all of her energy into her job, Williams's dress size shrank from a sixteen to a seven.

Years later, despite memories of those trying times, Williams was thrilled to learn that Kentucky's education reforms embraced the same techniques she had used in Tennessee. In 1990, when the ink was barely dry on the new education law, Williams randomly mixed her summer school students in a multi-age class, something the state wouldn't require schools to do for two more years. She also moved her students out of a strictly phonics-based language arts program that emphasizes sounding out lists of words as an activity separate from actual reading and writing. Instead, she used the whole language approach that integrates skill work with interesting literature and with children's own writing.

Williams later became the leader of a team of teachers at South Heights. The team worked together to plan appropriate lessons for about one hundred primary school students ages five to ten. Williams trained other teachers in Henderson County to use a technique called cooperative learning in which students solve problems in groups. She became a KERA Fellow, a sort of faculty member on loan to other schools in the state.

All that work, and Irmgard heard this comment from a colleague when the principal announced that she had been named a semifinalist for state Teacher of the Year: "Well," the teacher sniffed, "how did you get to do that?"

All that work, and Irmgard had to listen to her beautician—a woman who hadn't set foot in a public school in decades—rant about how Henderson teachers had lowered standards for students because of education reform.

All that work, and Irmgard had to learn from a reporter that she wasn't named Teacher of the Year. Her own notice from the state didn't arrive until a week later. The letter she received was polite but perfunctory. It didn't provide the extensive feedback she so desperately wanted.

"I keep wondering what I did wrong," she said.

Gladys Owens, coordinator of the Teacher of the Year program for the Kentucky Department of Education, said it wasn't possible for the judges to give teachers detailed evaluations of their applications and interviews.

"When they get this far, we know they're good," she said.

State officials thought it was obvious that they considered Williams special simply because they selected her as one of Kentucky's top teachers. But like many of her peers, Williams was unaccustomed to praise. Certainly, good teachers needed encouragement in the years before KERA. But with all the new demands and expectations, they yearned for recognition more than ever.

One of the ironies of education reform was that some of its strongest supporters needed the most assurance about their progress.

Education leaders in Kentucky tended to take the loyalty and the morale of converts for granted and to concentrate their efforts on resisters. As a result, active reformers often got few positive strokes, and trivial snubs became magnified.

That is where Williams found herself in the fifth year of Kentucky's education reforms. She believed so strongly in what she was doing and wanted so badly for the reforms to succeed, but she feared that hard-working teachers would stop trying to improve if people didn't acknowledge their efforts. Personally, she was feeling more depleted than fulfilled—and she had plenty of company.

In November 1994, a veteran teacher trudged into Bloomin' Things, the Henderson florist that Williams operates with her husband, Dewey, and told her colleague she "just couldn't take it anymore." She said she planned to quit at the end of the school year. The day before, Williams had received a letter from another veteran teacher who said that she, too, was overwhelmed by the pressures and intended to bail out the following spring. Although many new teachers were clamoring to take advantage of the opportunities reform presented, a record number of veteran teachers retired statewide in 1993 and 1994. Unhappiness with the education reform law was a major reason (Schaver 1994).

Some of the teachers who left probably needed to do so if they couldn't function effectively under KERA, Williams said. But she was more concerned about the spirit of those who chose to stay. "You can have the mechanics, but if you don't have teachers with heart and a passion to teach, what do you have?" Williams asked. "From the top down, there ought to be something we do to show people we're proud of them. It might make better teachers if more recognition was given."

Whatever pats on the back Williams missed in her years of teaching, she wasn't stingy with her praise for others. From the first day of the 1994–1995 school year, she set a tone of caring and consistency for her twenty-four students, a group that included mostly six- and seven-year-olds, among them a child with spina bifida, a child with autism, three children with attention-deficit hyperactivity disorders, a child with severe learning and behavior problems, and a child, she suspected, with Tourette's Syndrome. Four of the students took the drug Ritalin.

Under the multi-age primary program, Williams taught the same students for the equivalent of first and second grades. A full-time instructional assistant, Marlin Cobb, helped out because of the special education students in the class.

"Heather, how are you, girl?" Williams cooed at a returning student. "How's my writer?"

She pinned a name tag on a student she had taught in summer school. "I am so happy to see you, James. I tell you, you are special."

She wrapped another student in a bear hug, "Lamar, how are you, man? You look so sharp today. I'm so glad you're here."

Standing five feet two inches tall, Williams barely rose above some of her students. Yet, she was clearly in control of her classroom. She sang, she danced, she even donned costumes on occasion, but she never let fun and excitement give way to disorder. Like many grandmothers, Williams knows that children need soft laps to sit on and homemade cookies to soothe their hurts, but they also need steady hands to guide them. When a child misbehaved, Williams pulled the child close to her side and cupped the child's chin in her hand with a gesture that was meant to mix affection and discipline. She was effusive with praise, almost jolly at times, as she moved among her pupils during the day. But she was ever proper. Even when she laughed, Williams emitted little sound. Her eyes crinkled, her shoulders hunched, and her lips pursed in a grin that looked more guilty than gleeful.

She strongly believes that teachers should set good examples by their appearance and their actions. So, unlike many of her colleagues, Williams never wears pants to work, always a skirt or a dress and stockings. She prefers lace-trimmed collars, bold, flowered prints, and stylish business suits. She often covers her good clothes with a cotton apron to keep crayons and markers from ruining her wardrobe. Occasionally Williams will wear a South Heights Elementary T-shirt—with a skirt—for special events. But the trend toward dressing down in schools and offices is one she refuses to follow.

"I sometimes think that's why people have lost respect for teachers," she said. "Many of them dress worse than the students."

Over the years Williams watched the neighborhoods surrounding South Heights Elementary School change from solidly middle class to extremely poor, including a large number of subsidized housing tracts and public housing projects. The changing demographics brought more students to school who needed to catch up on skills they should have learned at home. Williams believes the growing gap in children's readiness for school probably did as much as the state education reforms to make teachers work harder.

Nearly 70 percent of the students at South Heights qualified for free or/and reduced-price lunches, a key indication of poverty, and a figure that was twice the district average and nearly one-third higher than the state average. South Heights typically posted among the lowest standardized test scores in the district. Williams acknowledged with sadness that she was teaching the children of some of her former students who were still teenagers. Yet she refused to see anything but potential in her students.

"I'm here to do a job," she said. "Whatever you give me, I'll handle it. I really feel like my classroom is my ministry."

Dorothy Meador, a retired reading instructor who regularly substituted for teachers at South Heights and Central Elementary Schools, recalled the first time she filled in for Williams. After the bell rang, signaling the start of school, Williams's students lined up quietly outside the door to the classroom. They neither moved nor spoke. Meador stood there for a few minutes and watched as other children walked into their classrooms and settled into their seats. Williams's students continued to wait quietly in the corridor. Bewildered, Meador asked one of the students why they hadn't entered the room.

"Well, Miz Williams always gives us a hug before we come in the room," he told Meador. "They were waiting for that hug," Meador said. "I've learned when I substitute for Irmgard to hug them before they come in the door."

Judy Whobrey watched Williams interact with students during the two years that her son, William, was in Williams's class. She said Williams had high expectations for her students and regularly honored their progress. Whobrey said she liked the changes resulting from the education reform law and believed critics hadn't spent enough time in classrooms to understand what was going on.

"I like it because they've got three or four years to progress at their own pace," she said. "There's no pass or fail. And yet, he's pushed, too. Last year, he had to do six words as a first-grader on spelling tests, but he always did two or more bonus words because the older children did it."

Jamie Woodard saw a difference in the way her two children progressed in school: Eric, who was a first-year student in Williams's class, and Dawn, a sixth-grader. Woodard believed Eric learned far more than Dawn did at his age.

"I'm impressed that he can come home and quote poetry and tell me the poet's name," she said. "It just seems to be much more than learning one plus one. It's a more broad spectrum of learning."

Woodard remembered that her own elementary teachers emphasized discipline and conformity above thinking and having fun. "In looking around this classroom, I have to say when I first walked in here I was shocked at the ideas and tools she uses to teach," Woodard said. "I don't know if new ideas are coming out and teachers are sharing them, or if she's just an exceptional teacher. I'm very impressed by the different ways they can teach the basics."

Williams acknowledged that her teaching methods were different—better, she thought—than they were years ago. She attributed it to the combination of new ideas generated through staff training and her own instincts about what works best for young children. She didn't follow education reform like a zealot, however. She preferred a balanced approach that didn't demand she toss tradition out with the trash. Williams still gave students weekly spelling tests, required them to read stories from textbooks every day, and controlled their behavior through a strict disciplinary code. She believed that the best way to teach children to read was to expose them regularly to good literature, but she also recognized that some children needed more help decoding sentences, a skill best emphasized through phonics instruction. "If some children can't learn one way, they can learn another," she said.

When teaching compound words, for example, she would give students visual, oral, and written cues. Williams would explain what a compound word was and ask students to read the words in print and to pronounce them out loud. Then she would put on an apron and pull one part of a cutout word (such as *hay*) from her left pocket and the other part of the word (such as *stack*) from the right. She would repeat the process through all the vocabulary words until the students understood the concept.

What Williams liked most about education reform was the permission it gave her to use the full range of her experience, judgment, and professional skill. She no longer had to follow a one-size-fits-all pattern that in her view never suited any student particularly well. Like a talented artist, Williams knows that good teaching requires a continual refinement of the craft, an ability to adjust techniques as circumstances change.

A glance at her lesson planning books over the years shows how she adapted her instruction from a narrow presentation of facts to a broad application of knowledge. Before the reform law, Williams's lesson plans contained neat, little boxes that compartmentalized each subject, gave the number of minutes the state required teachers to spend on each subject, and spelled out which pages of the textbook she would teach that day and which worksheets she would assign for homework. The planning guides had to be kept that way, Williams said, or her supervisors would mark her down during evaluations.

Now her lesson plans list general themes she intends to cover each week and major skills she wants her students to learn. "It's more practical," she said. "It's not segmented. It all fits together."

Planning takes considerably more time than it used to. Debbie Key, principal of South Heights, gave all the teachers keys to the school because most of them were working nights and weekends trying to keep up with new duties.

In recognition of these extra hours, the Henderson County school board began paying teachers for seven additional work days, on top of the nine paid training days that the state permitted—an unprecedented number in Kentucky. Each school council in Henderson County was supposed to decide how teachers could use the extra days, including attending workshops, meeting with parents, or planning lessons.

Williams seemed to plan on the run. At one time, she could take activities straight from the teacher's guides that accompanied textbooks. But now she had to pull materials from multiple sources each day, an almost non-stop routine that included consulting colleagues; scanning reference books at the library; seeking speakers from the community; reviewing computerized and tape-recorded lessons; and digging through file cabinets for resources she had collected over the years. In addition, all the lessons had to support the state's learning goals, relate to the themes her school and primary team had chosen for the year and, most of all, make real-life connections for students.

Williams devised lessons around broad, interdisciplinary themes; this school year it was people and places of the world. Each week she focused the topic more narrowly. During one five-day period, the theme was the earth's ecological changes. On Monday, she introduced some new vocabulary words—*earth*, *green*, *recycle*, *energy*, *protect*, *pollute*—which the children would have to spell correctly on Friday's test. She also taught them the importance of mathematical graphing and predictions for scientific exploration. On Tuesday, she used a lesson about synonyms and antonyms to teach more ecological terms—*clean* and *polluted*; *air* and *smog*; *life* and *death*.

On Wednesday, Williams asked her students to write in their daily journals. The topic was, "If I were a sea animal, I would like to be...." Then she sat in a rocking chair and read a book called *Dancing With Manatees* to her students (language arts). In the seamless discussion that followed, she asked students to show on a map where manatees live (geography), to discuss ways that pollution threatens the manatee's habitat (science), and to list some words from the manatee book that had singular and plural endings (spelling and grammar).

"How many months did I say it takes a manatee baby to be born?" Williams asked the class.

"Thirteen," the students answered.

Next Williams helped them figure out that thirteen months equals one year and one month, and that a female manatee, newly pregnant in October, would have a baby the following November (math).

"Okay, P2s (second year primary school students), I want you to write five good sentences about the manatee," Williams said. "P1s, I want you to write three good sentences. Don't just tell me that manatees are nice. Use your new vocabulary. Tell me about the manatee. Five sentences for the older ones, three for the younger ones, more if you want to" (language arts).

Later in the day Williams, asked the students to draw manatees in the ocean and to use a sponge-painting technique to create a three-dimensional picture (art). They also sang a song about the ocean (music) and wrote a cinquain, a five-line poem, about ocean life (language arts).

Williams's math lessons made similar connections. Each morning she had the children sit on the rug in a group and solve "Incredible Equations." In keeping with KERA's emphasis on fitting lessons to the students instead of the other way around, a bright five-year-old girl from the half-day kindergarten class usually joined the group of older students for the math lesson so she could be appropriately challenged. The students used plastic blocks, play money, calendars, sticks—a variety of tools to help them figure out mathematical problems. Williams taught part of the lesson in Spanish, not because she had to, but because she speaks Spanish and wanted to expose her students to a foreign language.

On the nineteenth day of one month, all the math equations featured the number nineteen. The class discussed odd and even numbers and agreed that nineteen is an odd number. Then Williams asked her students to prove it by counting by twos to twenty and using two stacks of blocks to see if they came up with equal or odd lengths.

"William, tell me what word equation you can make with these two stacks," she said to Judy Whobrey's son.

"Ten plus nine," he answered.

"Excellent," Williams said, then asked another student to spell the word *nineteen.*

"Brooke, can you tell me another way to make nineteen? Do you need to figure it out? Okay, here are the cubes. You work on that. Shane, what's another way to make nineteen with these coins?"

"Nineteen nickles," he answered.

"Now think a minute," Williams said. "What's a nickel worth?"

"Five," Shane said.

"So, is it nineteen times five?" she asked him then paused to give him more time to respond. "How many pennies are up there?"

"Nineteen," he said.

"Okay, so what's an equation with that?" she asked.

"Nineteen plus zero," Shane said.

"Good, I knew you could do it," she said, then led the children through a song that explains reversible equations.

"Okay, Nicole, give me another way to make nineteen," Williams said.

"One hundred times ten, take away seven hundred, take away two hundred minus ninety-nine, plus eighteen, equals nineteen," Nicole answered without a breath.

She said it so quickly that Williams asked Nicole to repeat the equation so she could copy it on a sheet of paper for the other students to see.

"Good job," Williams said. "Whew! You make me think! James?"

"Ten times ten times ten, take away one thousand, plus nineteen, equals nineteen," James answered.

"Okay," Williams said, "back it up so I can make sure you understand it. What's ten times ten?"

"Uh, one hundred," James said.

"Good," Williams said. "Times ten?"

"One thousand," he said.

"Good, now I know you know it," Williams said, beaming.

Students didn't always make such intellectual leaps in her classes. "I know this [reform] works," Williams said. "I now have first-graders who know times tables when I used to struggle to get third-graders to know them. I guess the biggest difference now is the children love to write. It's almost like they say, 'Do we get to?' I don't remember that from before. Used to be, all we did was copy work."

There is plenty of evidence to support her conclusions. In 1995, a team of researchers from the University of Kentucky replicated a 1982 study of elementary classroom writing practices to see what had changed as a result of KERA. Among the findings they reported in 1996:

- Elementary students and teachers spent twice as much time writing—more than one-fourth of the school day—than they did thirteen years before.
- The types of writing exercises that children performed changed significantly as well. In 1982, students spent most of their time copying texts and filling out worksheets. By 1995, they were engaged primarily in activities that required them to craft and revise their own writing.
- Teachers reported that additional staff training and the state's new tests, especially the writing portfolios and open-ended questions, had the greatest impact on their changing instruction.

"As many reformers have pointed out, the implementation of educational reform is largely a matter of teacher learning," the report concluded. "If any reform mandates are to be successfully implemented, the teachers whose job it is to implement them must be helped to acquire the requisite knowledge" (Bridge, Compton-Hall, and Cantrell 1996).

Williams was as eager to learn as her students. She recognized that for many of them school was the best part of the day. As a child, it had been that way for her, too.

Irmgard entered first grade at age five, nervous and unprepared, because her father hadn't thought it necessary to send her to kindergarten. She was so scared in the first weeks of school that in the mornings she sat on the fire escape outside her classroom and ate salami sandwiches while her mother, sitting beside her, tried to calm her daughter's fears.

Eventually school became a place where Irmgard excelled. It also offered temporary refuge from an alcoholic father who beat her as well as her brother and sister and who often made them wait for him in bars while he drank late into the night. Irmgard never discussed these problems with anyone outside the family. Her mother told her that "there are things you don't talk about," a message she would pass on later to her own three children.

Irmgard's father left her with a legacy of shame and self-doubt, and her need for outside approval grew so strong over the years that she tried to fill her emotionally empty spaces by serving others. Her natural instinct to please people evolved into a compulsion to put others' needs before her own.

"She'll give until it hurts," said Joel Williams, the second of her three children and a Christian music promoter who lives in Nashville, Tennessee. "You could walk over her and she would smile and say, 'Thank you.'"

Irmgard Williams's compliant behavior served her well as a pastor's wife. For twenty-six years, in three different churches, she followed her husband's lead as he ministered to his congregations. She planned weddings, accompanied Dewey when he visited parishioners at home and in the hospital, and counseled people through all the traumas of life.

Rachel Hester is the youngest child and only daughter of Dewey and Irmgard Williams. Rachel remembers how often her mother entertained people at church and at home. She kept a closetful of wrapped gifts in the house so no visitor would feel left out of the family's holiday celebrations. Her mother also distributed clothes and toys to children in Haiti and the Dominican Republic when the family traveled there for missionary work, and she encouraged her own children to donate some of their favorite possessions.

Hester, a program coordinator at a homeless shelter in Nashville, said she often rebelled against the family's standards of piety when she was younger; instead of going to Hispaniola in the summers to build new churches, she longed to visit Disney World. But over the years she learned to appreciate her parents' model of self-sacrifice. When a 1982 fire destroyed the family's home in Henderson, friends rallied to help and Hester began to understand the importance of charity.

"My mother always said, 'You only have what you give away,'" Hester said. "When we lost everything in the fire, the people we had helped helped us back."

There were limits to that generosity, however. Church life was demanding, and congregations could quickly become disenchanted with the minister and his family. They held the Williams family to extremely high standards. Any slipups, real or imagined, inspired reproaches from the flock, which aggravated Irmgard's insecurities. When she bought a red car, for example, some parishioners accused her of being ostentatious. When she waxed her hardwood floors, they said she was too preoccupied with wordly pleasures. When her husband built a church and home for his family in Henderson, people said the buildings were too extravagant. When the parishioners voted on her husband's contract every four years, as was then the custom in the Church of the Nazarene, Irmgard recoiled whenever her husband received a "No" vote. It didn't matter that most people supported him. She considered every negative message a personal attack.

"When you do your best and you still don't make people happy, it's hard," she said, adding that she and Dewey "never told our children anything about the people who were vicious. We thought they would not love the church."

Despite these occasional setbacks, the church and her family formed the center of Irmgard's life. They made her feel purposeful and necessary. Then, about a decade ago, the foundation started cracking. Dewey Williams had grown restless in his religious work. A few years before, he bought a florist shop in a bankruptcy sale. Some members of the congregation thought his new business was interfering with church duties, and they felt slighted. When Dewey Williams decided to leave that church, many parishioners turned their backs on the family.

Irmgard Williams felt as if her breath had been sucked out. All the familiar patterns were in disarray. Her two older children, Mark and Joel, had moved away, leaving a void in the family. Irmgard and Dewey had to move from the church parsonage, and Rachel, then in the eighth grade, was forced to change schools. The Williamses joined a new church, but it wasn't the same. Dewey Williams became distracted and unresponsive. His health deteriorated rapidly.

Irmgard Williams felt alone, adrift, and emotionally unfulfilled. In the months ahead, she spent more and more time at school, eventually channeling her unhappiness into energy she dedicated to her students. Instead of leaving school shortly after dismissal, as she usually did when she was tending to her family and church, she started staying behind until 6 P.M. or later. Often she returned to school after supper to grade papers and plan new lessons. She volunteered to serve on any school committee, attended a slew of education conferences out of town, and signed up for every professional workshop that was available. She immersed herself in work. And in the process, Irmgard Williams, always a good teacher, became an excellent one.

"She definitely changed in a good way," Joel Williams said. "I think she found a new life in school."

When Kentucky's education reform law came along, Irmgard Williams embraced its challenges. There was no limit to what she would do on a personal level. What she hadn't counted on was the demands KERA placed on teachers as a group. The expectation was that teachers would work together to collectively rise to a higher level, but the state didn't provide directions for accomplishing this goal. Most teachers had grown up in classrooms where individual initiative was the measure of success, and they continued rewarding independence in their own classrooms. Group responsibility was rarely encouraged or discussed.

The new emphasis on collective achievement forced Williams into an uncomfortable position. For most of her life she had been content to stay in the background. She didn't like to draw attention to herself, and she believed that others should mind their own business. Although she made certain she was personally accountable for her own actions, she never considered it her place to judge anyone. Now the state seemed to be suggesting she should.

When she opened the door to her classroom, after years of forced isolation, Williams couldn't help notice the difference between herself and some of her colleagues. They seemed to recognize the disparities, too, and often approached her for advice. When she became the leader of one of the primary teams, the questions multiplied. Williams always seemed to know what to do.

Yet, rarely did her guidance lead to improvements in other classrooms. Her colleagues had a tough time transferring her techniques, and Williams didn't have the luxury of coaching them on the spot. The lack of progress among the staff troubled her. She preferred to influence other teachers by example, not dictate to them. They were professionals, too. But despite her gentle reminders, some teachers had not heeded the message that they needed to make major improvements in their instruction—and fast.

The 1994–1995 school year was only six weeks old when Williams learned that some of her former students had become discipline problems for other teachers. The children seemed to spend more time in the hallway or in the principal's office than in the classroom. Her colleagues blamed it on the children's behavior, but Williams held a different view. The children had performed well in her classes. Maybe they were bored now. She believed if students were challenged and engaged in exciting work, they rarely misbehaved.

"I don't know if some [teachers] think KERA means no restraints," she said. "There are restraints. You go to church, there are restraints. You go to a restaurant, there are restraints. You have to give children structure. You can't blame the situation on the children."

How to help more teachers improve—that was one of the key questions of education reform. KERA expected all students to learn at high levels, but they would never succeed if teachers didn't give them the necessary skills. When teachers failed, who should intervene? And how?

Williams brooded about these questions for months. She analyzed her responsibilities as a teacher, as a team leader, and as a woman who knew firsthand the critical role instructors play in the lives of young children. KERA was based on the premise that no student should be left behind. Did that mean every educator had a stake in the success of every child?

What could Williams do about other teachers? What *should* she do? She was already so busy trying to address her own students' needs. Wasn't that enough? Certainly education reform required more of teachers, but did it mean they must expect more from one another? Were they obligated to confront incompetence, even if it meant challenging a friend across the hall?

"How can you tell another teacher how to teach?" Williams wondered.

Chapter Two

A Second Chance

Superintendent Gayle Ecton glanced across the conference table at the haggard, anxious face of one of Henderson County's best elementary school principals. Ecton was not looking forward to this meeting. He tried to give his principals plenty of latitude. He wanted to encourage innovation, not squash it with second-guessing. He liked risk-takers, people who went away and tried something before saying it could not be done.

Johnny Duckworth, principal at Chandler Elementary School, was a man who could run with a long leash. Always out in front, Duckworth was a hard-driving, flamboyant leader who expected a lot of himself and his staff. With the flood of mandates that streamed out of the Kentucky Education Reform Act, a principal was under constant pressure to keep the school staff afloat. Duckworth could be counted on to do his part.

But as much as Ecton disliked confrontations, he knew this one was overdue. Rumors were rampant about Duckworth's personal troubles. His boorish behavior at a recent education conference in Dallas, Texas, had embarrassed other school district employees. People reported that Duckworth was drunk at a dinner meeting and fell asleep at the table. He became so intoxicated on the airplane that he nearly missed his connecting flight. The blunt description was that he had "behaved like an ass." Although Ecton had no reason to believe Duckworth's drinking had ever been a problem on the job, he knew it was time to intervene.

On his side of the table, Duckworth tried to relax. He eased his clenched jaw and pressed his feet to the floor. He felt like a coil in a frayed armchair, waiting to pop through the upholstery and poke somebody where it hurt. He could handle criticism from his family. He had listened to plenty over the years. But this meeting with Ecton made him nervous. He knew it had to do with his job, the only part of his life Duckworth thought he could still control.

Ecton calmly laid out his agenda. "I'm concerned about you, Johnny," he said. "You don't look well."

Ecton reminded Duckworth about Stephen Covey's book, *The 7 Habits of Highly Effective People: Powerful Lessons in Personal Change*, which all the principals in the Henderson County school district had read and discussed. The book described the importance of having balance in one's life, Ecton said. It recommended taking advantage of the opportunities that change creates, to grow and engage in self-reflection. "You don't seem to have much balance in your life, Johnny," he said.

"Do you mean my drinking?" Duckworth asked quickly.

Ecton turned the question back on the questioner, giving him no way out. "Is your drinking a problem?" he asked.

Duckworth demurred. He had assumed that Ecton wanted to talk to him about his drinking. But, no, he didn't think he had a problem. He drank socially, he said, maybe more at night lately. He had dealt with several stressful situations in the past few years—opening a new school building, getting divorced, responding to education reform. He was tense and tired. But he thought he could handle everything. He was all right. "I don't think my drinking is a problem," Duckworth said. "But I'll see a counselor or somebody if you want me to."

It wasn't his right to pry into an employee's personal problems, Ecton said, or to order him to seek psychological help. "But I am concerned about your job," Ecton said.

The comment stung like a slap. Duckworth didn't hear much of anything after that. Nothing in his life—not sports, not his family, not his friendships—had ever given him the same sense of accomplishment as his job. He was good at it, he knew that. Take it away from him and he would have nothing, be nothing.

Duckworth knew he drank too much alcohol, although he never admitted it publicly. He kept telling himself that drinking was a reward for getting through another hard day. And God knows he had endured a lot of those lately.

He remembered drinking heavily on the trip to Dallas, but he couldn't recall much more. He had excused the drinking by rationalizing that he was afraid of flying. He had never been able to get on an airplane sober. Duckworth had grown up on a farm; he felt at peace on the land. If he had to travel, he preferred to go by car so he could see the countryside on either side of him. As a young man, he had even learned to plow at night by watching the moon and listening to the pitch of the tractor engine as the metal grooves massaged the soil. But when he heard similar engine sounds on an airplane, Duckworth panicked. He couldn't feel the earth beneath him. He wasn't the one steering the machine.

"Don't worry," Duckworth told Ecton. "I've got everything under control."

Who am I kidding, he thought to himself. He was forty-six years old, alone, and miserable. He could not get through the night without a drink, even though he waited until 4 P.M. on weekdays before imbibing. He was slipping, and everyone knew it. Henderson was a small city. People broadcast your problems no matter how you tried to hide them. Although he usually drove across the Ohio River to drink at bars in Evansville, Indiana, or meandered through the back roads of western Kentucky with a cooler full of beer in his car, Duckworth realized that people had heard about his indiscretions. Some of his colleagues had confronted him. His ex-wife, a teacher's aide at another local elementary school, left him because of his drinking and extra-marital affairs. His only child barely spoke to him. His mother thought he was an embarrassment.

But Ecton's opinion mattered more to him right now. Duckworth greatly respected the man. Ecton was one of his heroes—a smart, likeable leader who made Duckworth believe that he and the staff at Chandler Elementary could compete with anyone in the world. Had the superintendent lost faith in him, too?

Ecton reminded Duckworth that in education public perception often overpowers reality. Even if he didn't drink on the job, Duckworth had lost nearly all credibility as an educator because people had seen him inebriated in a public setting. Nobody wanted a drunk serving as a role model for children, no matter how distinguished his career. As long as he kept drinking, Duckworth's effectiveness as a principal was shot.

"This is an opportunity to get things straightened out," Ecton told him. He made no threats, but the repercussions were strongly implied. Then the superintendent left the principal alone to figure out a next step.

Over the next two days Duckworth thought of little else. Maybe he was not as good at his job as he believed. He had been so focused on doing the right *things* to improve education that he had neglected the *people* most affected by his decisions.

In the past few years Duckworth had become almost obsessed with education reform because he believed that changing was the only hope for Kentucky's malfunctioning public schools. In the early days of reform he had encouraged his teachers to store their textbooks and stop drilling students on facts. Instead, he urged them to start designing lessons that would help students see the connections between subjects and understand the practical applications of school work. He had taken a similar approach with tests. Duckworth forbid teachers to give students only traditional worksheets and multiple-choice tests, believing that these assessments merely measured a student's ability to regurgitate information, not use it in any meaningful way. Duckworth pushed his teachers to align their daily assessments with the state's new test by having students write regularly in every subject and solve complex problems alone and in groups.

He was proud of the changes at Chandler, but the truth was that he had bullied most of his teachers into compliance. They benefited from the new strategies, and so did the students. But the pace and the pressures exhausted everyone. The staff was wrung out.

For his part, Duckworth had completed all the new training that the state required of principals to help them better understand education reform. He had shared with his colleagues at conferences around the state and traveled around the country to learn from other administrators. Duckworth had involved his staff in decisions ranging from instruction to hiring long before the state mandated that principals delegate some of their power to an elected council of parents, teachers, and principals. But his inability to straighten out his own life had become a professional liability. Other administrators acknowledged that as an educator he was frequently brilliant. But as a human being, Duckworth often behaved like a jerk.

Disgusted with himself, Duckworth picked up his worn copy of *The 7 Habits of Highly Effective People* and started reading it again.

Three days after his meeting with Ecton, Duckworth gathered his staff together at Chandler. He told the faculty it was time to stop running from his problems. He acknowledged that he pushed staff members to confront their own fears about change but hadn't held himself to the same standard.

"I don't want to make any excuses for my behavior," Duckworth said. "But I've realized that I'm an alcoholic, and I need to get help. I'm going to check myself into a hospital in Louisville so I can dry out."

Staff members, male and female, wept. Few were surprised by the revelation—they had heard gossip about his drinking for years, although no one had ever seen him drunk at a school function. But they hadn't expected Duckworth to be so open about his problem.

Duckworth told the staff that he wasn't sure how long he would be away from school. He appointed Sharon Mattingly, a veteran teacher on the staff, to take charge during his absence. "I want to be real upfront about this so people won't talk," Duckworth said. "I'm even going to tell the kids."

For the next few hours he went class to class at Chandler and included all 220 students in his testimonial. He gathered the younger students around him on the floor. He addressed the older students by slouching next to their tables and chairs. "No matter how big or strong you are, sometimes you need help," he told the children. "Mr. Duck needs help."

They wrapped him in hugs and slapped him high-fives. Many children cried and held his hand. They told the principal about their relatives who had struggled with addictions to alcohol and drugs. They told him they hoped he would not have to drink again. They said they understood.

Duckworth left the school building that afternoon exhausted but relieved. He was electrified with a new understanding of the meaning of change. It wasn't just about putting programs in place or tossing out textbooks. It was a wake-up call to face the facts of a disappointing past. He could see clearly the parallels between his personal and professional lives. In the same way that he was trying to acknowledge his own misdeeds, Kentucky was trying to atone for its historical role in neglecting public education.

"We always knew learning wasn't going on. We just didn't say anything," Duckworth said. "Nothing changes when nothing changes. I think that's the biggest part of education reform. You don't just do it in your professional life. You do it in your personal life."

After he left Chandler, Duckworth drove into town and stopped by Benton-Glunt Funeral Home where his son, Lance, was working. He told Lance about his decision to seek treatment for alcoholism.

"If you're really willing to stop drinking," Lance, age twenty-one, told his father, "I'll help you any way I can." Lance did, too. He talked to his father on the telephone at least five times during his ten-day hospital stay, and he listened to his father pour out his pain. Lance honestly tried to be understanding. But inside, he raged. It was one thing to *say* you have changed, he thought to himself, but he wanted to *see* some results. Remorse was easier than remedy. No matter what his father did now, it would not make up for all the years he had neglected him.

Lance could not forget the memories of his childhood, including the days when he waited at the house with his baseball glove, hoping that his father, a hometown sports star, would finally teach him to play the game. Lance remembered the nights that he waited at school events and 4-H meetings, hoping to see his father clapping for him in the audience when he received awards for public speaking and leadership. But his father never came. He was too busy coaching school sports teams, working on a master's degree, or carousing with friends.

Lance couldn't help feeling more than a little skeptical about his father's intentions to turn his life around. His father had caused too much damage. He had broken too many promises. Lance firmly believed that even if his father managed to stop drinking, one thing would not change—Johnny Duckworth would still care about other people's children more than his own.

Although personal and institutional changes differ in some respects, they share at least one common element—the impact on individuals. A son's cynicism about his father's promise to straighten out his life arises from the same feeling of mistreatment that led Kentucky's parents and taxpayers to distrust the state's pledge to reform its schools. A history of indifference and bad decisions eroded so much good will that people did not want to believe. Like Lance, they learned to hear platitudes in every promise. They grew accustomed to being let down.

The importance of the population's support of KERA cannot be overstated. Behind every policy was a person who had to make it work—a teacher who had to change lesson plans, a principal who had to share power, a state official who had to stop drowning schools in regulatory paperwork, a parent who had to do more than glance periodically at a child's report card.

Change is not just about policies, or programs, or promises. It is an intensely personal decision to try something new. And to work, change depends on a broad belief that doing something differently will make it better.

Duckworth was only a bit player in the effort to turn around Kentucky's schools, but he knew he had a lot to prove both on the job and in his family. After completing a hospital stay in Louisville, he spent six months in an outpatient treatment program in

Henderson. He didn't participate in any formal therapy program after that. He considered Alcoholics Anonymous too limiting for his needs. These were signs that he was still trying to control his problems instead of allowing others to help. To stay sober, he was counting on public acknowledgement of his illness, regular discussions with friends, and a stack of self-help books.

Duckworth had a good track record for accomplishing tasks related to his work, but he had rarely succeeded in building and sustaining positive personal relationships. He acknowledged that he had been a lousy father. He just did not know how to make things right.

It was difficult to move beyond his son's irritations. Johnny always seemed to respond to Lance's resistance with more anger, and then father and son would stay stuck in the same painful place, both of them too stubborn to budge.

Johnny Duckworth always found it difficult to keep his anger in check. As a teacher, as a principal, as a man, he learned to define leadership and authority as control. For many years he was good at being the man in charge, demanding obedience and uniformity from the people he supervised. He coined a perjorative term to describe his past behavior. "I was the duck-tator," he said.

"What he said was what went, no matter what. He was the boss," said Sharon Mattingly, the Chandler teacher who took over for Duckworth when he went to the hospital. "He had a habit of walking away when you talked to him, saying, 'No,' before you even finished asking him something."

Jama Danhauer, a Chandler teacher, said Duckworth was not "open to listening and hearing different viewpoints" before he confronted his alcoholism. "He was talking about education reform but not really changing the way he managed."

Duckworth was groomed to follow in the tradition of Kentucky's paternalistic system of education, one which insisted that the principal should make all the decisions in the school, one that allowed only selected students to succeed. Duckworth had pledged allegiance to that system for many years. That he then tried to switch to a more democratic form of leadership says a lot about the ability of people to make difficult adjustments, even at mid-career, when they are motivated to change.

Duckworth credited Ecton with exposing him to new information about school leadership, such as the importance of collaborating with teachers instead of controlling them. Ecton also embodied the same management techniques he championed. Duckworth liked what he saw. He wanted to be more like the superintendent, but it would take years of practice before he could break free from his old habits.

KERA gave credibility to Ecton's penchant for shared management by stipulating that principals become less autocratic. It also boosted Duckworth's confidence; he could try a new role. Jan Kellen, a Chandler teacher, believes KERA gave everyone in Kentucky's schools a chance to start over. "I think the reform act has helped us all look at ourselves in new ways," she said. "Mr. Duck led us in that. He knew that he was going to have to change."

Duckworth's transformation was gradual. He started praising people more, actually thanked them for their contributions instead of assuming they already knew how he felt. Perhaps the most difficult adjustment was allowing other people to comment on a situation before giving his opinion or delivering an ultimatum.

He struggled to shake his authoritarian habits. At five feet ten inches tall with a belly grown rounder since quitting smoking at the same time he stopped drinking, Duckworth walked with a jock's intimidating swagger. He leaned into conversations, crowding people's personal space, making sure his points were clearly understood. He tended to use sarcasm when he felt threatened or overwhelmed. And although he tried hard to listen well before responding, he still wanted things done his way.

"Johnny doesn't allow people to hang back," said Ray Roth, a school psychologist who worked at Chandler and several other Henderson County schools. "He forces them to move on. Some of it is based on his old reputation. I think they're afraid not to do what he says. Apparently, he's been able to make people's lives hell before."

Even as a boy, growing up in the small Henderson County town of Cairo, Duckworth was known for being brash and opinionated. Virginia and John Edward Duckworth doted on their only child.

Johnny never had to study much in school. He got through most of his courses because he was good at memorizing information for tests. He was an average student but a superior athlete. In Kentucky that combination counts for a lot. In the 1950s and early 1960s, students either had what it took to pass each grade in school or they didn't. Students didn't take remedial classes if they fell behind; they just dropped out. "At my eighth-grade graduation, a lot of my friends' parents were happy they had made it that far," he said.

Because his elementary school was so small, Johnny was able to experience the classroom strategies that would be recommended by Kentucky's education reforms forty years later. Cairo Elementary operated like an extended family. Students in different grades shared the same teacher and older children helped younger ones. But in seventh grade, Johnny left comfortable Cairo for a larger, more structured domain—Weaverton Elementary. He made the switch because of sports; he wanted to increase his level of competition.

Johnny excelled at most sports, but his favorite was baseball. His father focused on making him a star. John Edward built a batting cage and a baseball diamond in the front yard of the family farm so his son could play ball every day. He also installed a gymnasium in the hayloft so his son could lift weights and increase his flexibility. From the time that he was three years old, Johnny practiced throwing baseballs at a heavy rug his father hung from the porch rafters. John Edward coached his son relentlessly.

Johnny peaked early as an athlete. At age twelve, he and his Henderson County teammates were runners-up in the 1959 Little League World Series. A shortstop and pitcher with a "sharply nosediving curveball," according to a local sportwriter, Johnny achieved three shutouts in his four World Series victories. He struck out fifty-five batters and posted an earned-run average of 0.00. Although he had some success on high school and summer league teams, Johnny never matched his accomplishments in the World Series. After graduating from high school, his dream of becoming a professional athlete dimmed. The recognition of his limitations started him on a long, slow fall from glory that led to years of disillusionment, self-pity, and binge drinking.

"When I look back on it, there was too much emphasis on sports," said his mother, Virginia, now divorced from John Edward. "They get all these honors and then school gets out and you don't get any more accolades. [Johnny] learned to want all that adoration."

In 1965, Johnny Duckworth accepted a baseball scholarship to Kentucky Wesleyan College in nearby Owensboro, Kentucky, becoming the first person in his entire extended family to go to college. After six weeks, he had a grade-point average of 1.2 on a scale of 4.0. He didn't know how to study because no one ever encouraged him to work hard in school. It had always been perfectly fine just to get by. Frustrated by new challenges, impulsive, and immature, Duckworth dropped out of college and married Cindy Berry, his high school sweetheart.

After a few weeks of work as a laborer and a grocery bagger, Duckworth decided to retrieve his scholarship and return to college. At age eighteen, he was attending classes full time, working two part-time jobs, playing second base on the college baseball team, and trying to be a husband.

During his sophomore year in college, Duckworth's disappointments increased. Playing in a game, he tripped over a base and separated his shoulder. His days as an athlete were over. He never played baseball seriously again.

Thwarted from achieving his only goal, Duckworth had to pick a new path. Versatility had served him well in sports, but rarely did he have to test himself off the field. He decided to turn his attentions to coaching. If he could not play sports anymore, he reasoned, coaching would at least keep him close to the action. Duckworth served as Kentucky Wesleyan's assistant baseball coach for three years. After graduating from college, he began teaching science and coaching basketball and football at North Junior High School in Henderson. Later, he moved to Henderson County High School. "The only way to coach was to teach," he said, clearly preferring the former job to the latter.

As a teacher, Duckworth was a no-nonsense classroom manager who was not afraid to paddle unruly students, put them in physical restraints, or slam them up against a classroom wall. Administrators regularly called on Duckworth to help keep order throughout the school. The duck-tator was building his reputation. "It was a terrible way to live," he said. "I felt that was the only worth I had, being in control. That was the expectation, that's what it meant back then to 'be a man.'"

In 1977, Duckworth switched jobs and became a physical education teacher who traveled to a different elementary school every day. When Bob Mitchell, then principal of Robards Elementary School, heard that Duckworth would be joining his staff, he was hesitant. Duckworth was known to be "loud, obnoxious, and harsh with students" at the secondary level, Mitchell said. He didn't think Duckworth was cut out to work with young children. But within two months, Mitchell said, "every kid there loved him."

Mitchell recalled how sweaty, excited children would run up to him in the hallway and breathlessly describe the games Duckworth had taught them in the gymnasium or on the playground. Mitchell said they loved the competition and the way Duckworth pushed them to meet new challenges.

"He's the only teacher I ever had who got a standing ovation from the children every time he walked into the building," Mitchell said. "He'd go across the cafeteria to get a cup of coffee and the kids would stand and cheer. I had the fewest discipline problems on Thursdays—physical education day—than any day of the week. He was the best damned P.E. teacher I ever had."

For Duckworth, the experience of working at so many schools helped him see how different principals performed their jobs. He observed some schools that pulsated with excitement and learning and others that resembled military barracks because principals barked orders and forced everyone to march in step.

In 1981, Duckworth decided to get into administration. He became principal of Corydon Elementary School, a promotion that he acknowledged had more to do with his reputation as a strict disciplinarian than his skill in the classroom. Corydon was thought to be "out of control" and in need of a firm manager. Coach Duckworth was physical and considered tough, so he got the job. His supervisors wrote down the school's address and tossed him a ring of keys. They never asked what he knew about curriculum, leadership, or teacher training. Duckworth acknowledges that he has tried to overcome that limited endorsement of his skills ever since.

Initially, Duckworth emulated the authoritarian principals that he had seen in action in so many schools. He didn't have the courage or the confidence to be different. Like many Kentucky principals of a certain age, Duckworth ruled his school like a feudal lord. He measured his success by how clean he kept the cafeteria, how often he got the school buses to run on time, and how well he kept the mostly female teaching staff on task. It was a macho world, built on discipline, stoicism, and a rigid adherence to rules. The good-old-boy network—long on ex-coaches—held the power in Kentucky school districts, and loyalty, not innovation, earned promotions. Principals ran the show, rarely consulting teachers or parents before making decisions. Nothing in the job description referred to collaboration. If a principal turned out to be good at working with people, it was a happy accident.

In Kentucky, principals almost always had at least a master's degree and the appropriate administrative certification, but their training had more to do with managing people than helping them adapt to change. Although the Kentucky Education Reform Act required principals to complete a special five-day session to update their skills, take forty-two hours of additional training every two years, and consult a mentor if they were new, the lessons still tended to cover traditional ground. A principal's first exposure to KERA included watching some unexciting videotapes produced by the state

Department of Education. In a show of hypocrisy that principals didn't fail to notice, state officials continued dictating the form and frequency of administrative training at the same time they required principals to give up control in their own schools.

In 1995, when Kentucky Department of Education officials surveyed three hundred principals who had been on the job less than three years, they discovered that the majority felt adequately prepared for their new responsibilities only in the areas of discipline and time management. Evaluating teachers, setting student achievement goals, engaging the school community in discussions about education, preparing a budget, working with teachers and parents to run the school as an elected council—these lessons rarely were included in a principal's training. The emphasis was still on what some have referred to perjoratively as "buses, budgets, and butts"—transportation, finances, and student discipline.

"Administrators are trained more to manage buildings than to lead and inspire teachers," California researcher Jane L. David noted in a 1994 report to the Prichard Committee for Academic Excellence on the progress of Kentucky's school-based decision-making councils. "They are certainly not professionally trained to lead a process of collaborative decision-making and organizational transformation—a task that is particularly difficult in schools where teachers are accustomed to working in isolation and parents are accustomed to maintaining their distance."

Since 1990, the responsibilities of Kentucky's principals had changed so dramatically that most were hard-pressed to define their new roles. Under KERA, each principal, in consultation with the faculty, was supposed to write a "school transformation plan"—basically an analysis of the school's strengths and weaknesses based on student test scores, dropout rates, and other factors. In addition, the principal was supposed to develop a plan for staff training that fit the specific needs of the faculty and a plan for integrating technology into the school's regular curriculum. Schools like Chandler, which served a high percentage of poor families, also were eligible to set up Family Resource or Youth Service Centers. All elementary schools had to reconfigure their classrooms to accommodate children of different ages, and many had to add preschool programs for students who were poor or disabled.

Given the added pressures, it was not surprising that education reform made the job of principal in Kentucky increasingly unpopular. Many administrators left their jobs as soon as they were eligible to retire. From 1990 to 1995, nearly 40 percent of the principalships in Kentucky changed hands.

"In the past, the principal needed to be more of a manager than a leader," said Wayne Young, executive director of the Kentucky Association of School Administrators. "They were responsible for taking care of *stuff*—ordering books, keeping the walls clean, making sure the student-teacher ratio was okay. Now, we've added a whole lot more skills for the job, but we haven't taken anything else away—the roof still leaks, the copier breaks down, and kids still misbehave. Something's got to give."

Duckworth always poured most of his energy into his job, so the additional responsibilities just meant he had to pick up his pace. Clearly, it was easier and quicker when he made all the decisions himself. Involving more people in the daily operations of the school took a lot of time. But most days, Duckworth believed to his surprise that the democratic process produced better results.

He thought back to the time a few years earlier when Ecton had asked him to describe his leadership style. "I told him I was a benevolent catalyst," Duckworth said. "I feel like my mission has been to effect change in a very humane way. Sometimes it has not been humane, more out of ignorance and habit than anything else. It's not easy to let go of the past, no matter how hard you're trying to be different."

Some parents and teachers did not want to accept the burden of shared power. They had grown accustomed to letting others call the shots. And for some, Duckworth's leadership was still suspect. "There's still some anxiety about him, I think," said Roth, the school psychologist and one of Duckworth's closest colleagues.

"I believe some people in the community lost respect for him" because of his drinking, said Joyce Hamilton, who taught at Chandler for six years. "I'm sure with many people that will never be gained back."

Duckworth and his staff struggled through an awkward transition. The principal had some good ideas, the staff thought, but he was rarely gracious or subtle about his plans. For example, in 1990, when state education leaders suggested that teachers use textbooks as classroom resources and not rely on them as the basis for every lesson, Duckworth walked into a faculty meeting and told the teachers they could not use textbooks for *any* reason during the school year.

"Leave them on the shelves," he said. "Don't touch them." Then he walked out of the room.

Some teachers panicked. They didn't know how to construct a lesson except to follow the textbook's lead. They didn't have anything else to use. "I had some misgivings," said Yvonne "Vonnie" Draper, then a kindergarten teacher. "I said, 'What will I teach if I can't use the textbook?'"

A few days later, a group of teachers urged Joyce Hamilton, who had a good relationship with Duckworth, to ask for leniency. Hamilton didn't think Duckworth was entirely serious about the textbook prohibition, but she still felt uneasy about the situation. "Mr. Duck," she said when she ventured into his office later that week, "now don't get mad. Can we just use our textbooks on Fridays?"

Duckworth hooted. He told Hamilton he had been waiting for someone to call his bluff. When he met again with the faculty, he emphasized that his point was not to deny teachers access to textbooks but to show them it was a new day in education, one where traditions had to be justified, not used as a crutch. He didn't care if the teachers turned to their textbooks some of the time, but he wanted them to draw lessons from a variety of sources—books, personal experience, computers, each other. The options were unlimited.

He reminded the staff that five of them had experience as kindergarten teachers. They already knew how to use activity centers and hands-on methods that made school so much fun for five-year-olds. They could do the same thing with older students, he said. Textbooks were not the only answer. "You know your students well," Duckworth told them. "You are professionals. Now go teach."

To some, Duckworth's method of modifying the use of textbooks might seem refreshingly bold in a profession that often moves slower than a tortoise—and with about as much grace. But to others inside and outside the system, his take-no-prisoners strategy indicated an autocratic manager who still had much to learn.

Duckworth believed that making teachers equal partners in management meant encouraging them to be as bull-headed as he was. In the next few months, he exhorted teachers to become savvy education consumers who would carefully study any new method before adopting it—even one the principal suggested. Over several years, he inundated teachers with research and sample lesson plans—filling up deep file drawers in many of their classrooms. "Don't you ever let anyone come in here and tell you to do anything unless they show you the research," Duckworth said.

The textbooks were returned to a room the teachers used for storing reference materials. The Chandler transformation had begun.

"Risk-taking was encouraged from the beginning," said Rebecca Duvean, a former Chandler teacher now serving as an elementary principal in nearby Union County. "He told us, 'It's not a failure that you tried something and it didn't work.' The key was trust. You knew you wouldn't get your hand slapped for doing something different."

Duckworth sent staff members to a variety of workshops and seminars so they could learn new teaching methods. After each session, the teachers were responsible for spreading the information to their colleagues. When they traveled around Kentucky and to other states, the Chandler teachers began to realize how much of a head start they had on others.

For example, Joyce Hamilton was working on a master's degree in education while teaching full time. Many nights, she ended up teaching the college classes because her personal experience was more relevant than the professor's prepared lectures. Still, it was unsettling for the Chandler teachers to realize they were so far out in front of others.

"The stress level of everyone was unreal," Hamilton said. "There was so much planning and paperwork. And we still had a lack of confidence about what we were doing. We were asked to dramatically change everything we did. Duck is the sort of person, when you jumped in, you jumped in all the way. We always did everything first and to a degree more than anyone else. He's a real perfectionist. He's very driven. And he's not going to ask more of you than he's willing to do himself. But he'll do it all—and he'll expect it all of you."

Some teachers initially balked at the changes Duckworth was pushing. "A lot of people, a lot of teachers, hoped this would blow over," said Chandler teacher Jan Kellen. "We were in denial. I denied it. Some of the things he was asking us to do sounded so drastic."

And the changes were happening so fast. At the same time he challenged the staff to use sources other than textbooks and to create new tests, Duckworth also asked them to compile collections of students' written work, capture student presentations on video, and develop individual education plans on the computer for each student. He encouraged the staff to discontinue the strictly phonics-based approach to teaching reading that drilled students on spelling and instructed them to sound out words by following simple texts. He emphasized a new reading approach that taught children to read by exposing them to literature and allowing them to write often, even before they had learned to read on their own.

State leaders had asked Kentucky teachers to make many of these changes, too, but on a more gradual schedule. Duckworth set his own deadlines for Chandler's staff. He didn't cut the teachers any slack.

When two teachers refused to adjust their lessons, Duckworth stuck some Kmart employment applications in their school mail boxes. It was a typical Duckworth strategy: back people into a corner where they either had to join his side or give up. One of the two teachers asked for a transfer. The other teacher decided to get on board.

The teacher who stayed, Gwen Fulkerson, was a veteran special education instructor whom Duckworth considered ineffective, as did many people in the district. He had to demand more of her, he said, because "we couldn't allow her to be less than excellent." The school's ability to meet its state goals depended on every staff member working for the same purpose.

Duckworth urged his staff to try inclusion, a method of teaching special education students in a regular classroom instead of separating them for most of the day. Inclusion enables a special education instructor to assist the regular teacher, paying close attention to students with disabilities.

Fulkerson initially resisted the switch in strategies. "I had done it the other way for so long that I wasn't convinced," she said. "I had my classroom in the basement. I wanted to pull them (the special education students) out. Mr. Duck would say, 'You need to be in the regular classroom. They are not *your* students. They are *our* students.' "He stuck to his guns. He was constantly telling me, 'Mrs. Fulkerson, you are not to pull them out of class.'"

Fulkerson acknowledged being set in her ways. She loved her students, and she feared they would get lost in a regular classroom with so many new distractions. Truthfully, she did not believe her students were capable of learning very much. Most years, she completed the federally required Individual Education Plans (IEP) for each child by November, assuming they would gain few new skills in the final six months of the school year.

That low level of learning was no longer acceptable in Kentucky, however. *All* students had to progress. Before 1990, it was common practice in Kentucky (and still is in most states) to exclude students with the most disabilities from state tests, thus increasing the chance that a school's average score would rise. "If all the special education kids were on a field trip that day, nobody checked," said Valerie Forti, assistant director of the Office of Educational Accountability, a Kentucky watchdog agency set up to monitor education reform.

The Kentucky reform law ended that practice, matching every student with a test score. A student who didn't take the test for any reason showed up as a zero on the school's report, which was even lower than the one point given to schools when a student scored in the novice, or lowest, category.

Reluctantly, Fulkerson started bringing her students to the classrooms of her colleagues. When she discovered that other teachers were willing to work with her and when she realized that her students were thriving in the new environment, she acknowledged that maybe Duckworth knew what he was talking about. "It's mind-boggling. It really works," she said. "Now I see where pulling them out has been such an injustice to the students. My expectations have never been as great as they are now. I enjoy teaching school a lot more now. I used to want out of special education in the worst possible way."

Over time, other teachers started appreciating the new methods espoused by Duckworth and Kentucky education reform. Like Fulkerson, they saw their students make leaps in achievement. And they realized that as professionals, they were gaining skills, too. "When I first started teaching, you taught from the textbook. The textbook companies told us what to do," Mattingly said. "It was quantity, not quality. It was easy. You read and answered questions at the end of the chapter. If you tested kids and they failed, big whoop. But it always bothered me."

The old teaching methods produced students who were robotic and passive, Mattingly thought. They didn't have to think very hard; they just had to learn how to please the teacher. "How many places do you know where twenty-five or thirty adults are in a classroom being quiet?" she asked. "How unrealistic is it for us to expect that from children when they're trying to learn? Before Mr. Duckworth came, there was a lot of talk and no action. As he stayed on and worked with us, all the talk became action. We learned together. We laughed and cried together. Like with his alcoholism, it made us stronger. It made us a special school."

But outside the Chandler community Duckworth didn't find much support. Other educators were reluctant to change their opinion of him, and they resented Chandler's growing reputation for innovation. Hamilton, who served on several school district committees, recalled "getting this look" of displeasure and eye-rolling when she suggested that others adopt some of Chandler's techniques. Mattingly was turned down when she applied for principal positions, rejections she and others believe had to do with her status as Duckworth's main assistant. Ray Roth recalled an elementary principal who urged him not to let Chandler be the first to try out a new counseling program the school district was testing because she didn't want Duckworth to get the credit. And when Duckworth made a presentation at a state education conference, he got only two negative written evaluations—from the Henderson County school leaders who were in the audience. "Why is *he* presenting?" one Henderson County principal sniped to a colleague.

Education reform was still viewed with suspicion by some Henderson County administrators. Although some school leaders actively supported change, others bided their time, secretly hoping this phase in education would fade away as so many previous initiatives already had. But Duckworth made this neutral position difficult. His activities at Chandler called attention to the apathy of his peers. They thought he constantly tooted his own horn, bragged about his staff, and publicly pointed out deficiencies at other schools. Duckworth's favorite outfit was a black dress shirt, black pants, black shoes, and a black and silver tie. He needed only a holster and a Stetson to make the outlaw image complete.

"Johnny has offended a lot of people over the years," said William "Ruie" Murphy, assistant superintendent in charge of school district operations. "He always seems to take two steps forward and one step backward. He'll be in a meeting and working well with people and then he comes up with something off the wall that reminds everyone about something he did in the past. And then they're all teed off again. He never gets the fire put out. He gets the flames lower and then the ashes pop up."

Resentment festered among Duckworth's administrative colleagues. Some of them had known him since elementary school and had watched him repeatedly bully his way into positions of power. When they looked at Duckworth now they saw an egomaniac, not someone whose bravado covered up his shame. They could not see past the messenger to the message.

So, instead of following Duckworth's lead, some circled their wagons and left their colleague out in the cold. If Johnny Duckworth was going to succeed with school reform, he was going to do it without help.

Chapter Three

A New School Year, the Same Old Excuses

This was my nineteenth year as a superintendent and, without question, my most difficult, frustrating, and crazy year. I don't feel like I ever worked any harder and . . . felt like I had accomplished less. But I have now come to realize that what we are seeing is the natural 'roll out' of restructuring our system as an empowered organization. We are in the midst of radically changing the culture of our organization. And it is tough, tough, tough!!!

It is also important to recognize that we are doing this in the context of a bizarre and hostile national climate. Public schools, public organizations, and all public officials are under attack like no time in our past. There is frustration over our economy and over the changing face of the workplace. There is real fear over the violence and moral decline in this country. Schools are a convenient scapegoat and target for placing the blame for our country's woes. Certainly, we have to accept our share and look at what we need to do differently. But, as we all know, the problems go deeper than our schools. Knowing these things doesn't change anything, but it does help us keep things in perspective and begin to understand what we need to do. We must get smarter and think and act strategically or we will fall victim to these things which are out of our control (Ecton 1994).

It was a Friday night in September 1994 when the members of the superintendent's advisory group gathered for the first time. They traveled the 150 miles, from Henderson to Louisville, giving up their weekend because the boss was upset and he needed their help.

Now Gayle Ecton, age fifty-three, head of the Henderson County Public Schools for eight years, stood at a conference table in the offices of an educational consulting firm that assisted the school district.

"This is a hand-picked group," Ecton said to those assembled. "Any time we hand pick, we run the risk that people will get upset because they weren't invited. But I'm taking that risk. I can assure you that you're here tonight because we have a lot of faith and trust in you."

The chosen thirteen included a junior high school principal, three elementary school principals, a junior high school teacher, a school board member, an elementary school psychologist, a school custodian, several central office administrators and an assistant high school principal. The teacher and the custodian were the leaders of their respective labor bargaining units.

Ecton exchanged his usual coat and tie for a flannel shirt, khaki pants, and brown Rocksports. He looked more like a model in a Lands' End catalog than a superintendent in charge of 984 employees and a $37 million annual budget. He was frustrated. The Henderson school system was in the fourth year of the Kentucky Education Reform Act, yet the campaign for better schools had produced few of the changes its creators envisioned.

Ecton did not want to overlook the school district's achievements. State and national education leaders considered the Henderson school system a reform leader. Henderson was one of the first districts in Kentucky to form councils of parents, teachers, and principals to run all of its schools. Indeed, it was one of the first school districts to try almost every feature of the state's model of school change, from primary school classrooms to high school restructuring. Fifteen of Henderson County's sixteen public schools expected to meet or exceed their two-year student achievement goals set by the state. As a district, Henderson County could boast about one of the best records in Kentucky.

But there were problems beneath the surface. Some administrators refused to share power with colleagues who wanted to try out new ideas. Teacher absences had risen to the highest level in years, primarily because of the stress of trying to incorporate so many new instructional changes. Parents complained they couldn't get consistent answers about what their children were learning—and why. As a result, in the 1993–1994 school year, 209 Henderson County students left for private and home schools, about ten times the number that left in 1991. The withdrawals meant the school system would lose about $600,000 in state aid based on student attendance.

To Ecton, the challenge was threefold: to implement the state-mandated changes quickly, to prove to parents that the reforms worked, and to give his staff time to adjust to new responsibilities.

He was most concerned about his top administrators. Despite having substantial professional training, some of them still seemed unsure about the mission of school reform. If school leaders were still so hazy about their objectives, there was no telling what teachers believed.

Month after month, Ecton watched as some county school administrators sat in meetings, nodded in agreement, then returned to their offices and ignored everything they had heard. Give the school staffs support, Ecton would preach. Involve more people in decisions. Quit intimidating people by looking over their shoulders and waiting for them to fail. Focus on the kids. If whatever you're working on does not help students learn, replace it with something that does. And then he would discover that an administrator had designed a new form to fill out or had made subordinates jump through more hoops.

These types of bureaucratic chokeholds made Ecton want to tear his hair out. As superintendent, *he* might have to comply with the ridiculous regulations fired off by the Kentucky Department of Education, but he would not repeat the process in each school. He had spent his career showing people how to focus on the big picture, a personalized form of management by objective—concentrate on your goals, show some results, but don't get bogged down in the details.

Ecton believed the foot-dragging was all about power. Those who had it did not want to give it up. There were two forces competing for control of the Henderson public schools: the reformers and the resisters. And then there were the fence-sitters, perhaps the biggest group, who waited to see which side blinked first.

"Last week, my frustration reached its highest level," Ecton told the group. "At the (bi-weekly) principals' meeting, when we tried to recap where we were. When I looked around the room, I saw people who looked like they were in pain, people who looked confused, like I was speaking a foreign language. And I thought, 'How many people still don't see the need for change?'"

Ecton wanted the advisory group to help him figure out how to put people on track. The participants talked about administrators who repeatedly stifled innovations by responding with "No," "Don't bother me," or "But we've always done it this way." They discussed the need to move beyond conventional school communications—newspaper supplements and notices sent home in students' folders—because they weren't reaching members of the public who had reservations about school reform. "I accept responsibility that somewhere along the line I have not explained or communicated this well enough," Ecton said, sighing.

Mike Waller, a school board member and factory manager from Henderson, said most of the resistance could be traced to confusion. It's not enough to have commitment from some school leaders, he said. Everyone needs to know what to do, and when.

"There is truly a lack of understanding out there (about KERA)—why it's being done, why it should be done, and why we should change," Waller said. "We've done a lot of communicating, but people aren't sure whether they're supposed to be playing shortstop or center field."

Group members acknowledged that parents still didn't understand the changes in classrooms. Johnny Duckworth described a meeting with a mother who wanted to remove her daughter from Chandler Elementary because she thought her daughter wasn't getting any math instruction. Duckworth observed the child's teacher and discovered she was using quilting patterns to teach six- and seven-year-olds about geometry and the historical uses of math. "I asked the children, 'Did you learn any math today?'" Duckworth said. "'Oh, no,' they said, 'We had fun. We didn't do math.'"

Meanwhile, Chandler's students "knocked the charts off" the math portion of the state test. "These kids are going home and Mom says, 'What did you do in math today?' And they say, 'Nothing,'" Duckworth said. "Parents can't understand that math can be fun."

Jackita Snelling, the school district's director of instruction, recalled meeting with parents who didn't want their child, a fourth-grader, to take the state test because the parents believed it focused on social values, not academics. "I sat down with all the [Kentucky education] goals and said, 'Are there any here you don't agree with?' They couldn't find any." The parents left without signing the paper excusing the child from participating.

Debbie Key, an exuberant Doris Day look-alike who was principal of South Heights Elementary School, was quiet during most of the discussion. Now she leaned forward on her elbows and spoke passionately. She reminded her colleagues that over the past year they had tossed around the problems confronting the school district at meeting after meeting. They had pointed enough accusing fingers, she said. They knew what needed to be done—each of them had to stop waiting for someone else to fix the problems. "We've always talked about involving parents and the public. But we've gotten so caught up in the routine of getting everything done," Key said. "We really do have a lot of committed people. If a small number of people can make a difference" by pulling their children out of public schools, "why can't a small number of people make a difference the other way?"

Duckworth nodded in agreement. "We have identified the problem," he said, paraphrasing Pogo, "and it is us."

Ecton looked around the table and made eye contact with each member of the group. From the waist up—the picture he presented to his colleagues—he seemed confident and serene. Underneath the table, however, his crossed right leg shook uncontrollably like a buoy caught in a wake. He kept a supply of Pepto Bismol in his car to control recurring stomach distress. He had hypertension and gallbladder trouble.

Ecton knew he had to make headway quickly with this group. If they could see solutions, they could lead their colleagues. "Let's get a plan to *do* something. Let's don't keep *talking* about it," he said. "If we can't agree as a group where we're going, I can forget about going ahead with other initiatives. I don't think we've got a prayer with the rest of the people."

He stopped talking and looked at his team, searching for some sign of recognition and support. He felt like a coach who had called a time out to ask his best players, already bruised, muddied, and tired, to ignore the heckling in the stands and press on. Defeat was as close as victory. And the clock was ticking.

That Gayle Ecton was feeling depressed about the pace of reform at the start of the 1994–1995 school year was cause for concern. As one of the state's leading proponents of school change, he was a barometer of success. For eight years, before the birth of Kentucky's education reform initiative, Ecton had tried to alert a complacent Henderson community that its school system was deficient—too many students left school unprepared to hold steady jobs, much less pursue college or careers. Teachers filled students' heads with facts instead of helping them understand what they had learned. The old methods of instruction might work for highly motivated students, but those methods missed an increasing number of students who felt alienated from school. Truthfully, Ecton didn't believe in the traditional ways of teaching that assumed students were empty-headed children whose job was to parrot adults, not to think on their own. Their expectations for all students were just too low. "I've told people, a lot of the things that we're doing with KERA we would have done anyway, should have done, would have wanted to do," he said. "People have all focused on the fact that we *had* to do all these things instead of what was good about them."

Because Ecton believed so strongly that Kentucky must raise its standards, he supported the state law that promised to do it. With encouragement from the five-member Henderson County Board of Education, Ecton led the school district to the front of every initiative on the crowded state reform lineup. Years before, Ecton had seriously considered a career change. The superintendent's job then was more about buses and buildings than leadership. KERA had rejuvenated him. "Now I'm back to the point where I feel like I'm finally utilizing the skills I was trained to use," he said. "I thrive on change, tough as it is. I enjoy the process and working on teams. More than that, I feel like we're making a difference. I think if people just don't give up on this we'll really show some great results."

Ecton served on every state committee that asked for his support. In 1992, he was named Superintendent of the Year by both the Kentucky School Boards Association and the Kentucky Congress of Parents and Teachers (Parent Teacher Association). In 1995, he was named Kentucky's top superintendent by the American Association of School Administrators. That same year, his colleagues around the state encouraged Ecton to apply to succeed Thomas Boysen as state Education Commissioner. But the Kentucky Board of Education signalled an early preference for hiring someone from outside the state, and Ecton wasn't really interested in the job. He would have had to live in a fishbowl, he said, his every action subject to public scrutiny even more so than in his current job.

John Carnes, an administrator with the Bullitt County Public Schools and Ecton's boyhood friend, said he couldn't count the times that mention of Ecton's name brought the same response from educators around the state: "He's the best superintendent in Kentucky."

Despite his support for education reform, however, Ecton had serious misgivings about the state's hurry-up timetable and its threat of sanctions for poor performers. In KERA, the state had obliterated a public education system that once operated like the military, with performance measured not by quality but by an individual's adherence to rules. Now Kentucky was emphasizing quality, but the bureaucrats still tried to enforce a complex set of regulations.

For years, Kentucky required teachers to spend a specified number of minutes per week on each academic subject and follow approved textbooks in lockstep. The state evaluated teachers' performance based on their ability to cover subjects, not on whether students learned the material. Now, almost overnight, Kentucky expected teachers to integrate several subjects into well-connected, thematic lessons rarely demonstrated in traditional textbooks. Teachers were encouraged to develop an individual education plan for each student that corresponded with a child's abilities and interests. No longer could teachers shoot straight down the middle of the class. Moreover, for the first time, teachers had to answer for how well their students performed on the state achievement test.

Some teachers embraced the new challenges. Others refused to do anything differently. All of them needed guidance during the transition. State curriculum specialists did what they could to help, but they were still trying to sort out the various requirements of the reform law at the same time teachers were putting them into practice. The resulting confusion threatened to poison the attitudes of everyone who was caught up in KERA, from the enthusiastic reformer who was tired of being out in front of such a risky venture to the frightened resister who never wanted to change.

In 1992, officials distributed a thick curriculum guide, called "Transformations," that listed the major goals of education reform, gave some general suggestions, and included sample classroom activities. "Transformations" was fairly comprehensive, but also dense and unwieldy. Teachers and principals received limited assistance in using it. "There was a deliberate attempt to not have the state Department of Education be in the business of prescribing what teachers should do in the classroom," said Jim Parks, the department's press secretary.

KERA assumed that children came to school with a mixed bag of skills and preparation. The state expected educators to sort out students' various needs and find ways to address them. But the law made no such allowances for the different talents and training of teachers. The failure to recognize and respond to these gaps of understanding would prove to be the most serious mistake of Kentucky's reforms.

State officials talked about relaxing restrictions, but they continued showering schools with regulatory paperwork. At the same time, they expected teachers to be creative. It was as if the state had chained teachers to empty desks, placed alarm clocks in front of them, and told them to write stunning new symphonies, without the help of instruments or assistants, by the time the bell sounded. At best, the composers' music would be conventional. At worst, they would give up. "Basically everything they did with the reform act ignored everything we know about the change process—people need to come along slowly," Ecton said. "It's almost as if we're driven by a panic mentality. I don't know that we'll make the best long-term decisions as a result."

Thomas Boysen, who served as Kentucky's Education Commissioner from 1991 to mid-1995, acknowledged that the magnitude of the changes and the tight time lines put everyone in education on edge. But he also believed the pressure—especially the controversial test that triggered rewards and sanctions for schools—produced progress much more quickly than voluntary compliance would have done.

"There needs to be a sense of urgency," Boysen said. "I think people don't get ready until they have to."

In response to concerns that the reform law asked teachers to do too much too soon, the legislature decided in 1994 to postpone the most severe sanctions for failure from 1995 to 1997. The practical effect of the decision was nil. Only one of the state's 1,247 schools met the criteria to be considered "in crisis" during the first biennium. Once a school earned this crisis label, an appointed "distinguished educator" started working with staff members and eventually would recommend whether to keep, fire, or reassign them. The appointed guardian's ruling was binding; the superintendent and school board had no appeal. During the first biennium, an additional one hundred schools fell short of their state-mandated goals by smaller margins. These schools also received help from a distinguished educator and had to write improvement plans. But the guardian could not require the staff to accept the changes; neither could the guardian fire them.

Ecton believed government deadlines had more to do with efficiency than effectiveness. He knew from experience the best way to get people to change was to explain the reasoning behind it, provide suggestions and on-going support, then get out of the way. When people have some control over their destinies, they will go to great lengths to do the right thing, he believed. Force them, and they will resist. Ecton was caught between the need to have his school district meet the state's timelines and the fear that in their haste, schools would botch well-regarded teaching methods and, in turn, give critics reason to discredit them.

Although he resented the fast pace of KERA, Ecton also thought the state's school reforms didn't go far enough to promote change. Kentucky's education reform law told a lot of different groups what to do, but not how they should work together. For example, the state gave the newly elected school councils the right to make curriculum and budget decisions, but said nothing about what to do when those choices ran counter to the interests of the school district as a whole. What should the superintendent and school board do when a school celebrates its good test scores by giving students a day off at the same time the public complained students already spent too few hours in the classroom? How should a school district respond when the state refuses to let classified employees, such as janitors and teachers' aides, serve as voting members of school councils even though they already served for years on Henderson County's councils? What should the superintendent and the school board do when a school schedules expensive field trips that some students can't afford at the same time the district was making every effort to ensure that all children receive equal opportunities? "It's like we've re-created the United States. We've got states' rights and then the need for central government," Ecton said. "The district has to have the same latitude as individual schools have." The state's interpretation of the law is "too arbitrary. It's too controlled."

Ecton believed in shared leadership, but he knew that technique required plenty of patience and finesse. He liked working with committees and delegating responsibility. He thought cooperation and consensus were essential to effective management. Yet, however sound these strategies are, people still need to practice them regularly. He thought KERA might have moved faster if everyone involved had taken a crash course in civics so they would understand how to participate fully in a democracy.

At first glance Ecton didn't seem like a man who willingly shared power. At five feet nine inches tall with a cleft chin, erect posture, and a haircut just a few snips away from a buzz, he still resembled the distinguished military graduate of his college Army ROTC program. He kept his trousers neatly pressed. His shoes were buffed to a shine. A diet and exercise plan within the past few months put him close to his old training weight. If not for strands of gray in his hair and worry lines around his eyes, the superintendent could have served as a model for military recruiters.

Ecton's managerial style had little in common with a boot camp drill sergeant, however. He didn't rule by intimidation. He rarely dictated. He never bullied or ridiculed his colleagues. He preferred to set personal standards for civility and integrity and lead others by example. "He's just not an ego man," said Scottie Long, principal of North Junior High School in Henderson. "There's nothing vengeful about him. When somebody does something wrong, he doesn't make a big issue out of it. He knows they know they screwed up."

Duckworth said there had been times when "a lot of us thought he should have gotten on people. But he doesn't. Sometimes he's sitting over there [in a meeting] and you can just tell that he's biting his tongue. But to build trust you have to be trusting, and he always trusts you to do the right thing. He's the best I ever saw at getting people to follow his lead. He'll be standing there dribbling the ball, and the next thing you know you're dribbling the ball, and you never even saw him make the pass."

Still, Ecton worried privately that his laid-back leadership style was not helping Henderson County meet KERA's relentless demands. If he followed his instinct to give people time to change gradually, they might not meet the short-term goals set by the state. Some of the confusion about the proper approach could be traced to the misinformation Ecton received from his subordinates. They were not always truthful about the pace of change in Henderson County. Ecton was so nice that people hated to let him down. They put him on a pedestal. And they told the superintendent what they thought he wanted to hear, whether they intended to follow through with his plans or not. "One of his problems is that he doesn't like to hurt anyone," said Assistant Superintendent Ruie Murphy. "He doesn't want to kick butt. Sometimes you have to."

What Ecton wanted from Henderson County—and what KERA also sought—was support for equity in education. He believed all children deserve a rigorous education. It wasn't good enough to sort them by their perceived abilities and give some algebra and others consumer math. Nor was it okay for a teacher to simply cover all the required lessons in a textbook and consider the school year a success. "We did a real number on people over the years," he said. "We taught kids all this *stuff,* but we didn't teach them how to use it."

Although KERA required schools to help all students meet higher academic standards, the public remained unconvinced that it was the right thing to do. In 1993, the Lexington marketing firm Roberts and Kay Incorporated asked focus groups in Kentucky about a key tenet of the reform law—that all children can learn at high levels—and found that most people believed some students were destined to fail. Educators were among the biggest skeptics. As one teacher told the researchers about her students, "I don't care if you had the best teacher in the world, they cannot all do algebra." Or as one school administrator said: "What's a high level for someone may not be for somebody else. I mean, there have got to be people to work at McDonald's, and if everybody is a genius, who is going to be the genius who is going to want to work at McDonald's?"

A 1994 survey by the Kentucky Institute for Education Research found that only 52 percent of principals, 35 percent of teachers, and 40 percent of the general public believed all children can learn "at a relatively high level." The percentage of principals and teachers who believed the state should set high standards of achievement for all children was even lower.

Such comments and beliefs made Ecton realize how much he underestimated the challenge of reorganizing schools to move all children ahead. "It's not a real comfortable feeling for a lot of people," he said. "We've created a system of 'haves' and 'have nots' in education, and now we're focusing on the ones who haven't been successful. The changes have been difficult for many people."

As a student in Kentucky's schools, Ecton was one of the "haves." Although he earned good grades, he knew his education was inadequate. The memory made him cringe to think of the meager diet served to those who fell below him in the academic pecking order.

Born in Winchester, Kentucky, in 1941, Ecton moved to Mt. Washington, a small town twenty miles south of Louisville, when his widowed mother married an agricultural and vocational education teacher who taught at the local high school. His mother worked as a bookkeeper at the Bullitt County Board of Education. In Mt. Washington, Ecton received straight A's in school without too much effort. Teachers labeled him "smart" and never made him work hard. Even as a teenager he knew that wasn't quite right.

John Carnes, Ecton's boyhood friend, said Ecton always stood out academically. He remembers him reading encyclopedias for fun in the fourth grade when other children still struggled to read their primers. As a boy, Ecton amused himself by reading textbooks in the school district offices while he waited for his mother to finish work. He played most major sports in high school—basketball was his favorite. He was a good athlete, although never a star, but he earned the respect of his teammates and coaches because of his strong work ethic. "He had the ability and the leadership to do anything," said Lloyd Mullins, Ecton's former basketball coach and later a superintendent in Spencer County, Kentucky. "He was an exceptional young man."

In 1959, Ecton graduated from Mt. Washington High School as senior class president and salutatorian. Then he went off to the University of Kentucky and promptly flunked algebra and chemistry. He did so poorly in most of his classes—he had been placed in advanced courses based on his high college entrance examination scores—that at the end of the first semester he posted a 1.1 grade-point average on a 4.0 scale. For a man accustomed to praise for academic achievement, the experience was devastating. By the time he graduated, Ecton had boosted his grade-point average to 3.0. But he would spend the rest of his life trying to avoid the stigma of more failure.

Ecton's small high school offered no foreign languages, no lab sciences, and algebra classes so poorly taught that Ecton asked a local pharmacist to tutor him after school. Although Ecton had several standout instructors, he also remembered being among a group of high school seniors who were "reamed out" by the principal because they asked too many questions in class; the teacher complained because she did not know all the answers. Ecton was bright, but he had been poorly prepared for higher education. He later earned a doctorate in educational administration from the University of Kentucky. He received accolades and awards as a soldier, a teacher, a coach, and an administrator. But Ecton never forgot the feeling that his public school education hadn't measured up. "I'm very sensitive about seeing that children get a good education," he said. "And that they have teachers who are well qualified in their fields."

He looked away and seemed transfixed by an unpleasant memory. Then he returned to the conversation. "I'm very sensitive to those issues," he repeated.

In his junior year at the University of Kentucky, Gayle married Barbara Collier. Barbara had graduated from a hospital nursing program and already worked full time. Gayle stayed in school for two years to finish a master's degree in secondary education. Then he spent two years in the Army (and later completed four years in the Army Reserve) to fulfill the requirements of his college ROTC scholarship. The Ectons' first child, Stacy, was born within a year of their marriage, and Scott and Susan followed in quick succession.

In the hubbub of college, new careers, and a rapidly growing family, Barbara didn't worry much that her husband always stayed so busy. Both were young and active, and they enjoyed being around other people. Her husband's compassion and his interest in public service had attracted her from the start. "He was honest and sincere, and he cared about people," she said. "That was evident when I met him." As they matured, however, Barbara would learn to resent the personal cost of her husband's humanitarian interests.

Gayle Ecton planned to earn a doctorate and teach at the college level, but a series of coaching and teaching jobs at junior and senior high schools linked his future to elementary and secondary education. From 1966 to 1970 he worked as a physical education teacher and assistant principal at The Lincoln School in Simpsonville, Kentucky, an experimental public boarding school for disadvantaged teenagers who were academically gifted. The Kentucky legislature appropriated $250,000 to start the school; Governor Edward T. "Ned" Breathitt later added $207,000 from his contingency fund. The backers hoped that, over time, The Lincoln School would attract more funds from foundations and private sources. Ecton wrote his doctoral dissertation about his experiences at the school, and the events he described parallel the current task of recreating Kentucky's beleaguered school system along more equitable lines.

During its first year, The Lincoln School served sixty-four adolescents who came from severely deprived backgrounds, including families with limited incomes, families with absent or poorly educated parents, and families who lived in substandard or crowded housing. The goal was to give these gifted students a public education as challenging as the programs offered at private college-prep schools, with time for independent study and opportunities to work with committed teachers beyond the classroom. Without the restraints of a typical public school calendar, The Lincoln School staff could schedule some courses, such as art and music, in the late afternoon and evening, keep class sizes to an average of twelve students per teacher, and let students progress at their own pace. "The awesomeness and the challenge of the task soon became apparent," Ecton wrote in his dissertation. "The teachers anticipated a group of bright youngsters who would immediately become enthused with learning once the obstacles from their former environments were removed." It wasn't that simple. Just as Kentucky's teachers and students had to reach for higher academic standards in the advent of education reform, The Lincoln School's students had to learn how to learn. The legacy of low expectations kept both teachers and students behind.

"Upon entering [The] Lincoln School as ninth- or tenth-graders, most students are undermotivated or indifferent to learning. They do not know how to study or how to organize their work," one observer wrote. "They are very much oriented toward short-range goals. There is a great deal of irregularity in the academic and intellectual profiles of most students. They tend to show a desire for concrete, rather than abstract, learning experiences, and teachers view this as more of a habit than an inability. Probably no more than 10 to 15 percent of the students in an entering class are motivated learners with stable interest patterns, planned general life goals, and positive ideas concerning the long-range advantages of education" (Tisdall 1968).

The Lincoln School's staff disagreed about the best way to reach these struggling students. Some advocated few restrictions, arguing that disadvantaged children needed to be free to develop their capabilities. Others believed that such students must have a great deal of structure and direction. This philosophical split became more troublesome over time. Once they had freedom, students rebelled when the staff later tried to take it away. The proper structure of the school program "was to become a continuing point of debate throughout the three years of The Lincoln School's operation," Ecton wrote. "The entire time the school was in operation it was under close scrutiny."

For his part, Ecton passed inspection. Dr. Samuel Robinson, the principal, was so impressed by Ecton's diligence and his rapport with students that he promoted him to assistant principal in his second year at the school. Ecton was twenty-seven.

"He played a major role in bringing about the type of standards we wanted for our children," said Robinson, now president of the Lincoln Foundation in Louisville and a member of the state Board of Education. "He felt that young people could achieve given the right resources and creativity. I think he feels at home with disadvantaged children."

Many other people were not so enamored of The Lincoln School's students. Because some students were African-American, the hysteria of racism magnified the community's suspicions about the school. Critics resented giving these students preferential treatment with state tax dollars. "The crisis of education today concerns the masses, how to educate millions of children as well as possible without bankrupting the taxpayers," a local editorial writer argued. "It thus seems an ill-advised luxury, that, in the face of this increasingly critical problem, hundreds of acres of land and many well-equipped buildings could be given over to the education, at state and federal expense, of a relatively few hand-picked students by a highly-trained faculty. All that money and high-powered faculty for the new Lincoln School while just a few miles away our city and county school administrators struggle with the tortuous problems of not enough money, too few teachers, and not enough classrooms" (*The Shelby Sentinel* 1967).

Like KERA, The Lincoln School also represented a radical departure from traditional thinking about education, which made it difficult to attract followers. Only two other programs in the country were similar to the one offered at Lincoln, and these operated only during the summer. The Lincoln School attracted a great deal of national attention but inspired little local support. "State schools for the handicapped are one thing. But a state school for the gifted is quite another," the *Christian Science Monitor* intoned on May 7, 1968. "And Kentucky, unused to acclaim as a leader in education, is pioneering an idea which may set a pattern for the rest of the United States." The assessment sounded strangely similar to remarks made in early stories about KERA. It seemed that anytime anyone linked "educational innovation" and "Kentucky," national pundits couldn't wait to reflect on the paradox.

Ultimately, the legislature not only removed the proposed $1.7 million biennial appropriation for the school but also repealed the law that created it, which eliminated the possibility that private funders would continue the program. On May 31, 1970, The Lincoln School graduated its first and last class, shutting down after just three years.

Ecton became an assistant principal, a principal, and then a superintendent in several Kentucky school districts. But his experiences at The Lincoln School taught him a great deal about the reluctance of the privileged to share with the deprived and about the deep suspicions many Kentuckians have for educational innovation.

From 1970 through 1973 Ecton served as an assistant principal and a principal in two junior high schools in Louisville's inner city. He was one of several young administrators who sharpened skills under the direction of Superintendent Newman Walker, a Missouri native who already had demonstrated a flair for classroom change and shared leadership when he was superintendent of the Bowling Green, Kentucky, public schools.

As Ecton would years later, Walker coached his staff to solve problems together, sent them on weekend retreats, and exposed them to massive amounts of educational research and training. He then stepped back and let them do their jobs with minimal supervision.

Walker, now retired and living in Palo Alto, California, said he and others quickly recognized Ecton's leadership potential. In 1970, Ecton became assistant principal of DuValle Junior High School, a huge institutional-looking building located in one of Louisville's toughest and poorest neighborhoods. A year later, Ecton moved to the principal's job at nearby Woerner Junior High School, and several teachers from DuValle followed him. Ecton had just turned thirty.

In 1973, Ecton took a leave from his job to participate in a special doctoral program, "Developing Managers of Educational Change," that the Louisville school system organized with federal funds. The twenty-six participants could earn advanced degrees in educational administration from the University of Louisville or the University of Kentucky, and at the same time they could spend a considerable amount of time applying theory to practice during internships in the Louisville schools. The year-long program enabled Ecton to continue receiving three-fourths of his salary (tax free) while he completed the major requirements for the degree. He returned to Woerner for the 1974–1975 school year, eager to try out new skills.

Within several months, however, the Louisville school system was sucked into the maelstrom of a merger with the county system and a court-ordered desegragation plan that would splinter the community for years to come. Everything else, including education, seemed to take a back seat to the challenge of filling schools with the requisite number of black and white students. Gloomy about his prospects during the turmoil, Ecton began shopping for other jobs. A former professor at the University of Kentucky, who was on the search committee for a new superintendent in Owen County, Kentucky, encouraged Ecton to seek the position.

"To be honest," Ecton said, "I didn't have too many ideas what a superintendent did." Nevertheless, he got the job. At age thirty-four, he had the opportunity to push his leadership skills to a higher level. His apprenticeship was over.

Eleven years later, when he accepted the superintendent's job in Henderson County, Ecton discovered that many people in the community considered their schools superior to those in other parts of the state. Teachers had ample books and resources. The school board wasn't highly political. Many educated professionals sent their children to public schools, and they volunteered in them, too. Given the low standards in many Kentucky school districts, however, being better than most was hardly cause for celebration. And inside

Henderson County's school buildings, the educational experience was unequal for some children.

While many people in Henderson seemed content with the symbols of educational success—high average college-entrance exam scores, a fairly steady crop of National Merit scholars, and competitive athletic and band programs—statistics showed that for every Henderson resident who attended college, another hadn't made it through the twelfth grade. In the 1989–1990 school year, which preceded KERA, only 74 percent of the students who started ninth grade graduated from high school. The district's figure was slightly higher than the statewide rate of 67 percent.

Henderson's per-capita income of $15,623 was well below the national average of $17,592, but it exceeded the state average of $13,823, making it one of the wealthiest counties in Kentucky. Yet, while about one in seven white residents in Henderson lived below the poverty level, nearly two-thirds of black residents did.

Like relatives hiding family troubles, people in Henderson and throughout Kentucky kept pretending that no one knew their shameful secrets. They looked the other way, ignoring all the signs that the family foundation was crumbling from neglect. The strongest resisters of change included people who benefitted from the old system of education. This group included teachers and administrators who refused to try new strategies despite convincing evidence that their traditional methods hadn't helped all students learn.

Teachers and administrators were among the most highly educated people in every Kentucky community. However, having advanced degrees did not mean they were all qualified to teach rigorous academic courses. The preparation of teachers at the college and university level was built on the same mediocre foundation as the state's elementary and secondary system. In general, Kentucky expected little of teachers, so in turn they expected little of students. Many teachers did not understand the conditions that caused students to fail in traditional school settings. One of the ironies of KERA is that people who enjoyed school so much they decided to make a career of it were in charge of changing the very system that made them feel safe and valued. Furthermore, they had to make those changes in the name of students who traditionally had the least success in school, the students with whom they had the least in common. Not surprisingly, the motivation of these educators to make classrooms more inclusive, and their understanding about how to do so, were extremely low.

Jack Edwards, an associate with the Center for Leadership in School Reform, a Louisville consulting firm that worked extensively with Henderson County, said Ecton "spends a lot of time talking about" the need to help all students reach high standards. "But a high percentage of people do not get it and are not interested in getting it," Edwards said. "That's pretty typical of Kentucky. A whole lot of educators will say, 'Our job is to help kids realize their potential.' But they assume that something like an IQ test can determine that potential. They don't believe that all children can learn. The big question is: How does a school district build up enough momentum to overcome that (resistance)?"

High school educators, in particular, were cynical about school reform. In May 1994, when Ecton conducted a workshop about different ways to meet the various needs of students, he discovered that many Henderson County high school teachers weren't interested in changing their lessons. They expected students to adapt to them, not the other way around. Ecton later learned that some high school administrators, in the first years of the state's education reforms, actually encouraged troubled students to drop out and attend home schools in an attempt to boost the high school's overall test scores. "They had on a set of blinders that didn't look at the lowest half of kids," he said. "They didn't think it was their fault if some kids didn't learn," but they did accept the credit when other students succeeded.

Getting Henderson County High School unstuck was one of Ecton's greatest challenges in the early years of education reform. Although pockets of resistance existed throughout the school district, the high school employed the largest population of critics. If Ecton could persuade this group to change its habits, then others might fall in line. The high school staff's support of KERA was important for two major reasons. First, the high school students would be in college or the work force soon, giving the public an opportunity to inspect the quality of their education. The results, good or bad, would be attributed to the effects of KERA, even if their teachers hadn't given the school reforms a fair trial. Second, if high school teachers refused to adapt their practices, they could thwart progress students made in the early grades where KERA's push for more individualized instruction was starting to pay dividends.

Howard Crittenden, the long-time principal of Henderson County High School, acknowledged that he sulked for about a year after KERA was passed. In 1990, Crittenden was named state Principal of the Year by his peers, and he considered his school on top of progressive movements in education. He resented being "condemned unjustly" by the implication that nearly everything in Kentucky schools needed to be fixed. He also took offense at the legislature's decision to create layers and layers of demanding reforms without having had deep conversations with the teachers and administrators charged with making them succeed.

It took three years for the Henderson County High School staff to approve the election of a council of teachers and parents to run the school with the principal, as the state required all schools to do by 1996. The resolution passed by one vote. Although the vote was not late by the state's standards, the high school was the last school in Henderson County to come on board. A group of teachers already served on participatory management committees at the high school, and they did not like "outsiders" from the state telling them to change their setup.

"We thought we were doing a good job," said Crittenden, a rangy, silver-haired former basketball coach who spent thirty-six years in education, including a number of years heading one of the largest high schools in the state. "It hurts your self-esteem to be thought of as not skilled in your profession."

In 1992, when the state released the school's starting point for measuring all future changes in achievement—a figure, based on a hundred-point scale, that shows how far a school is from reaching the state standards—Henderson County High School topped off at 36.9, not exactly an A. More uncomfortable to a competitive person like Crittenden was the realization that Henderson County High scored lower than several schools in the region, schools the principal informally compared to his over the years.

Crittenden said he began to realize that his negative attitude had rubbed off on the staff, so he decided to stop complaining about education reform. Crittenden served on a state committee looking at ways to change secondary education and persuaded the staff to become one of twenty-seven Kentucky high schools that would try out the recommendations. This partly reflected his desire for self-preservation; if the school had to change, he wanted to at least have a voice in shaping it.

Many faculty members at the high school resisted the changes, however, and they made poor decisions that gave education reform a bad name. For example, Kentucky now required students to submit extensive writing portfolios as part of the new state tests in fourth, eighth, and twelfth grades. These essay collections included different forms of writing, such as narrative and persuasive papers, as well as examples from classes other than English. Ideally, teachers in every subject would assign a series of papers throughout the year; help students understand how to draft, edit, and revise their work; and then collaborate with English instructors to select the best entries. In most cases, students submitted their writing portfolios by mid-February so teachers could grade them and turn them over to the state in early spring.

However, in 1993, the first year of the new test cycle, the Henderson County High School staff did not follow the plan. Teachers outside the English department didn't think they should have to make students write in their classes. Instead of including the portfolio assignments as part of their regular course work, most teachers waited until January to request essays, forcing students to write and revise several papers simultaneously, in addition to completing their regular assignments. Then, a few weeks later, the same students had to complete the short-essay and problem-solving portions of the state test, a process that consumed several days. The stress at Henderson County High School was palpable, and KERA—not the teachers' rigidity—got the blame. Based on the students' poor performance on these assessments, the school's accountability score in the first year of the biennium dropped to 33.9. Henderson County High School was in danger of being declared "in crisis" by the state.

In addition to their distaste for portfolios, the high school teachers grumbled about a new school schedule that included longer class periods. Instead of guiding independent research projects, planning related lessons with other staff members, and giving students time to practice new skills, many teachers used the extra time to deliver longer lectures. Some teachers remembered the eighty-minute class periods they had been forced to adopt in Henderson County's junior high schools twenty years before, an experiment that failed because none of the teachers had been trained to do anything other than stand in front of a group of students and preach. KERA gave the staff similar opportunities to use a variety of teaching methods but also a similar lack of guidance about how to do so.

At Ecton's initiative, the Henderson County Board of Education agreed in 1994 to adjust the high school's schedule so teachers would have more time to plan lessons and meet with each other. Lengthening the school day by ten minutes enabled the staff to dismiss students early once every three weeks and use the two-and-one-half-hour block of time for staff training and planning. Ecton also urged Crittenden to focus more training on the specific skills teachers needed instead of letting them choose workshops and topics at random.

As he listened to Crittenden address the staff at a back-to-school faculty meeting in 1994, Ecton acknowledged that the "dynamics of moving this size group" was an incredible challenge. Yet, while many teachers still resisted the changes, their opposition wasn't as vocal or intense as before. The slight improvement in their attitudes gave Ecton hope that school reform eventually would work at Henderson County High School. Progress was apparent—it just wasn't widespread.

"Teachers for years have complained that they wanted things to change. Now here's their opportunity to change, but they're backing off of it," explained David Ettensohn, an art teacher who became one of the leaders of the high school reorganization. "They want to be told what to do, but they don't want to be told what to do. It's human nature."

The state didn't help things, Ettensohn said. Instead of sending a team of experts to each school to help teachers through the transition, state leaders mailed a thick book of curriculum goals with very few directions. The book bulged with reformers' jargon, terms such as "rubric" and "culminating events," that teachers didn't understand.

Nevertheless, Ettensohn, a thirty-one-year teaching veteran, said he felt renewed by the suggested teaching strategies. Although some of his colleagues balked at having their students write portfolio entries in classes other than English, Ettensohn developed some intriguing assignments. For one assignment he asked his students to explain how they would create in pencil a "value scale"—the contrasts between light and dark shades—and explain how to use it in drawing composition. For another assignment he displayed pictures of famous artists and their works, then asked students to write fictional accounts of the artists' lives based on their interpretation of the art. His students also used computer programs to draw and to write about what people might see in outer space. "I think this is the best thing we ever did," Ettensohn said. "For years in art we didn't do much writing. Then in 1991, I served on the cluster team that graded the senior portfolios. I didn't realize how poor [student] writing had gotten. Their spelling had gotten pathetic. A lot of them couldn't formulate sentences. A couple I read rambled on and on without punctuation."

The writing portfolios tell students and parents much more about academic progress than a grade on a report card, Ettensohn said. He believed that requiring students to write more in every subject had improved their skills. But Ettensohn stopped short of agreeing with the reform law's premise that all children are capable of learning at high levels. "Our good students are far better than they've ever been," he said. "They're brilliant. The ones with the low IQs are having all the babies. The only way they can learn at high levels is if you put them on a high stool. They have limitations. It's wrong to hold teachers accountable for that."

Robert Lyons had a different view. In 1990, the same year the state's education reforms started, Crittenden hired Lyons right out of college to teach science and math at Henderson County High School. At the time, the school had only one physics class with ten students, all of them enrolled in the advanced placement program. By 1994, thanks to Lyons's reputation and recruiting, 280 students had enrolled in a total of eleven physics classes and only one class contained advanced placement students. By actively demystifying his favorite subject, this Pied Piper of physics had persuaded a large number of students that science was not just a subject for nerds.

Although Lyons had just graduated with a teaching degree from Murray State University, a few hours south of Henderson, he had little experience working outside the confines of a textbook. But the straight lecture approach didn't satisfy him. Lyons started reading about alternative instruction, attended conferences, and consulted other teachers. In 1990, he worked as an assistant at the Kentucky Governor's Scholar program, which brings the state's top high school students together at college campuses each summer for six weeks of intensive study. The instructors there favored group problem-solving, discussions, and projects.

"It really rejuvenated me," Lyons said. "I saw the potential."

In Henderson County, Lyons successfully lobbied for new science equipment because most of the school's supplies were thirty years old. He also set up the high school's first physics lab, believing that more hands-on experiments would help those students who learn best through visual instruction. He collaborated with an Algebra II teacher to coordinate lessons so students would understand the integration of math and science. Lyons also asked his students to keep journals, design projects, and write research papers defending scientific positions. One such assignment asked students to research

Congressional funding for space exploration and homeless shelters and debate the economic implications of both.

"Can all kids learn? Sure, if they're interested," Lyons said. "I believe they can all learn at a lot higher level than we give them credit for. I've never thought about physics being elitist. Everybody can do it." To persuade more teenagers to study science, Lyons considers it essential to show them the practical applications of their lessons. Apparently, the students agree. Jamie Courtney, a Henderson County High School student, said she decided to take an extra year of science—chemistry—because of her positive experiences in Lyons's physics class. "Most teachers don't show you how to do things. They just tell you," she said. "He does experiments. He has a toy collection and uses it to explain the principles of physics." A model train track with two cars simulates velocity and force. A baseball bat demonstrates impulse. A bowling ball and hooks hung by a cable in the ceiling explains the conservation of energy. Student Chris Wesner said Lyons's physics course is "one of the only classes I look forward to" (Holland 1995b).

Although Lyons and Ettensohn were far ahead of many of their colleagues in seizing the opportunities KERA presented for extended learning, the rest of the high school staff eventually stopped actively fighting change and began to participate more fully. In the fall of 1994, their efforts succeeded. The school's score on the state test soared from 33.9 to 50.1, earning the staff financial rewards for exceeding the school's two-year goal. Henderson County High School had rebounded in a big way. Crittenden paid for a full-page advertisement in the local newspaper to celebrate the triumph and held an assembly where the graduates received a standing ovation from other students and teachers. "We have come so far here in accepting the change," Crittenden said. "But we have so much more to do."

The drama unfolding at the high school was just one of many passion plays staged in the Henderson County school district during the 1994–1995 school year. For the superintendent it was a constant challenge to monitor each school's triumphs and tragedies and to understand how all these related to the school district as a whole. Like the harried director of a repertory company, Ecton had to repeatedly shift his attention from one group of actors to another, from one play to another.

To give order to the commotion, he began insisting on consistent behavior from the administrative team. The week after he met with the advisory group in Louisville, he called the entire central office staff together for a frank conversation. He told those assembled about the weekend meeting, identified the people who attended it, and explained why he had chosen them. The group was not exclusive, Ecton said. Anyone who wanted to be a leader in the school reform movement could join.

Ecton explained that as part of the follow-up to the Louisville meeting, each member of the advisory group had agreed to call ten parents a week during October and ask them what they thought the school system could do to improve the education of their children. "We need to get a better handle on the concerns and needs of our customers," he said. Secondly, Ecton said, the advisory group had identified staff behaviors that impeded progress—apathy and cynicism, duplicity and insensitivity. "These are behaviors we feel are tearing our family up and affecting our ability to work effectively together," Ecton said. "We love the people, but we don't like their behaviors."

The advisory group agreed they would no longer tolerate gossip, deception, or slacking off from colleagues. As a group they were committed to confronting conflict before it festered. Ecton put the entire staff on notice: it was time to shape up. "We've got to walk our talk," Ecton said. "You can either lead, follow, or get out of the way." From this day forward, he said, "We are going to hold people accountable for their actions."

Chapter Four

The Challenges of Change

Getting two dozen children to pay attention and learn for six hours every day took all the imagination, concentration, and planning Irmgard Williams could muster. Sometimes it also demanded courage. Good teachers like Williams made the work look like a cinch. But people who believed that anyone could do the job obviously had never tried to teach.

School reform seemed to make everything in education just a little bit harder. Nothing ever let up. All the new initiatives and requirements simply piled on top of old ones like the accumulation of household goods in an overcrowded closet.

After KERA, Williams found teaching had more highs and lows than usual. In the fall of 1994, there was the exhilaration of being named a semifinalist in the competition for Kentucky's Teacher of the Year. Then came the letdown of losing to a younger colleague, a woman from Elizabethtown. The euphoria of being set free to challenge students with thoughtful lessons that didn't need to come from a prescribed textbook was followed by the depressing knowledge that some of her colleagues at South Heights Elementary School couldn't make the switch. The excitement of being able to motivate students to solve problems that drew on their knowledge of many subjects was followed by deflating complaints from the public that teachers were ignoring the basics.

Often, her energy was drained by things unrelated to teaching. One day after Williams had returned to school following a family funeral in Cincinnati, she was accosted by a parent. "I'll get you!"

the mother shouted, marching down the hall toward Williams and spewing profanity that made the former pastor's wife cringe.

"Please don't curse in front of the children," Willliams said, embarrassed but still calm. She shooed her students into the library so she could deal with the enraged parent in the hallway.

"What in the world is going on?" Williams asked.

"You caused Derek to have chicken pox," the mother shouted, pointing her finger accusingly at her son's teacher. "You sat him next to a child with chicken pox."

Williams was too stunned to speak. She couldn't even laugh at the absurd situation. Teachers get blamed for everything else, she mused, why not infectious diseases? She sighed and tried to collect her thoughts. "I wasn't even here," Williams explained. "I've been out of town." Her high heels clicking as she walked briskly down the hall, Williams escorted the mother to the school office and let Debbie Key, the principal, take over. This was one battle Williams did not wish to fight.

The school day had barely begun, and she was exhausted. Most of the time, Williams dismissed her nagging fatigue as the result of menopause, the stress of caring for a husband with severe heart problems, and worry about her mother who had moved recently to a nursing home because of Alzheimer's disease. On days like this, however, Williams also had to acknowledge that school, her long-time refuge, was starting to wear her down. "You only have so many hours in the day," she said. Because of school reform, she already worked ten or more hours a day. And Williams noted, "then I come back a lot of nights. I finally get to the place where I can't come back at night. I do get burned out."

The reward for her efforts was more hard work. Often, administrators simply weren't aware of how much the increasing demands could negatively affect a teacher's performance. But their seeming indifference rankled Williams. She became frustrated at supervisors, including Ecton, who tried to motivate teachers to do more by preaching pithy phrases about education reform such as, "Don't work harder, work smarter."

"You *have* to work harder," Williams said, exasperated. "It's not just because of reform. We have so many more problems in children to combat. And yet, I still have an obligation to the best student in the class." She reflected for a moment about what she had said. Did it sound too harsh, she wondered, covering her mouth and grimacing. She didn't like to be confrontational. Like so many times before,

Williams vacillated between blaming the circumstances and blaming herself for the difficulty of change.

"Maybe I'm too serious," she said. "My husband always teases me, 'The school will close without you.'"

But rarely did it open without her. South Heights, a modern, one-story brick and concrete building, usually was dark from the outside when Williams pulled into the parking lot just before 6 A.M. She would leave the car near her classroom in the front of the building, then walk around to the rear and enter the kitchen where the cooks were preparing breakfast. After exchanging pleasantries with the women, she usually spent a few minutes striding along the school corridors for exercise. She then visited briefly with Sharon Stull, another primary team leader who also used the quiet time before school started to catch up on work.

On a cool, rainy Friday in mid-November, Williams entered her classroom about 6:10 A.M., flicked on the lights, and stashed her purse on the top shelf of a closet. She dropped both her book bag and assorted folders on the carpeted floor behind her desk.

Williams's classroom "office" consisted of a three sides of a square. Her desk served as one border, a large cart on wheels formed the middle edge, and a small table against a wall provided the third boundary. The fourth side was open to the students. The table contained assorted mementos and knickknacks, including a half dozen teacher's "apples" fashioned from pottery, wood, and glass; a small American flag stuck in a wooden base; several wooden plaques that students had given Williams over the years, and a worn, red Bible divided with a bookmark labeled with a child's printing—"To my teacher. Learning from you is lots of fun. Thanks for being such a great teacher. Heather Speaks. 6-10-93."

The rolling cart that represented one side of the "office" demonstrated Williams's organizational habits. It contained twenty-four identical, cream-colored plastic bins—stacked end to end on three shelves—with neat purple labels identifying the contents: "flash cards," "language arts," "math manipulatives," "team planning," and others. Bookcases full of first- and second-grade textbooks and three sets of encyclopedias lined the wall across from the rolling cart.

Williams had decorated the window in the back of the room with blue and white gingham curtains on which she had sewn gold stars. In front of the window stood a child-sized wooden locomotive next to a pedestal sign that said, "Successville Train—Arrival: 7:45 A.M. Departure: 2:30 P.M. Round trip only." Close to the train sat the

"Little Red Schoolhouse," a six-foot cardboard display filled with children's books. The only computer in the room rested on a table in the back corner near the restroom. In the front of the classroom, running the length of a wall-mounted green chalkboard, Williams had arranged the students' desks in four groups of six with paper flags identifying them as the East, West, North, or South teams.

After surveying the room and seeing that everything was shipshape, Williams turned her attention to the morning's tasks. She corrected some papers, walked to the office to make copies of a meeting agenda, and returned to her classroom to select books for a reading exercise later in the day.

At 7 A.M., William Whobrey, a seven-year-old student who has spina bifida, wheeled himself into the classroom and began lifting chairs from the table tops and putting them in place on the floor. "There's my muscle man," Williams said, greeting him with a smile.

She hurried out to the hall to begin supervising the arrival of other students. After escorting the children to the cafeteria for breakfast, she returned to the classroom with a cup of coffee and completed preparations for her team meeting later that morning. She scribbled in a notebook then furiously erased the writing. "Oops, wrong thing," Williams said, slapping her forehead with a manicured hand. "Where's my mind today?"

The exertion made her cheeks flush bright pink, a shade that nearly matched the lipstick she had carefully applied that morning. Her reddish brown hair, permed and styled in a middle-aged fluff, was the color of a fox's tail. Williams adjusted her oversized eyeglasses and scanned the memos and announcements that Key had passed on to team leaders at a recent meeting. Before education reform, this information almost always came directly from the principal at an all-faculty session. But now Key, like many Kentucky principals, delegated more responsibility to lead teachers. Williams viewed this as an important sign of the growing role of teachers in educational leadership, but on a personal level, it meant one more obligation during the school day. "It's harder now, maybe because it's newer," Williams said. "We're having to do so many things to get it together. It's like when you first start a new job."

At 7:35 A.M., Williams brought her students into the classroom from the hall where they had been sitting single file against the wall. "Give me five," she called out, holding her outstretched hand in the air. The students raised their hands in unison. They understood the five-finger signal for quiet.

One by one, Williams hugged her students before letting them into the room. After putting their backpacks and coats away, the children quietly lined up at the pencil sharpener. They knew without being reminded to get ready for the weekly spelling test. "Put your name on your paper and number your words," Williams instructed.

"Number one, *away*. We went *away* on a field trip," she said.

"Number two, *back*. We came *back* the same day."

"Number three, *be*. I want you to *be* a good speller."

"Number four, *because*. I want you to be a good speller *because* you can be a good writer."

A bell sounding over the intercom interrupted the test, and the students stood to recite the Pledge of Allegiance and sing a patriotic song. Williams led them in her choir-trained soprano: "We love our flag, the beautiful flag, the red, the white, and blue."

"Number five," Williams said, resuming the test. She called out a total of fifteen words, including several related to the upcoming Thanksgiving holiday—*Pilgrim*, *tribe*, and *feast*. She had tapped two sources, a basal reader and the monthly themes her primary team had adopted.

After she collected the papers, Williams took the students to the library for the start of a two-hour rotation of classes, including physical education, music, and computer technology, that would enable her team of primary teachers to get together for a planning meeting. Back in her room, Williams quickly corrected a few spelling tests. Then she scooped up a plastic tub full of papers and left for the meeting precisely at 8 A.M.

Team planning "is as taxing as teaching to me," she said as she walked out of the room. "I feel like I have to make everyone happy and please everyone."

Sitting on chairs designed for five-year-olds, members of the Super, Talented, and Responsible Students (STARS) team gathered around a table in the spacious kindergarten room at the end of the hall. Despite a state recommendation that kindergarten students be mixed together with older children in primary classrooms, the STARS team chose to keep the five-year-olds separate for most of the school day. Initially, the teachers placed five-year-olds and six-year-olds together, but later agreed that this was an imperfect arrangement. They considered it too difficult to include the youngest students in the full primary program because they attended school only half a day, typically lacked academic skills, and had shorter attention spans than the older, more experienced kids. As the five-year-olds learned to read sentences and understand basic math computations, they joined the six- and seven-year-olds for longer intervals.

Williams passed out copies of the agenda that included hand-written items listed under typewritten subject headings. Even where she had written notes in the margins, her penmanship was as precise as the letters on the green and white cursive writing charts that elementary school teachers staple to bulletin boards all over the country.

At 8:15 A.M., two of the ten teachers and aides were still missing, but Williams, irritated by their tardiness, decided not to wait any longer. From a plastic tub, she pulled out a glass container shaped like an apple that she had filled with candy corn. She told her colleagues about a Thanksgiving tradition in which members of her family gave candy to one another and shared something special about the person next to them.

"I want to tell you something good about you," Williams said, turning to Laura Courtney, a primary teacher and long-time member of the South Heights staff. "Laura, I appreciate your perseverance throughout the year. You've hung in there."

Courtney thanked her, popped the candy corn in her mouth, and turned to Diane Holmes, a special education teacher. "Diane keeps my blood pressure low," said Courtney, nervously pulling her long, brown hair into a hand-held ponytail. "Sometimes I get so mad at the kids and want to boil, and I look at her and we just laugh. Well, I could go on and on."

One by one, they passed around candy and compliments, some women choking with emotion when it came their turn to speak. As the last person in the exercise, Jeannette Banken turned to Williams. "My dreams came true after two years of teaching at South Junior High in the basement in the welding room under the gym," said Banken, a teacher who speaks with a soft Texas drawl. "I have followed Irmgard into the primary program. We've shared some good times together. She's special among our team. We're a team that's had silly times and serious times. I'm going to have surgery later this year. I'm going to need some prayers and somebody to lean on."

"We really do need each other," Williams said, smiling at her colleague. "KERA can't work without it."

Williams had used similar trust-building activities at nearly every team meeting during the past three months, hoping to reduce some of the staff's stress. The team members shared their "favorite teacher" stories, recalled the greatest "gifts" from students, and talked about their reasons for choosing a career in education.

"I think it's better to clean the heart and soul," Williams said, "then get down to work."

Key said Williams had been particularly good at building collegiality and trust among the staff, something Key believed must occur before reluctant reformers would move forward with change. Key recalled one teacher who had considered becoming a reading specialist but later changed her mind because she didn't want to leave the STARS team. "Irmgard has done that," Key said. "She knew they needed to come together."

During this week's team meeting, the teachers discussed their plans for December—lessons about holiday traditions practiced around the world, final projects for a unit on American Indians, and an ecology fair. They talked about possible rewards for students who had demonstrated good achievement and attendance.

"Okay, about the multicultural Christmas, several of you talked about your ideas for doing it," Williams said. "Rather than just taking a country, let's work on customs and research them. Remember, we said we were going to decorate trees in the hall. The other thing we talked about was what kind of projects [the students] could work on with their families."

The teachers became animated as they shared ideas for involving parents in the lessons about multicultural holiday traditions. They talked about the team's recent field trip to Evansville to view a display of multicultural holiday decorations. Although the city is located just across the Ohio River from Henderson, many students had never visited Evansville, or the bridge that connected the two cities or, for that matter, the river.

"Okay, January plans," Williams announced. "Native American Indians and the Alaskan heritage. We want to extend that to January. Is that okay? Or, how else do you want to do that?"

"We did this last year at another school," said teacher Dolores Todd.

"Do you know of any resources?" Williams asked.

When she didn't get much feedback from her colleagues, Williams moved on to the other items on the agenda: computer software purchases, an upcoming bus safety program, and storage space for new science kits.

In her classroom after the team meeting, Williams said she was pleased with the spirit of cooperation at the meeting but disappointed with some of the content. It was difficult to plan theme-based lessons for the team when some teachers couldn't get organized enough to share the load. She had tried to delegate more responsibility for tracking down speakers and finding other resources. But frequently, her colleagues waited until it was too late.

Williams hesitated to be more demanding because she believed each teacher should decide how to best implement KERA's mandates. Yet, she was concerned that some colleagues seemed more interested in using "cutesy" activities mass-produced from a workbook than taking the time to develop challenging academic lessons. From her perspective, other teachers relied too much on dull ditto sheets and unimaginative textbook exercises to keep students under control instead of encouraging a sense of discovery and allowing children to solve problems in groups. At a staff training session the day before school started in August, Williams told her colleagues that the primary school curriculum should be laid out like the pattern pieces of the dresses she once made with her mother—everything should fit together. "Sometimes it's difficult for teachers to find the time to tie it all together," she said. "I don't think they're negative. They're just struggling."

All things considered, Williams thought the school year was progressing well. Her colleagues seemed to have better attitudes than last year about teaching in the new primary school setup, whether or not they understood all that it entailed. After four years of almost non-stop changes forced by the state, teachers finally had the chance to practice some of what they had learned.

The teachers and aides also seemed more comfortable working together. One sign was the frequency with which the five primary teachers on the STARS team kept their classroom doors open. With only a few feet separating four of the five classrooms, it was easy to observe other teachers and students in action—a change Williams admitted she wasn't entirely comfortable with when the noise in other classrooms exceeded a level she considered appropriate.

Still, she was glad that most of the personality clashes and tensions from previous team meetings had begun to dissolve. The previous spring, for example, the team squabbled about how to spend a $2,400 annual allotment for books and supplies. Some wanted the money distributed equally to each teacher so she could make her own decisions in isolation as in years past. Williams suggested the team consider everyone's needs as part of the overall academic plan for the year, even if it meant an unequal distribution of funds. That led to arguments about which teacher had to contend with the most difficult students.

In August, Dolores Todd complained that she had more poor and unskilled students than any other teacher on the team. She joined the staff just before the start of the school year—transferring from a school that served a more affluent population than South Heights. Todd assumed that because she had not participated in the student assignment process, the other teachers had stuck her with the toughest group of children.

Initially, Todd took the problem to Key instead of consulting Williams, the team leader. It was a breach of protocol that caused some hurt feelings. Key told Todd to work out the problem with the team. After some discussions with her colleagues, Todd realized that because nearly three-fourths of the students at South Heights came from poor families, the chance that any teacher would get a group of students with learning disabilities and behavior problems was fairly high. Her colleagues had not hand-picked the brightest, most motivated students and given her what was left. Her students were typical of what South Heights had to offer.

Todd was grateful to be at South Heights and believed the early misunderstandings with her colleagues had been resolved. After working for twenty-one years at East Heights Elementary School, a run-in with a new principal caused her to transfer. Her experience at the former school made her a little defensive, she said.

Todd, a tall, robust woman with short black hair going gray, started crying as she described her affection for her new team members. "You don't know how happy I am. I tell my team members at least once a month how much they help me," she said. "Here I can work with KERA and feel good about it and what I'm doing with the children. It's the teamwork—we care for the children and for each other."

Most teachers weren't accustomed to working together on projects or consulting each other about lessons any more than they were used to letting their students move out of straight rows of desks. With KERA's emphasis on collaboration, the principal often played the peacekeeper's role. Instead of scheduling infrequent observations at approved times, principals under the reform plan were expected to drop by routinely to stay on top of each teacher's progress. All this new exposure heightened the anxiety of many teachers. They felt vulnerable and defensive.

It had been only a few years since Key led her own classroom, so she wasn't much of a threat. At forty-four, the trim, elegant woman with the soft, cheerful voice was much more likely to hug her teachers than to scold them. But she could be forceful when necessary. In September, Key intervened when some members of the STARS team complained that they, not the teachers on the school's other primary team, kept getting new students in their classrooms several weeks after the start of the term. Key, who considered the issue "a piddly little problem," wanted to turn it back to the teachers to settle. But she also realized that it was the kind of concern that could lead to more disputes if left unresolved.

Key was aware of the lingering perception that she favored the members of the Totally Outstanding, Awesome, Dynamic Students (TOADS) team. During the 1991–1992 school year, Key's second year in charge, three of those teachers—Sharon Stull, Carolin Abbott, and Nadine Harris—volunteered to be one of the first teams in the district to formally adopt the primary school model; a team from Chandler Elementary was the other. Although several teachers, including Williams, tried the new techniques on their own, the TOADS team members got a great deal of training and attention. They received a $4,000 grant from the state to buy new materials for their classrooms and to take students on special field trips. Reporters and researchers flocked to their classrooms for an early look at Kentucky's education experiment. *Education Week* included the team's experiences in a front-page article and in a 1993 book, *From Risk to Renewal*, which focused on school reform nationwide.

"In the very beginning of our program, just when we were beginning to wonder if large group multi-aging would really work for the children, we happened to notice their behavior on the playground one day," Stull wrote about the first year's experiment in the school district's 1992 annual report to the community. "The whole group of six-, seven-, eight- and nine-year-olds had gone to the playground for recess. Without adult organization and direction, we noticed the children had formed teams and were leading their own softball games. They had successfully organized themselves and had cooperated on their own to achieve a common goal. Sixes were playing next to eights and nines and were loving every minute of it. Primary school had given these children more choices, more freedom, and more responsibility than they perhaps ever had before."

Although the children blended without too much trouble, their teachers had a tougher time working together. In a situation that experts acknowledge is common around the country, teachers at South Heights and other Henderson County schools started resenting their pioneering colleagues for standing out from the crowd, just as some later became jealous when Williams was named a semifinalist for

Kentucky Teacher of the Year. Their envy occasionally spilled over into the classroom; some of the South Heights teachers initially refused to share lessons and strategies with each other.

"It was really difficult for everybody to celebrate success," Key said. "I would hear comments such as 'How did *you* get that [accolade]?' I think sometimes we showed that [jealousy] in front of the children. They can sense conflict." Key likened the experience to the first years of a marriage when one partner tries to adjust to the other's personality and eccentricities. The most difficult part of any relationship involves trust, a belief that being together is better than being alone.

Initially, Key let the teachers choose their own teams. Later she reduced the school's primary teams from three to two and put the groups together in one wing of the school so the teachers would have more opportunities to work together. The relationships improved—Stull and Williams, the team leaders, grew especially close—and Key didn't want to return to the tensions of days past.

So, when presented with the conflict about assigning new students, she called a meeting of the ten primary teachers on both teams and presented the facts about the school's enrollment: South Heights had a high transient rate; students moved in and out of school frequently during the year. Key assigned newcomers to the classrooms that had space. "I'll leave the numbers with you," Key said. "If you want to do something different, that's fine."

The teachers didn't make any changes.

Another time, Key pleaded with the staff to reduce the number of photocopies they made on the three office machines. The school's copying expenses far exceeded the budget—something that was true for the district as a whole. Key knew some of the increase was legitimate. Because they used textbooks less often now, teachers had to find and design more lessons on their own. Tailoring instruction to different groups of students also meant developing multiple assignments for the same lesson, and that required copying small batches, whether tests or homework. But Key thought some teachers still used traditional lessons and assignments under the guise of reform—too often the copy machine duplicated fill-in-the-blank exercises from workbooks and textbooks.

Key didn't object to the staff periodically using those popular tools of the trade. Like Williams, she believed teachers needed a mix of educational schemes—some new, some old—to reach every child. What worked well for one student might not suit another. Like any good coach, a teacher needed to consult a detailed playbook that included multiple offensive and defensive strategies. What worried Key were the teachers who insisted on running the same plays over and over, no matter what the scouting report said.

For example, primary teacher Jeannette Banken still relied almost exclusively on worksheets and textbooks. Binders and folders containing hundreds of mimeographed and photocopied exercises lined the shelves in her classroom. Next to each student's desk was a decorated metal canister containing worksheets past, present, and those yet to come. Although Banken had plenty of other strategies and supplies at her disposal—her classroom contained a computer station, a science center, and plenty of puzzles, games, and activity mats—she rarely used them.

A twenty-one-year veteran of the Henderson County school district, Banken said she tried to follow Williams's lead by adopting interdisciplinary lessons and group projects, but she fell back on old methods when the students became unruly. She said she liked KERA in theory but found it difficult in practice. Her students, mostly eight- and nine-year-olds, represented at least three ability levels on any given subject. In spelling, for example, she admitted that it was just "easier on the teacher if she can give one level of words." She got frustrated spending so much time with the few students who couldn't read when other students needed more challenging work. During one class, she worked with younger students who were learning how to put words in alphabetical order while a group of mostly older students worked at their desks—completing a unit on prefixes by filling in the answers on worksheets and copying and answering questions from their language arts textbook. "They should be more motivated," Banken said, motioning to the students. "I have computer and tape recorders and more things for them to use. But they don't seem very motivated to learn."

Banken served on a district-wide curriculum committee and was pushing for some uniform course of study for elementary schools. Without that, she feared children would leave the primary grades with such a mishmash of skills that teachers up the line wouldn't know where to begin.

"We need some kind of guide to go by," she said. "Nobody in the state seems to have that. I'm afraid our students are not learning their skills. Some of them are going to fourth grade without knowing their multiplication tables. In other ways, I think this is marvelous. We used to teach reading and push and push. This way, with whole language, we read a book about baking a cake, and then we bake the cake."

Banken thought there was too little flexibility within the team. She believed students should be moved around among the teachers depending on the child's skill level, but that rarely happened because Williams thought each teacher should be able to reach all the children in her care.

Key tried to find some middle ground with her staff. She offered suggestions for improvement, and she tried to sell them on new ideas while still allowing them to hold on to traditional methods they thought were effective with children. Under state law, she was supposed to formally evaluate new teachers every year, and evaluate those with at least four years of experience on a three-year cycle. KERA hadn't changed the procedure except to require principals to fill out a form indicating how many times a month they visited each classroom.

Key's observations revealed that some teachers couldn't get the hang of their new roles as classroom leaders who taught children *how* to learn, not just *what* to learn. Like travelers who were afraid of venturing anywhere without a tour guide, these staff members didn't trust themselves to deviate from their familiar scripts—typically well-worn textbooks that did everything for the teacher, from highlighting key words and phrases to suggesting questions for tests. "The fear—I think that's what Jeannette's talking about," Key said. "'I want to have my x's and o's so I know I'm doing right for the kids. It's easier with a textbook. It's easier to plan. You need to teach this and this and this in that order. Some people need that comfort."

Key recognized that people move at different speeds, and she tried to give them extra time and resources. But she also feared that unless she exerted more pressure, some teachers might never catch on. "Some sincerely *think* they've changed," she said. "With some, I think I'll be long gone before they've changed. I try to think about it in these terms: Are they still effective with kids? Sometimes they are, sometimes they aren't. I struggle with that a lot. Where are the kids going to be when they leave those classrooms?"

The route each teacher followed made the primary school experience different for nearly every child in Kentucky. Just as in years past, some lucky youngsters found themselves with teachers who made learning challenging and fun, while some had the misfortune of being assigned to instructors who were boring and lax. But where incompetence could hide behind a mandated textbook in the old educational system, it was thrust into the open under KERA.

Unfortunately, the education reform law was no better than the old system at removing bad teachers. In theory, school sanctions would become the stick that prodded people to either change or retire. But by threatening the entire staff when a school's test scores failed to improve over time—an option that was not carried out in the first five years of KERA—the law did nothing to distinguish one teacher from another. It tarred everyone with the same brush.

The staff at South Heights had not found a way to bring students up to speed. The school's test scores, lowest in the district in the 1991–1992 school year, had improved only marginally. Almost every other school in Henderson County was on target to earn financial rewards; South Heights was not. At an individual level, teachers didn't know if their techniques worked or had somehow contributed to the school's inability to earn cash rewards. Williams wanted to track her former students to see if she had prepared them well for the state's fourth-grade test, but because she only taught the children for two years or less, she was never really sure about her influence. Teachers in the upper grades told her that her former students were "such good writers." Williams didn't have much else to go on.

Teachers in the primary grades had to make more adjustments in the first few years of school reform than instructors at any other level in Kentucky, but their colleagues in the intermediate grades had the major responsibility for getting students ready for their first formal state evaluation. Many fourth-grade teachers focused on coaching students to write the essays for their state-required portfolios. These teachers also had to coach children to take the timed portions of the state's test. This section included responding to writing prompts; answering multiple-choice and short-essay questions; and solving problems in groups, after which the children had to write their responses individually. Primary teachers could make the whole process easier by introducing these concepts before students advanced to the fourth grade, but at many schools cooperation between primary and intermediate teachers was weak. The two groups tended to blame each other for any gap in a student's skills, instead of working together to fill it.

For the children, the transition between primary and intermediate grades was exacerbated by the difference in teaching styles between the two groups. In many cases, intermediate teachers reverted to more traditional practices such as requiring students to work independently at their desks and to write formal papers, a big adjustment for children accustomed to reading for pleasure on bean bag chairs and consulting their classmates about assignments. On the whole, intermediate teachers thought their colleagues in the primary grades were too soft on children and let them play in class instead of work. Primary teachers considered the intermediate instructors too rigid, as if the major focus of their school year was pushing children to grow up quickly.

At South Heights, Key tried to smooth the divisions between primary and intermediate grades by exposing each group to the other's responsibilities. She considered full knowledge of the state's objectives part of every teacher's homework. During the previous summer, committees representing teachers from several Henderson County elementary schools took the state's curriculum guidebook and broke down the academic expectations for fourth grade into skills that students should learn each year of primary school. To prepare for the writing portfolio, for example, the staff guide suggested that five-year-olds should be able to tell a story using pictures and words and that six-year-olds should be able to write complete sentences. By the time they were seven, students should be able to write a paragraph of five sentences, including a topic sentence; address an open-ended question with multiple parts, including restatement of the question in the answer; write a friendly letter; and write a brief description. In their last year of primary school, students should be able to refine all the previous tasks as well as write a paragraph defending a position, including examples and reasons, and write a personal narrative using two or three paragraphs.

Students in the last year of primary school were expected to know a range of math concepts, including numbers (place value through one thousand, multiplication and division, fractions, comparing and ordering, estimation, and addition and subtraction through one thousand); space and dimensionality (recognizing, drawing, and using several geometric figures); and measurement (standard and metric units of distance, capacity, weight, temperature, time, and money).

In all cases, basic skills were considered essential building blocks, but Kentucky wanted students to use those skills to solve complex problems, recognizing their relevance outside the classroom. For example, a science question on the state's fourth-grade test asked students to help the lunchroom staff plan nutritional meals for a hypothetical class field trip. In their answer, students would have to chart their food choices for each meal and explain their decisions. Answers considered at the "proficient," or passing, level would demonstrate the student's knowledge of all the food groups and an understanding of the importance of fats, proteins, and carbohydrates in a person's daily food intake. A "distinguished," or excellent, answer also would include clear explanations for the health concerns involved in choosing the foods listed for each meal.

From the start, Kentucky's youngest students received the most attention from education reformers. They realized that if the state's children were going to compete with students throughout the United States—indeed, the world—remediation had to happen at the start of their schooling, not the end. To boost each student's academic skills, Kentucky required teachers to incorporate seven major characteristics in primary classrooms, including lessons geared toward the developmental needs of each child and a method for mixing students of different ages and abilities. However, the law allowed schools to choose their own configurations—blending two, three, or four traditional grade levels in the same classroom, for example—and to decide how often to cluster children this way. The legislature amended the law in 1994 to make it clear that schools had a great deal of flexibility in grouping students. But the Kentucky Board of Elementary and Secondary Education said the amendment did not permit schools to abandon the new approach entirely.

Many teachers were confused about what was appropriate. In 1992, California researcher Jane L. David uncovered six different ways of grouping kindergarten students in primary school—"from ten minutes a week to every minute of every day of the week. Each person sharing her views vouched for their accuracy by citing an official of the Kentucky State Department of Education."

In 1995, researchers at the University of Kentucky found that just 8 percent of the state's elementary classrooms included students from three or four traditional grade levels throughout the school day and that 41 percent included two age groups for the entire school day—the two patterns most "compatible with the original recommendations of the planners of the primary program in Kentucky." Teachers most often grouped five-year-olds with one other traditional grade level—usually first-graders. But as with the STARS team at South Heights Elementary, about 20 percent of kindergarten classrooms were self-contained.

The Kentucky law required schools to let young children advance through the early elementary grades at their own pace, and not be held back or moved ahead simply because of their chronological ages. To gauge each student's progress, teachers were expected to use a variety of measurements, including work samples and classroom observations, not just grades on tests. The new objectives were based on sound research and practice in the field, but the methods were foreign to many teachers and parents who had learned in an entirely different environment.

"I really think we may have done an injustice the first year," said Sharon Stull, the leader of the TOADS primary team at South Heights. "We moved so fast. We took away all the structures parents knew. Suddenly they had no yardstick to gauge progress. If I hadn't been a teacher [in addition to being a parent], I probably would have been panicky. "That first year in [parent] conferences, I think parents thought I was really flying by the seat of my pants."

The state's deadlines rushed everyone. If legislators and state bureaucrats had listened more and dictated less, they would have found a population of teachers whose allegiance to education reform shifted almost daily, depending on their training, support, and success. As researchers noted in 1992, the groups included teachers who embraced the changes because they seemed similar to those adopted during the open-education movement of the late 1960s, and teachers who feared the changes for the same reason. Another group of teachers, "who for years have been celebrated as expert and excellent in their craft, held natural concerns about how their teaching might be re-evaluated under the new mandates. Others who felt successful in traditional schools were taking an 'if it ain't broke, don't fix it' attitude'" (Raths, Katz, and Fanning 1993, 27, 28, 30).

The philosophy of the primary school seemed reasonable to most teachers. It was the practice that stymied them. In the first five years, researchers found that most teachers had made only minor changes. These included giving students a variety of materials to help them understand basic skills, encouraging active exploration instead of making children sit with their feet planted on the floor while they filled in worksheets, and providing positive discipline that included frequent praise and rewards.

On the down side, many teachers did not use recommended practices in science, social studies, and art—those subjects got very little attention in the average classroom, as test scores revealed. Many teachers failed to recognize the various adaptations students might need to be successful—some children grasp meanings most clearly by seeing things in print, for example, while other children need oral or physical cues. Many primary classrooms also lacked well-developed lessons that integrated several subjects, such as the ecology lesson that Irmgard Williams had designed with links to science, social studies, English, art, and math. In addition, teachers rarely involved parents in significant classroom activities or consulted with other education specialists outside their teaching teams (Bridge 1994, ix).

Although teachers made a good-faith effort to develop effective primary classrooms, they tended to concentrate on one or two parts of the program instead of all. Researchers found that many teachers, like Jeannette Banken, slipped back into old habits after spending only a short time practicing new ones. In surveys, teachers—including those judged to be successful with primary school practices—said they needed much more training, time, and support to get it right. That Kentucky teachers were struggling with educational change was obvious. The challenge was figuring out how to help them.

"The reform has changed the ground rules," G. Williamson McDiarmid, co-director of the National Center for Research on Teacher Learning at Michigan State University, wrote in a 1994 report on KERA. "Many teachers prepared to teach at a time when teaching subject matter was viewed . . . as presenting information and procedures—usually set forth in textbooks, worksheets, workbooks, and on tests." That objective was no longer sufficient, he said. The aim of the reform was to help all children learn and apply knowledge in sophisticated ways—expectations once reserved only for the brightest students. "The experiences that most teachers had as students in school and college classrooms did not prepare them for this agenda," McDiarmid said.

The report recommended giving Kentucky teachers time to try out new ideas, assess the results, make adjustments, and assess progress again. Teachers needed opportunities to work with colleagues and to observe and demonstrate the best practices, the report said. Above all, teachers coping with a massive amount of change needed support, encouragement, and understanding from principals, parents, and the general public.

The Kentucky General Assembly disagreed. It moved up the required date for primary school implementation from the 1993–1994 school year to the 1992–1993 school year because of complaints from state leaders that teachers were progressing too slowly. Legislators did little to find out why foot-dragging had occurred and what might stop it, before turning up the speed.

"Some days I get so stressed out with all the things they expect," said Nadine Harris, a primary teacher and a member of the TOADS team. "You've got to fill out the list of homeless kids, do the fire [prevention] program and the drug [prevention] program, and the math-a-thon, on top of all the KERA responsibilities . . . I can't get to the bathroom until the end of the day. I'm so exhausted when I go home. Nobody understands. They say, 'Well, you just teach school.'"

Members of the TOADS team had repeatedly invited their state legislators to visit South Heights to see what the staff had accomplished. The teachers were not surprised that no elected official had bothered to show up, but they were enraged all the same. "We have to sell this program every day to everybody. I'm frankly tired of it," said Carolin Abbott, a twenty-year veteran of the Henderson County system. "You're in a group of people and the first question is: 'What do you think of primary school?' Well, I like it. It scares me to think it might change. This is good for kids."

For Abbott, primary school was about embracing "teachable moments" instead of following an inflexible schedule. A squat woman who favors dangly earrings, loose-fitting T-shirts, and multicolored socks, Abbott taught in a classroom resembling a circus tent. A menagerie of pets—including a rabbit, a guinea pig, and a cat—roamed the room. Colorful banners and awnings draped from the ceiling. Abbott arranged the students' desks in two semi-circles, parentheses that framed her desk in the center.

Abbott once followed textbook lessons page by page, but now she sought opportunities to connect assignments to the world outside the classroom. During a unit on nutrition and economics, for example, Abbott and her team members decided to put the students' pretend lessons to a test. The team asked groups of six- through nine-year-olds to write individual and group shopping lists, estimate their expenses, and plan budgets. Then the teachers took the students to a local discount store and a supermarket to find the items, count out enough play money to purchase them, and stay within the budget. On the way back to school from the field trip, teachers gave each child three dollars (of real money), took them to a McDonald's restaurant to buy lunch, then watched as the students debated the merits of paying nine cents more to get a toy instead of cookies with their Happy Meals. "I think we are finally teaching them to think," Abbott said. "One of the kids said, 'Hey, we don't do anything without a reason now, do we?'"

She recalled another youngster who brought a caterpillar to school one day to show the class. Abbott said she could have told the student to put the caterpillar away because she hadn't planned a science lesson that day, but she decided instead to cater to the children's curiosity. "The kids were so fired up," Abbott said. "We went to the cafeteria and library and researched that thing for an hour and a half. We observed it for days. We learned all about caterpillars and moths.

Later, when it developed into a cocoon, the child who had brought it to class went to consult with a junior high science teacher. It was the most wonderful unplanned lesson I ever did."

Another time, Janet Jones, a teacher on the TOADS team, turned a fiasco with Abbott's pet rabbit into a math lesson. The bunny, who roams freely throughout the classrooms of the team members, made a mess on Jones's floor. Instead of getting angry, Jones seized the moment, a dust pan, and a broom, and said to her five-year-old students: "Now, if I scoop up three bunny foo-foos and then five bunny foo-foos, how many is that?" The children shouted out the answer, "Eight."

Although she loved most of the changes resulting from school reform, Abbott spoke for many teachers when she said she had had enough. She wanted some time to reflect and refine, not tackle another new project or fill out one more new form.

Key sensed that the staff had reached the saturation point when she started having trouble getting teachers and parents to serve on school committees. She saw how quickly the staff dismissed a promising new anecdotal report card because each student's evaluation involved more than an hour of additional paperwork.

Always eager to be involved in a new project, Key wanted to write a grant to pay for a new reading lab that would train some of the teachers to better understand the needs of children with linguistic problems. She also hoped to join four other Henderson elementary schools participating in the Effective Schools movement, a national network of schools working to develop characteristics shown to help all students achieve academic success. But the teachers "were overwhelmed, and I backed off," Key said. "I can tell when my teachers have had too much. I switch back and forth from, 'Golly, we've come so far,' to 'Gee, we have so far to go.' Sometimes I still feel we're at a standstill, like we're at the edge and, you know, if you'd just go further, but you don't know how to get there. Maybe it's that we all need to adjust to the change. They've had all they can take for a while. You push and you push and you push. Maybe it's adjustment time. We need time to look at this and see if it's okay."

Laura Courtney was one teacher who was still sitting on the fence. An introverted woman who joined the South Heights staff after she graduated college twenty-six years earlier, Courtney had been unsure about primary school from the beginning. "It's been a challenge for me," she acknowledged. "I think it would have been different if I was [sic] a young teacher. This is the only school I've worked in. I don't like to make changes."

Courtney lacked confidence in her ability to succeed with an objective that had so few guidelines. She wanted a plan that would tell her how to move students from point A to point B, a checklist that would let her know when she had covered the necessary material. When she followed a textbook, Courtney knew what she was supposed to do. Someone more knowledgeable than she had decided what was important for students to know. It was her job to convey the lessons to them. She taught, and students listened.

But KERA was all about choices, for Courtney and her students. It suggested a frightening lack of control. She liked some of the suggested strategies such as cooperative learning groups and calendar-based math lessons. But she still was testing the waters; she was unsure about how far she could wade without sinking.

On her most courageous days, Courtney recognized that her attempts to use different activities with students stimulated them. Williams was her inspiration, she said, someone she could count on for encouragement and advice. She had listened as Williams extolled the benefits of moving away from a traditional curriculum that was as unyielding as concrete. "She's more of a leader type. I'm more of a follower type," Courtney said. "I'm glad she's next door so I can run over and ask things."

Williams gave generously to Courtney and any other colleague who dropped by her classroom several times each day to ask questions, borrow materials, and seek approval. She shared every important learning tool she could find. But truthfully, she was tired of the one-way flow of information. Williams would return from a workshop or a meeting, eager to share ideas and insights with other teachers, only to find that they were more interested in getting through another day than in having an intellectual discussion about education. They would accept anything she had to give, but most rarely passed anything back.

Perhaps they thought she didn't need any help. Williams was so efficient, so organized, so sure about her craft. She epitomized the kind of teacher most of her colleagues yearned to be. But for all her confidence, Williams often felt deficient. She knew she was a good teacher. It wasn't that. Her anxiety focused on her level of improvement. How far could she go? What more could she do? And who could show her how?

Despite all the new collaborations, the team meetings, and the new leadership opportunities, the frustrating thing about education reform was that teachers still spent most of the day alone with their students. Some people probably liked it that way, but not Williams. She would have preferred to work in a glass-enclosed room where experts could regularly observe her from the outside, then meet with her later to evaluate her progress. As a group, they would discuss what worked, what didn't, and why. Then, armed with that new information, Williams could go back the next day and practice.

Essentially, she wanted someone to model for her what she modeled for her students. Williams watched as her students exceeded her expectations, year after year. She was their coach, constantly moving the goal line just a little bit farther away from their reach. The children stumbled, but they kept getting back up and trying. Williams wanted a coach, too. She longed for a mentor who would cheer from the sidelines and give her pointers in the huddle. She wished someone would value her work enough to praise her, yes, but better yet, teach her how to move ahead.

Three decades in the classroom had made Williams a versatile, resourceful, and insightful teacher. But experience counted for little when it came to the emotional challenges of change.

Chapter Five

Jackpot

To get to Chandler Elementary School from the city of Henderson, you drive west on Green Street through the heart of town until the road narrows from four lanes to two and leaves the cluttered shopping strips behind. Small farms poke out of the horizon as the road meanders past Henderson Community College, climbs a steep hill, then drops down amid rolling pastures leading up to scattered country estates. Eight miles from the Henderson city limits, on the outskirts of Corydon (population 850), Chandler pops up on the right side of the road, the view partially obscured by a glade.

The school, a one-story, red brick building shaped like the letter H, sits at the top of a small knob. A plexiglass sign identifies the school. In front of the building is a circular driveway; in back a playground and woods. To the left of the school's driveway is another sign, an unobtrusive, rectangular piece of plywood attached to a stake stuck into the ground. Visitors to the school can see it only as they leave the property. "Duckworth Drive," it says, nothing more. The sign, a gift from the school council to Principal Johnny Duckworth, is as understated as its namesake is bold.

Johnny Duckworth built Chandler, a new school with an innovative mission led by a man desperate to make his own life new again. He put his professional reputation on the line by supporting changes that he believes will give him and the Chandler faculty a second chance at success. But similar to others trying to remake Kentucky's troubled public school system, Duckworth often finds it difficult to live down the past. "He's failed at a lot of things—his marriage, his relationships," said Ray Roth, the school psychologist. "This is something he doesn't want to fail at."

In January 1992, Duckworth got a chance to start over when the Henderson County school district replaced the aging, environmentally hazardous Corydon Elementary School with a new building in a new location. Officials decided to rename the school after Henderson's favorite son, the late A.B. "Happy" Chandler, the two-term governor and U.S. Senator who helped integrate Major League baseball when he served as its commissioner from 1945–1951.

The new school building sits on fifty-five acres deeded to the district through a trust. Duckworth saw the property as an opportunity to emphasize exploratory learning. He used a state grant to create an outdoor classroom near a pond. The grant enabled the school to build four tiers of wooden benches set into a hill overlooking the pond, an arrangement that resembles a small amphitheatre, and to erect two docks next to the pond. Students from Chandler and other schools gather at the outdoor classroom to learn about fish and wildlife.

With inspiration and guidance from Chandler's head custodian, Charles Meyer, Chandler's staff and students also cleared three hiking trails in the woods behind the school. Students researched dozens of plant and tree species, studied with state biologists and foresters, and uncovered a graveyard formerly used by slaves. Chandler's teachers and students routinely use the trails and pond to observe the change of seasons, measure plant growth, and study animal and insect habitats. "It's a whole lot easier when you're studying spiders to go out and actually see the webs," explained teacher Sharon Mattingly. "We've had major units out there—fossil digs, and a 'monster mania' where students had to research monster legends and movies. We've had math portfolio entries based on the graveyard—measuring the dimensions of tombstones and discussing the economics of their sizes. It's a living textbook out there."

Duckworth spends as much time as he can outdoors with student groups. He keeps sweat pants, T-shirts, and an old pair of sneakers in his office closet. Walking through the hallway one day in his outdoor gear, Duckworth took time to hug children and give them high-five handshakes. His banter was a mixture of cornpone and no-nonsense authority. "Trail guides, you are not talking today," he said to a noisy group of fifth-graders preparing to lead nature tours for other school groups. "Remember, knowledge comes to those who open their ears. Before you can *give* knowledge, you have to *have* knowledge."

He also offered a few tips about exploring in the woods. "Don't put any frogs in your pockets," he joked. "Also, we don't allow people to eat worms. But if you want to get your teacher to model some worm-eating, that's okay." The children squealed and groaned at the suggestion.

Chandler's outdoor classroom is a backdrop for the larger lessons the staff seeks to convey to the students on a daily basis: The world is theirs to explore. The school building is not the only place for learning. And no matter what their backgrounds, all of them can excel.

About 44 percent of Chandler's students come from poor families, a figure slightly higher than the district average. The school also contains a special program for elementary students from around the district who have severe emotional and behavior problems. In a typical year at Chandler, the staff will discover that about a dozen students have been physically or sexually abused outside of school. Children's vision, dental, and medical problems routinely go untreated in many of Chandler's families. There are no health care facilities within ten miles of the school. "People look at this pastoral setting and think that our children have no problems," Duckworth said. "It's hard being a kid today. It ain't no picnic."

He recalled the morning in mid-October when he tried to track down a child who was missing from school. The child's mother had moved to Corydon from Evansville to escape the child's father who beat the child and burned down the family's house. Now, Duckworth discovered, the police had arrested the mother on drug charges and the child had disappeared. Duckworth kept checking on the boy, shuddering at the thought of what the police might find.

At the beginning of each school year, Duckworth rides all the school buses home from Chandler to see where every student lives. He does it to show his interest in the children as individuals, but also to learn more about them. "I find out that no matter what kind of physical structure they come from they have pride in their homes," he said. "They only lose that pride when they compare themselves to others."

It was the same way in education. When the goal in Kentucky was to rank students along a bell-shaped curve, some inevitably fell to the bottom. Even if every child achieved the desired academic standard, the traditional sorting and grading procedures in schools ensured that some students would be labeled failures. Duckworth believed that KERA had improved that practice by trying to measure progress, not just average scores, on the state test. However, because Kentucky's test evaluated a different group of students each year, it couldn't determine with a great deal of accuracy what each child had learned over time.

But the major message of the state's reform law—that all students are capable of learning at higher levels—was one that Duckworth and his staff took to heart. Ever since the new school building opened, Duckworth asked students to repeat the school's goal when they recited the Pledge of Allegiance each morning: "The mission of Albert Benjamin Chandler Elementary School is to provide for each child an internationally superior education to ensure a lifetime of success within the home, school, and community." Teachers believed the persistent messages about high expectations had influenced students. Teachers noticed a profound shift of attitudes among the children, a new can-do spirit, a greater willingness to try. "Kids are beginning to realize we've got something different here," teacher Jane Esche said.

The impact of those differences was put to the test in the fall of 1993. A situation that initially shook the staff's confidence in education reform became a defining moment in Chandler's support for school change.

In October of that year, Duckworth and his staff received the results of the state test that Chandler's fourth-grade students took the previous spring. Most teachers were not particularly concerned about the scores. They had worked hard to prepare students throughout the year. They saw daily progress in student achievement and believed those gains would carry over.

Statewide, the results released in the fall of 1993 provided public schools the first indication of their progress under KERA. During the 1991–1992 school year, the state gave each school a baseline score that represented the starting point for measuring changes in achievement over the next twenty years. The state calculated the baseline by combining student scores on the first round of exams with statistics, such as attendance rates. Depending on how well students score on the test, which covers several subjects, they receive ratings of either "novice," "apprentice," "proficient," or "distinguished," the highest rating.

In 1991–1992, Chandler's baseline score was 32.5 on a 100 point scale—one hundred indicating the goal of having every student at the proficient level of learning. Based on its initial test results,

Chandler's two-year goal was 39.3. By October 1993, however, the marker had barely budged. When Duckworth opened the package of test materials from the state, the school's score seemed to leap off the page—a lowly 32.9, representing a gain of less than 1 percent. Chandler was closer to becoming a school "in crisis" than a model of education reform.

The school's reading scores showed the most improvement. A few students had moved up from the novice, or lowest category, to the apprentice level, and some had moved up from apprentice to proficient. But in math, science, and social studies, the scores were generally worse than before. "You talk about rocking our world," Duckworth said. "We weren't thinking about [a cash] reward at all. We were trying to stay out of the mud puddle."

Duckworth took the biggest gulp of humility. Much of his anxiety was bound up in ego. He had flaunted the school's success with education reform and urged others to follow Chandler's lead. He had forced his staff down the path to change, laggards beware. Now it seemed his brazenness had blown up in his face.

At a series of formal and informal staff meetings, each of them thick with tension, Duckworth and his staff looked for answers. They had passionate discussions about whether to resume using textbooks on a daily basis. They questioned whether the outdoor lessons in science and social studies had been rigorous enough. Should they place students in more ability groups? Were they teaching children enough basic skills?

"We had to decide quickly, would we go ahead, or do we need to shut this down and go back," Duckworth said. "It came down to whether we were going to walk our talk and keep on, or say this is all we can do and stop."

The teachers brooded. They believed they were doing so many things right. They had read all the educational research. They had completed all the training. They had investigated and practiced new techniques for challenging students to apply their knowledge of basic skills. Why were the test results so inconsistent with the staff's experiences and beliefs?

Primary teacher Vonnie Draper went home and cried for nights at a stretch. She kept asking herself why she had failed. Although she taught five- and six-year-olds at the time, Draper felt responsible for every student in the school, including the ones who left her classroom and moved up the pipeline to fourth grade.

Sharon Mattingly, who taught fourth- and fifth-graders, speculated that Chandler's baseline score might have been artificially high. Even before the state's education reform law required it, the staff had been teaching students how to respond to open-ended questions and to solve problems in groups. Perhaps the initial group of test-takers had performed too well. "We knew what we were doing was best for kids," Mattingly said. "That made it worse. It was not showing up in the results."

The staff complained about the validity of the test. It was too long, they said, and too narrow in scope. Some of the questions, such as the one that asked fourth-graders how they would look for a job, seemed inappropriate. Then the teachers started comparing the caliber of the two groups of fourth-grade students who had taken the test in different years. The first group—whose scores established the baseline—included a larger number of academically gifted students than was typical for Chandler. The second group included more students who had learning disabilities. In a small school, with only about twenty-five students taking the tests in a given year, a slight swing either way could make a huge difference.

Duckworth lay awake at night trying to figure out what to do. Some evenings he drove for hours along western Kentucky's back roads, mulling his options, feeling alternately remorseful and defensive. It was one of the most somber periods of his life. Finally, he decided on an approach. It seemed so obvious in retrospect that he wanted to kick himself for having overlooked it. He was so accustomed to feeling bad about everything that he had neglected to see the good news right in front of him.

At a faculty meeting, Duckworth tossed the test results on a table and stared at his staff. "Look at the tremendous job you did," he said emphatically. "You held your ground even though some people would say these kids are not capable."

He explained that the staff had taken students whose learning disabilities slowed their achievement and had helped them better the marks earned by the previous group—students whom other educators would have considered inherently superior. The staff believed in all the students, and the students had come through. Chandler hadn't posted much of a gain, Duckworth acknowledged that. But the school's score was higher than the year before, and there was still time to catch up.

The former coach likened it to the two halves of a football game. The final score mattered most. Unlike previous years, one set of marks did not make a school a failure. The state averaged the scores from two years of test results. If the Chandler teachers believed that what they were doing was best for children, then they must stay on course.

Duckworth said tests were important but frequently misused and misinterpreted. A personal example made the point clear. He recalled a boyhood friend who wanted to go to college and "hauled hay for two years to earn the money." Both Duckworth and his friend subsequently took a test to get an academic deferment from serving in the military during the Vietnam War. "He didn't pass, and six months later he was killed in the war," Duckworth said. "It changed my whole view on test-taking. That was the ultimate negative result of scoring poorly on a test."

Most tests merely fulfilled expectations, he said. If you considered some students incapable of learning, you could design a test to prove it. But if you believed all students could master material—allowing for the right kind of support and different ways of expressing their knowledge—you could create a test to prove that, too.

He recalled an American literature class he took in college. The professor told him he couldn't possibly succeed because he was on the college baseball team; no athlete had ever received a passing grade in the class. Defying the odds, Duckworth earned a B-plus. "My whole life has been based on people telling me I can't do things," he said. "In sports, I was too small. In education, they told me I was just a jock." Duckworth did his best to ignore the dismissive comments over the years, but he acknowledged that they stung. For much of his life he had carried a chip on his shoulder, always daring anyone to knock it off.

Chandler's teachers were surprised but also pleased by Duckworth's remarks. He had affirmed the value of their work. They *had* made a difference with their students. The important thing now was to analyze the test results so they could do an even better job.

Over the next few weeks, the staff started looking for clues by dissecting the scores, subject by subject and student by student. The analysis became the basis of the school's annual transformation plan, a two hundred-page compendium of goals and strategies required by the state. In reading, for example, the teachers determined that students needed more help understanding stories in context. In math, they needed to concentrate on space, dimensions, and measurement. In science, they needed to pay more attention to the solar system and biology. In social studies, they needed to understand more about the relationship between geography and human history.

The entire staff suggested lessons the primary teachers could use to prepare students for the fourth-grade test.

Two issues drove the staff's response. The first was a shared belief that children have very different ways of learning. Some have trouble understanding traditional academic lessons that favor students who are linguistically or mathematically inclined. The second issue concerned academic labels. If a student had significant learning disabilities, he or she could go through a battery of tests and receive federally required special education services. The child would receive an individual education plan and classroom adaptations as needed. But what about children whose difficulties in school were not severe enough to warrant special education services, yet still distracted them from learning? Shouldn't the classroom be adjusted to suit them, too?

Using multiple resources, Chandler's staff started compiling and using adapted lessons. For example, when teachers set up learning centers (activities at a variety of locations around the room that give students opportunities to explore topics in depth) they made sure to include materials that would stimulate all of the children's senses, not just sight. Teachers let some students turn in assignments on cassette tapes. Younger children who needed to touch and see things to aid learning wrote with shaving cream on their desks or shaped letters with Play-Doh.

Chandler's teachers demonstrated assignments for students, videotaped the children's attempts to repeat them, then used the tapes to help the children see both what had been accomplished and what areas still warranted improvement. In a few cases, the teachers learned that children had failed tests, not because they didn't know the material but because they couldn't focus their attention on more than one question at a time. So, the teachers intervened by standing next to the children during tests and repeating this phrase whenever the youngsters completed a problem: "Answer the next question."

"We made a variety of adaptations so they could be successful," Draper said. "Duck presented us with a lot of research and let us practice."

Chandler's staff focused most intently on the students who had started school with limited academic skills, typically children whose parents were poorly educated. The teachers wanted to motivate these children by challenging them and letting them taste success, not view them as helpless or incapable of assisting in their own learning. Chandler's school council (the elected group of teachers and parents that KERA created to run a school along with the principal) decided to trade a full-time teaching position for two full-time instructional assistants, recognizing that the staff needed more adult hands in the classrooms. The school council also found money in the budget to increase the number of hours a part-time special education teacher could work with regular classroom teachers to adapt their instruction for children with disabilities.

In the second semester of the 1993–1994 school year, Chandler's teachers felt confident and purposeful. They were tired, but also relieved. Students seemed ready for the next state test that spring. The staff had not retreated or yielded to despair. Instead, Chandler's faculty had pulled out all the stops. And yet, the same question lingered in everyone's mind—was it enough to raise the school's accountability score?

Chandler's experience with Kentucky's new assessment reveals the love-hate relationship that many people, locally and nationally, have with standardized tests. On one hand, the public believes schools should be accountable for making sure students learn required material. On the other hand, few people agree about the best way to measure that achievement. People who score well on one kind of test generally insist that everyone should take it, while those who have some difficulty with a particular test usually seek another avenue through which they might demonstrate their knowledge. In the last half of the twentieth century, this disagreement has caused policymakers to change standardized tests so many times that no one can say with any accuracy whether students today are learning more or less than previous generations.

"Good tests, which are reliable, fair, and legally defensible, are difficult and time-consuming to produce," Robert Sexton, executive director of the Prichard Committee for Academic Excellence, wrote in the group's newsletter, *Perspective*, in 1995. "Such standardized tests are also unpopular." In a 1990 poll, the Prichard Committee found that accountability was the most popular element of the entire education reform law. The same poll found that standardized tests were last on the list. At great taxpayer expense, Kentucky adopted and then threw out three multiple-choice tests between 1979 and 1989 because they indicated the state's children were above average and because parents said those particular tests didn't reveal enough about how their children were learning.

In 1993, the General Accounting Office found that schools in the United States were spending about $516 million a year for standardized tests, about $14 per pupil. From 1960 to 1989, sales of standardized tests doubled while enrollments increased only 15 percent.

"Much of the increase in testing is in response to a very legitimate demand on the part of parents and the public for a measurement of how schools are doing," Michael J. Feuer, director of the National Academy of Sciences' Board on Testing and Assessment, explained in a 1996 *Washington Post* article. "But the risk associated with all this testing is that it tends to become too much of a focal point. We have substantial evidence that too much reliance on testing for accountability can lead to inaccurate conclusions about student learning. It is not a rare occurrence to find test scores going up and erroneously infer from that that kids are learning more, when in fact they are just doing better on tests."

The Kentucky Education Reform Act rode the new wave in testing, one that hoped to address concerns that students had become slaves to multiple-choice exams. Studies showed that in trying to raise test scores, many teachers drilled students —particularly children from poor families—in these repetitive exercises to the exclusion of almost everything else. While teachers of advanced classes frequently supplemented textbook assignments with debates, complex research, and out-of-school explorations, teachers of remedial classes tended to drag students through the same sequence of fill-in-the-blank problems year after year.

Kentucky's new test—which included "performance-based" questions that asked students to solve problems in groups as they might later do in a business setting—was supposed to alter that practice. The shift in emphasis stemmed from the belief that the deepest layer of knowledge is the ability to demonstrate or use what is learned. Memorizing multiplication or periodic tables is the first step. Using that information to find solutions or conduct experiments is the next step. And moving beyond academic exercises to solve practical problems is the ultimate achievement. Students need to learn to work alone and with others to perform successfully in the modern era.

The popularity of these new demonstration questions increased rapidly in the early 1990s, but the public's understanding lagged far behind their use in schools. By the 1992–1993 school year, thirty-eight states evaluated student writing samples, seventeen used "performance events" and six required students to submit collections of their writing in addition to passing a series of multiple-choice exams.

Studies showed that in states such as Kentucky and Vermont (the two that deviated the most from traditional tests) the innovative techniques had improved instruction, particularly in reading and writing. But because of the frequent switching of state tests and the reluctance to track the same group of students over time, much of the achievement data was incomplete.

Another problem was the public's uneven support for national standards: states wanted to hold their students up as equal to any in the country, but resisted efforts to impose national benchmarks or graduation exams that would let them know if they were right. Impatience prevailed. By the middle part of the decade, many people were questioning whether the new type of tests had lived up to their hype. "There was an initial period of enormous enthusiasm which, in my judgment, was often unrealistic," said Daniel M. Koretz, a senior social scientist at the RAND Corporation. "And now people are going to have to start asking: Are we getting what we're paying for?" (Olson 1995).

Kentucky's new annual test—formally known as the Kentucky Instructional Results Information System (KIRIS)—was designed to demonstrate what students could do with basic skills. For example, one math problem asked eighth-graders to calculate the number of people getting on and off a train from Paducah, in western Kentucky, to Ashland, on the northeastern edge of the state. Given some information, students were supposed to develop an algebraic formula that would show all the values for the number of people arriving at the final destination, instead of just figuring out the answer. Under Kentucky's system, such open-response questions initially accounted for 80 percent of a student's score in most subjects and "performance-based" events counted for 20 percent. Portfolios, the collections of student essays, accounted for 100 percent of the writing score.

Multiple-choice tests, which ask students to choose the right answer from among several provided, generally are believed to measure understanding of a limited range of facts. Kentucky's education reformers sought to probe deeper. The theory got tripped up in practice, however. Teachers, students, and parents did not have enough training to help them understand, prepare for, or interpret the new tests. Another problem was the long lag time in reporting the KIRIS test results to schools—six months to a year compared to about six weeks for a national standardized test. The new test also cost more than the old ones ($50 million in the first five years, which represented about

$60 per student) because it required people to grade the results by hand. Commercially prepared standardized tests could be graded by machine for about one-tenth that amount.

Kentucky's new test was so different than anything on a national level that the public had no way of knowing how well the state's students stacked up against their peers around the country. In 1994, at the request of the Kentucky Department of Education, the American College Testing Research Division (ACT) compared the scores of Kentucky's high school seniors on both the state's assessment and the ACT's college-entrance exam. Although ACT officials found a "substantial overlap" in the scores, they also noted some disturbing inconsistencies. A fairly large number of students who scored in the bottom categories on Kentucky's exam scored in the top quartiles on the ACT exam, while a much smaller number of students who scored in the top categories on Kentucky's exam scored in the bottom quartiles on the ACT exam. State leaders couldn't explain the discrepancies, although they suggested that students who are good at answering multiple-choice questions, such as those found on the ACT exam, are not necessarily good at applying that knowledge, as Kentucky's test requires. Nevertheless, the study seemed to give credence to arguments from opponents that the state's test does not prepare students for the traditional, multiple-choice exams they must take to enter college.

Another indication of the state test's questionable reliability was the reading scores of Kentucky fourth-graders. On the National Assessment of Educational Progress, the only longitudinal measure of student achievement across the country, the reading scores of Kentucky fourth-graders remained flat at the same time the state test results showed large gains.

Furthermore, school districts that had supplemented Kentucky's mandated test with the Comprehensive Test of Basic Skills (CTBS)—a test designed to evaluate student progress against national averages—reported some flat or declining scores during the 1994–1995 school year. In response, state and local school officials said students no longer understood the multiple-choice format of the CTBS and had taken the test too early in the year to effectively measure achievement. But the results were misleading for another reason. When officials with the Kentucky Office of Educational Accountability, a state watchdog agency, examined the CTBS results, they discovered that only 8 of the 177 school districts had tested every student in both cycles. KERA had outlawed the routine practice of exempting the academically weakest students from the test, an exclusion that had inflated scores of many schools in previous years. Thus, there was no valid way to compare the pre-KERA and post-KERA CTBS scores. Even when the analysis was limited to the eight school districts that had included every student in both tests, the results were inconclusive: in half the districts the CTBS scores rose, but in the other half they declined.

The most damaging news about KIRIS, however, was released in mid-1995. A panel of national testing experts reviewed Kentucky's new assessment and called it "seriously flawed." Commissioned by the state legislature, the 272-page report said the test was not a valid measure of student achievement. "As a result of the serious measurement flaws, 1) the public is being misinformed about the extent to which student achievement has improved statewide," the report said. "And 2) the public is being misled by being given information about the accomplishments of individual students that may be inaccurate." The panelists revealed that scores on the open-response part of the test were being determined on the basis of only three questions per subject and grade, much too limited a sampling. The margin of error was so great that some schools were improperly classified in reward and sanctions categories—a common occurrence at small institutions such as Chandler Elementary. Such discrepancies undoubtedly accounted for some of the sharply different test scores from year to year at the same schools.

In addition, the report raised concerns that the scoring of writing portfolios was too subjective and "remains too flawed for use in a high-stakes system." In particular, the writing portfolio scores provided by teachers in the students' own schools appeared to be inflated. The panelists also complained that the test questions, especially those in science and social studies, didn't require students to demonstrate much knowledge of a subject to earn a good score. "It was almost as though the student did not have to attend science or social studies classes to be able to answer the questions," the report said. "Consider this eighth-grade item: 'Manifest Destiny was a belief in the mid-1800s that the United States was destined to extend its borders from the Atlantic to the Pacific. Discuss whether fulfillment of this belief was a success. Explain the effects that Manifest Destiny had on Native Americans at that time.' The report continued, "One panel member, dazzled by the words Manifest Destiny, concluded that this item clearly requires knowledge of social studies. Closer scrutiny shows that the concept was defined for the student and that the top two score categories did not require the student to know or discuss" the term.

The panelists made several recommendations to Kentucky policymakers, including removing the writing portfolio scores from the accountability index, adding multiple-choice questions to the test, and conducting regular audits of the test results because of the high stakes involved.

The report wounded state officials who had stuck their necks out to support the test against mounting opposition. Some agreed the report made valid points that must be addressed to gain the public's confidence. Others, such as Education Commissioner Thomas Boysen, argued that the panelists had judged a radically new test by traditional measures—a mismatch that was destined to bear bad news.

But while policymakers debated the merits of the test, teachers and principals had no choice but to keep trying to improve the scores at the schools where they worked. The controversy did nothing to relieve tensions or resolve doubts. Valid or not, the test remained the only public measure of success with students. For some, it became a whip; for others, it was a bouquet.

In late September 1994, schools around the state received a preliminary report about their progress on the state test. Although some data was still to be released, the bulk of the scores had been calculated and schools had a fairly accurate sense of where they stood. At Chandler Elementary, the news was all good. Students bettered the school's previous score by nearly sixteen points, jumping from 32.9 to 48.8. The two-year average of 40.9 exceeded the school's goal and was good enough for a cash reward.

By focusing on students who were performing at the lowest level, Chandler had moved a substantial percentage of children up the scale. In reading, science, and social studies fewer than one-fifth of Chandler's students were still in the "novice," or lowest, category. In social studies, one-fourth of the students moved into the top two levels, up from 7 percent in each of the previous two years. A student with severe learning disabilities earned a "distinguished" score in math. For the Chandler teachers, it seemed, the cash was in the bag.

In February 1995, state officials announced that about 13,500 teachers at 479 public schools would share $26 million in rewards. Officials said 50 percent of the state's public elementary schools, 25 percent of middle schools, and 12 percent of high schools were on the list—about one-third of all public schools in the state. In one of the most important signs of the education reform law's ability to reverse past financial inequities, school districts serving predominantly poor populations were just as likely to earn rewards as districts serving more affluent families (May 1995). Overall, the number of schools receiving bonuses proved greater than anticipated, meaning the pie would have to be sliced into smaller pieces. Chandler's cut was $26,000.

Although the checks would not arrive until April, schools had to decide by the end of February which staff members would share the cash. The law stated only that a majority of teachers at each school should decide how to split up the money, and state officials refused to issue clear directives.

Neal Kingston, an associate commissioner of education in charge of the state's testing program at the time, told *The Courier-Journal* in 1995 that he expected teachers "to deal with this professionally and celebrate their success together. You can't legislate every fine point in the law. You need to give people an opportunity to figure out what works best in their situation."

Others, such as Wayne Young, executive director of the Kentucky Association of School Administrators, were not as optimistic. These skeptics expected complaints from the community, perhaps even lawsuits, over decisions about spending the reward money.

"Money brings out the worst in people," Young told *The Courier-Journal* in 1995. "I've seen too many brothers and sisters fight over $1,000 of daddy's money. I don't see this as being any different. I think it's a recipe for some really distasteful things happening."

At Chandler, questions about what to do with the reward put the school's democratic principles to the test. The first item on the agenda was deciding who should vote. In a tense, three-hour meeting after school, Duckworth and the teachers hashed it out. Some teachers wondered why state officials wouldn't just tell them what to do. Duckworth reminded them that shared decision-making carries both opportunities and responsibilities. You couldn't accept one without the other.

Other teachers asked whether they should vote by secret ballot. The law was not clear on that point. Also, the group recognized that some teachers had moved on to other jobs, while new teachers had recently joined the staff. Which ones should be included in the vote? Mattingly said she was bothered that staff members such as teacher's aides weren't included in the closed meeting. Their exclusion seemed to discount the staff's efforts to think of everyone as part of the school team.

Her colleagues disagreed. At 6 P.M. the meeting broke up. The teachers decided that any teacher or administrator who worked at Chandler in the biennium and who was still with the Henderson County school system would help decide how to distribute the reward. Other staff members would be left out.

In April, when the check arrived from the state, the Chandler staff met for a second time. Present were fifteen current and former teachers. A few teachers who previously worked at the school sent informal proxies, saying they trusted the group to make a good decision.

Duckworth, whose vote was equal to the others, went around the room asking each person to express an opinion. Mattingly spoke first, pleading with her colleagues to be magnanimous. A compassionate teacher with a well-known soft spot for troubled kids, Mattingly argued that everyone who had some contact with Chandler students should get a share of the money. If staff members truly believed all the adults in the building were important to the school's success, then they must back up those views with action. "To have the school run well, every person in the building has to do a good job," she said. "We can't leave anyone out."

"That's very egalitarian," Draper said, not unkindly. "But the way the law was written, it was to reward good teaching and sanction those who weren't performing. If we were sanctioned, the teachers and Mr. Duck would be affected, not the custodians and bus drivers. We could lose our jobs. I think it's right to share with people because we're all in this together, but their stakes are not as high."

Draper struggled with what to do. As a member of the teacher's union, she knew she had a right to a share of the money. But she felt so uncomfortable voting to reward herself. No one had ever entrusted her with that kind of decision before. A passionate, kindhearted teacher, she had always been a person who gave more than she received. Only recently she had returned to school after recuperating from donating a kidney to her father. Other teachers teased her because she was so sensitive and was frequently moved to tears from empathizing with someone else's plight.

At first, Draper wanted to donate all the money to the school because teachers never had enough cash for supplies and field trips. Later, she changed her mind, believing the award was an acknowledgement of the service she and other teachers had performed in the name of reform. Although she didn't teach fourth grade during the biennium, she believed the fourth-grade teachers should get a bigger share of the money because they had prepared students for the test. The fourth-grade teachers declined. If the primary teachers had not worked so well with the children initially, the students never would have succeeded later on.

Steve Waller, a special education teacher, agreed with Draper that teachers should receive the largest share of the money because they had been on the firing line. Undaunted, Mattingly tried again. She acknowledged that teachers played the biggest role in Chandler's turnaround. But who could say which adult had helped a child score well on the test, she asked. For three years, nearly every adult in the school, including the secretary and the head custodian, had been paired with a child to serve as a writing portfolio coach. These buddies worked with children on their essays. They asked questions and clarified sentences. They provided feedback and encouragement. The reward money belonged to all of them.

"To be successful on the assessments, it takes a bus driver getting the children off to a good start, the cooks in the cafeteria smiling at them at lunch, and the work Vonnie did with them when they were five- and six-years old," Mattingly said.

The room fell silent. Some people held their heads in their hands. The stress was suffocating. Joyce Hamilton spoke up, saying she would rather not have any of the money if it was going to cause hurt feelings among the staff. They had worked too hard to build collegiality and trust.

Someone suggested that $5,000 of the money be set aside to start a college scholarship fund for Chandler's students, a recommendation the staff unanimously endorsed. Only $21,000 to go.

How would the community interpret their decision if they kept all the money for themselves, the teachers asked next. Duckworth told them not to worry about the public. Businesses frequently rewarded top performers with bonuses, he said. Teachers shouldn't be treated any differently.

After about an hour, the group reached a unanimous decision—to share the bonus with everyone who had helped Chandler earn the reward. To divide the money, they agreed to use a complicated mathematical formula Waller scribbled on a piece of paper. He based the formula on the number of hours each day that a staff member had worked with Chandler's students. He then factored in each person's years of experience and salary level. Those who were most involved in planning and teaching lessons, those who stood to lose the most if the school was sanctioned, received the largest share. Teachers got an average of $800 each. Duckworth's take was about $2,000. Smaller shares went to the bus drivers, cooks, and secretaries, and to the district specialists who occasionally worked at Chandler. Some of the amounts were negligible. For example, the district's gifted education teacher, who worked one day a week with Chandler's students in a special district-wide program, received 0.1 percent—about $130. But the money carried a message that each person counted at Chandler. Mattingly's bid had prevailed.

Duckworth sat back and beamed. He had never been so proud of the staff. They had affirmed his belief that talented educators working toward a common goal would collectively make better choices than any one person could. "Thank goodness there was this input," he said, laughing, "so the administrator didn't have to make this decision."

Most other schools in the state that received cash rewards handled the financial dilemma with similar aplomb. Like Chandler's staff, many teachers elected to distribute the money to everyone who had worked in the school during the two-year period, tailoring the amounts to the person's specific level of influence and experience. At one high school, teachers used the money to buy steak dinners for everyone on the staff and donated some funds to the eleventh-grade students whose test scores had earned the reward. At several schools, the staffs created scholarship funds for students.

Other staffs weren't as generous, however. State education officials reported that some teachers called the department's Frankfort office, asking if they could "blackball" colleagues who had stood in the way of change. In a few communities, school employees such as bus drivers and custodians publicly complained that they were entitled to some money. Several teachers and principals who had moved to other jobs filed lawsuits when their former colleagues voted to include only current teachers in the cash distribution (Harp 1995).

Many educators would have preferred to pass back to the state the responsibility for dividing up the money. They wondered whether the new emphasis on local control was really worth the hassle. In 1995, Wilkerson and Associates, Ltd., of Louisville asked Kentucky education groups whether they favored standard statewide guidelines for how the reward money should be spent: 65 percent of principals, 62 percent of school council parents, and 45 percent of teacher's said yes. Teachers were slightly more divided—45 percent said yes, 56 percent said no. And in a 1995 survey of seventy-four schools that received cash bonuses, the Kentucky Department of Education found that 32 percent wanted the state to regulate the distribution of funds and 19 percent wanted more guidelines for what to do.

In a 1995 interview with *The Courier-Journal*, Democratic State Senator Joe Meyer, the chairman of the Senate Education Committee, said he wasn't surprised that the first round of rewards produced some awkward moments. Kentucky was the first state in the country to link bonuses to a testing system that was part of a broader education reform initiative. It was a learning experience for teachers, an example of the responsibilities that typically accompanied independence. If teachers made poor choices about splitting up the pie, he said, it could hurt their ability to earn rewards in the next round. But that didn't mean they should "pitch the whole system."

Although they weren't able to link the reactions directly to the rewards, researchers found sharp differences between the attitudes of teachers who earned bonuses and teachers who did not. According to a 1996 study, P. Winograd, E. Anderman, and T. Bliss conducted for the Kentucky Institute for Education Research, teachers who received rewards were much more confident than teachers who did not about their ability to help even the most difficult students learn. By much greater margins, teachers who had not earned rewards believed some students would not succeed no matter what they did. Strong majorities of both groups agreed the rewards did not motivate them either to work harder or to become better teachers.

Back at Chandler, Duckworth and the staff sighed with relief and then got back to work. The faculty had endured its trial by fire and emerged barely singed, but there was little time to celebrate. By the time the staff members received the bonus checks for the previous year's state test results, the next round of exams was already in progress. Chandler's success was still being measured one report card at a time.

As Duckworth and the teachers went about their business, head custodian Charles Meyer stood back and marveled. He had such respect for the work ethic at the school. To Meyer, the staff's diligence provided one more example of Duckworth's "unique" and "farsighted" management. Under the principal's leadership, everyone focused on helping Chandler's students succeed. All the adults played important roles at the school. The shared reward money was a formal acknowledgement of that philosophy, but it wouldn't have made a difference to Meyer either way. He would continue offering support to the students and staff, no matter what.

Meyer had worked with Duckworth since 1986. During the past several years, Meyer's duties had included helping Chandler's students complete their writing portfolios. The mentoring role proved a comfortable fit for the sixty-one-year-old janitor with the bushy white hair and gruff manner every child in the school knew could be melted with a hug. From January through March each year, Meyer would meet one to three times a week with his fourth-grade buddy. Usually, he would escort the child to the cafeteria for a soft drink while they sat together and discussed the child's writing samples, taking turns reading the passages aloud. Meyer didn't like to immediately point out the child's errors. To help his buddy learn how to make independent discoveries, Meyer preferred to ask a few leading questions: a nudge toward more character development, a little encouragement to include additional examples, a suggestion about checking punctuation.

The more he got to know the children, the more Meyer learned to appreciate their talents. He recalled how one of his portfolio buddies, a little girl whom he initially considered rather dull, had dazzled him with her insights. These children held such promise, he thought.

Sometimes Meyer played dumb, telling his partners that if *he* could understand what they had written, then the essays would be clear to anyone. The children didn't know that Meyer had a degree in engineering and a successful career in business before he started working for the Henderson school district. His own children were grown, and Meyer was tired of traveling so often for business. He wanted to settle in his hometown and step off the corporate treadmill. It had been a smart decision. He loved his job at Chandler.

Being a custodian at the school wasn't just about emptying trash, sweeping hallways, and keeping the boiler in shape. Meyer's job was serving children. Like every other adult in the school building, he played a part in molding futures. Duckworth had helped him understand the importance of his assignment. "He is a leader," Meyer said, "not a boss."

Chapter Six

Democracy Is a Messy Business

Kenny Tegethoff kept trying to swallow his anger. An assistant superintendent in charge of transportation and school operations, Tegethoff did not attend Gayle Ecton's advisory group meeting in Louisville in late September, nor was he asked to go. But when Tegethoff and other uninvited administrators showed up at the follow-up staff meeting in Henderson—as requested—they received a tongue-lashing from the superintendent for impeding the school district's initiatives. Tegethoff still didn't understand what, if anything, he had done wrong. Ecton talked about back-stabbing and cynicism and people who were blocking change and all Tegethoff wanted to do was return to his job. What did any of this have to do with bus schedules and building maintenance?

Although Tegethoff enjoyed working for Ecton and was grateful he didn't try to micromanage the staff on a regular basis, Tegethoff agreed with others who thought the superintendent needed to get tough with some administrators, particularly principals who refused to follow rules. But this meeting showed Tegethoff that being an authoritarian manager wasn't Ecton's style. Tegethoff resented the "Hitler-type approach to discipline"; Ecton seemed to be tarring everyone with the same brush.

Some of Tegethoff's colleagues privately suggested that he was a major opponent of school reform, but in an interview Tegethoff refused to accept the rap. A short, ruddy-faced man built like a high school football tackle, he had spent twenty-eight years in the

Henderson school system as a teacher, coach, principal, and central office administrator. He acknowledged that KERA, like other major changes, had created factions within the school system. Tegethoff said he stayed above the fray by "trying to do what I thought was right. I have a philosophy that, if I'm not doing what I need to be doing, I need to hear that directly."

Bob Hall, the school district's mild-mannered finance director, also wasn't sure why Ecton was so annoyed. Hall did not attend the Louisville meeting either. He conceded Ecton's point about people who sabotaged progress by delaying approval of simple projects, ignoring mandates, and pushing more paperwork than was necessary. But Hall just couldn't get worked up about other people's problems.

Truthfully, Hall was bewildered by some of Ecton's recommendations. Although Hall tried to go along with the changes required by KERA, he really didn't understand why the initiatives should concern him. He wasn't involved in instruction. He sat in a windowless office and filled out financial reports, moving from one meticulous stack of papers to another. Hall's biggest headache came from having to revise the school district's budget every time the state issued a new revenue forecast—sometimes ten or more times in a single school year.

Hall thought he probably should do more personally to help the superintendent carry out his mission. But with retirement looming, he planned to continue ignoring, instead of confronting, the negative behavior of his colleagues. And as for his own adaptability, well, Hall figured his warranty had long since expired. "The older you get, the harder it is to change," he said.

Ruie Murphy thought Ecton had gone too far this time. During the past eight years, Murphy considered himself not only one of Ecton's chief lieutenants, but also the deckmate who kept the superintendent's sails from blowing the boat off course with his gusts of enthusiasm. Although Murphy acknowledged that some people considered him "a foot-dragger" on school reform, he thought he was just being pragmatic. "It's easier to go in there and tell him what he wants to hear," the assistant superintendent said, adding that some principals seemed to wait in line to second Ecton's suggestions. As a result, Murphy said, those who didn't speak up or those who disagreed with the superintendent were labeled wet blankets when all they were trying to do was size up the situation.

Although Murphy was about the same age as Ecton, he seemed older than his boss. Murphy's thick, coarse hair was as gray as steel. His meaty hands and snug sports jackets suggested a man who spent a lot of time sitting behind a desk, ordering others to action. Colleagues said they had revered Murphy when he was in his prime. Over the years, he had shown an uncanny ability to recommend the right person for a job, and he had worked hard to help people succeed. More recently, however, some of them thought he had lost his edge.

Murphy conceded that he wasn't easily swayed by arguments for change. After thirty years as a teacher, principal, and district administrator, he thought he knew a thing or two about education. Some of the old ways were worth preserving. His daughter taught at a local elementary school and his grandchild would be in the school system soon. He cared deeply about progress in education. But Murphy didn't want to jump on every new bandwagon. He thought school reform was just another trend that should slow down and take a good look at itself before moving on. "Do the changes benefit who they're supposed to—the children?" he asked. "I think we lose sight of that. I think many changes end up being adult-focused."

For example, Murphy thought Ecton had pushed schools to elect governing councils too soon. He suggested that the superintendent might have been more interested in being first than being best. As a result, the councils suffered serious growing pains. Council members, principals, and central office administrators weren't sure of their roles. Initially, the state suggested that the councils concentrate on instruction. But they quickly had to shift their focus to include budgets, long-term planning, and larger school district decisions. Meanwhile, administrators in the central office seemed to move in a dozen different directions simultaneously—advising the councils and responding to their varied agendas while trying to maintain some consistency in policy and purchasing decisions. In that kind of chaos, Murphy doubted that anyone routinely made the best choices for children.

Murphy recognized that much of his discomfort had to do with Ecton's laid-back leadership style. The previous superintendent was a hands-on administrator who wanted to be part of, if not make, most of the decisions in the school district. Ecton liked to delegate. He gave his employees the freedom to handle their own departments. Murphy wondered if the superintendent really understood the day-to-day operations of the school district. He judged him to be inexperienced in some matters—Ecton had jumped from the principal's chair to the superintendency without having held other positions in the central office. Murphy believed you had to work in a job before you could really appreciate its function in an organization.

Like some of his colleagues, Murphy also was tired, frankly, of having to attend a seemingly endless series of leadership training seminars and workshops about navigating the change process. Ecton put a lot of faith in the teachings of management consultants; Murphy thought most of them had made a financial killing by preaching common sense.

"If I'm uncomfortable with anything, I feel like we've reached a point where we've been exposed to a great deal of training...[but] we're not implementing enough," Murphy said. "We do not complete a task or bring closure before we go on to something else." He shared these thoughts with Ecton, who agreed things occasionally moved too fast in Henderson. But "the next thing you know," Murphy said, "we're off to something else."

Johnny Duckworth reacted to such second-guessing about Ecton's leadership by suggesting people were looking for a scapegoat. They were tired of the new demands on their time, they were indecisive, and they were angry. So they searched for someone to blame. Ecton was a convenient target.

"It was not his job to bring all these issues to closure. His job was to open doors," Duckworth said. "People won't say this, but what they really want is for someone to tell them what to do and when to do it and when to quit doing it."

When people implied that Ecton moved too fast, Duckworth interpreted it as an admission that *they* didn't know what to do next. The superintendent had stretched their comfort zones. "If you're striving for mediocrity, you need pragmatic people," Duckworth said. "But if you're in your car and you have to hit the brakes every mile, what kind of trip are you going to have? You'll blow out your engine and nobody will follow you. All you're doing is blocking the road."

Murphy had his own issues with Duckworth. He considered him a sycophant and an opportunist. Moreover, he thought Duckworth was wrong about the pace of change—education reform in Kentucky was moving at breakneck speed and heading toward a crash. That's one of the reasons Murphy disagreed with Ecton's decision to criticize those he deemed recalcitrant about school change. The whole chain of events in the past few weeks had been based on a misunderstanding, he said. Murphy recalled the earlier meeting where Ecton met with the school district's principals to discuss their progress on Henderson's reform agenda. The staff responded to the superintendent's speech with silent stares, which Ecton interpreted as signs of apathy and disagreement. Instead, Murphy believed people were genuinely confused about Ecton's message.

In Murphy's view, Ecton and Sue Williams (an assistant superintendent in charge of curriculum, staff development, and communications), seemed uncharacteristically disorganized during the meeting. Their discussion lacked focus. Later, when Ecton and Williams shared their frustration about the group's unresponsiveness, Murphy told them they were overreacting. He thought they had compounded the mistake by subsequently taking a select group of people to Louisville to discuss the district's problems. That meeting only widened the divisions among the staff. Resentment over Ecton's perceived display of favoritism festered after he accused the other staff members of resisting change. "It created a real cool atmosphere in the district for a while," Murphy said. "To me, he needed to bash sometimes, but this was not the time."

If it were possible to subtract the inevitable personality clashes, hurt feelings, and emotional outbursts that accompanied change, school reform in Kentucky might have marched along unimpeded. But policy is nothing without people. And many of them were too disgruntled and disoriented to give KERA a chance.

Indeed, before the first frost fell, it seemed clear that Ecton's reform agenda for the 1994–1995 school year had been knocked off course. He kept talking about the vision for the school district; administrators and teachers kept talking about individual programs. He hadn't persuaded most people of the need for educational change. He hadn't really come close. And he was beginning to take the rejection personally.

By this point in the semester, the superintendent hoped his staff would be more comfortable working toward common goals of improvement and growth. Instead, many still fought to preserve their parochial interests. Administrators did it. Teachers did it. School councils did it. Every group focused on one project and then another, not comprehending how everything fit together to produce collective success. Their uncertainty was understandable to a degree, he thought. People were overwhelmed. Because the state had issued so many new requirements simultaneously, educators needed to break them down into discrete tasks just to make sense of them all. However, if that's all you did, the rationale got lost in the process. And without a reason for change, each new assignment became a burden that people would try to dump at the first opportunity. Old habits never give way without plenty of practice.

A few weeks after telling his administrative team that he was going to start holding people "accountable for their actions," for example, Ecton encountered more inertia. When the time came to review the progress made by the advisory group, almost all the members said they were too busy to get together. Just six of the thirteen people who attended the meeting had telephoned parents as promised; only four had completed the forty contacts for which each had accepted responsibility. Ecton made only six phone calls himself. Clearly, the group wouldn't meet its goal of communicating with nearly every parent in the district by the end of the year.

The comments from the parents who shared their views were generally positive; the highest compliments came from those who had recently moved to Kentucky. Some parents said they had initial concerns about the state's education reform plan, but experience made them more appreciative of the classroom changes. Parents said they liked the family resource centers that tried to eliminate pressures outside school that could hinder a student's success; and they liked the extended school services program that provided tutoring to children who needed extra help. Many Henderson County parents wanted to talk about issues unrelated to school reform: racial tensions at the high school, the awkward transition from elementary school to secondary schools, the need for crossing guards when kindergarten sessions changed at noon, and the desire to reinstitute corporal punishment. In most cases, people said they were grateful that someone had asked for their opinions.

Ecton wished his own staff was as eager to engage in a dialogue about education. He blamed himself for some of the strained silence that seemed to reverberate throughout the halls of the small, one-story administrative office building. Instead of forcing some issues out in the open, particularly the lack of consensus about school reform, Ecton's impassioned pleadings during the past few weeks had caused some administrators to retreat even further. A few wouldn't look him in the eye when he passed them in the hall.

He conceded that he might have misjudged the mood of his staff. In hindsight, he said, he probably should have handled things differently. After the last meeting, he decided to confront some people individually, recognizing that he had a greater chance to break through their reserve when they didn't feel threatened in a group.

"He came around mending fences after that, which he is good at," Ruie Murphy said.

Because some people were just too set in their ways to change, Ecton began searching for opportunities to use their skills without allowing them to jeopardize his mission. With several veteran administrators preparing to retire within the next year— including Murphy—Ecton started transferring some of their duties to younger, more flexible, staff members. He allowed the older administrators to concentrate on the areas they knew best. He moved Murphy into a new advisory role where he could share his considerable expertise but not block reform initiatives or stifle communication among his staff as he had in the past.

"Ruie and I have had a lot of discussions about this," Ecton said. "He acknowledges that he disagrees with a lot of what we're doing. At this stage, it's not about debating with him or winning him over. But he's also a valuable player."

Although some people considered Ecton's inclusive leadership style a strength, others viewed it as a weakness and had taken advantage of his trust. He regretted, for example, that he hadn't ensured that all the principals were working as hard to push education reform with their staffs as he was working to push it with the principals. He thought he should have built in more ways to monitor their progress. "I probably let them go too far in hopes that they would learn and grow," Ecton said. "In a way, it was easier to confront Johnny's alcoholism than it is to confront an administrator's [negative] attitude. There's not the same kind of rehabilitation clinic to send somebody to so you can follow up on their progress."

A normally confident and cheerful person, Ecton grew more pensive with each passing month. He kept trying to reach out to the community by attending weekly Rotary Club meetings at the local Days Inn, by serving as chairman of Henderson's United Way fund drive, and by taking questions on radio talk shows. But he often wondered if had penetrated the surface civility to reach people's hearts and minds. Eight years in Henderson did not mean the community accepted Ecton like a native.

At home, he didn't find much release from the stress. His wife, Barbara, a licensed practical nurse at Henderson County High School, had enrolled in evening and summer courses in college to complete a bachelor's degree in nursing. After enduring thirty-four years of her husband's preoccupation with his job, Barbara had decided to invest more time in her own interests.

The Ectons once enjoyed shopping for antiques and attending high school basketball games together. For many years they bought season tickets to the University of Kentucky's men's basketball games in Lexington. Barbara used to think she and Gayle had so much in common. Now they rarely did anything together. "I haven't had a lot of the good times because of the time [he has] spent with his work," she said, crying softly. "By the time he gets home, sometimes I don't see him at his best."

Barbara respected her husband's commitment to improving education in Kentucky. She knew him to be a generous, good-hearted man who succeeded in everything he did professionally. But it was difficult not to grieve about the knowledge that she and her children had been cheated by his life's work. Gayle proudly passed around photographs of his grandchildren at school district staff meetings, but when he spent time with his family he often seemed impatient to be somewhere else.

"I know what kind of job he does. I know how much he cares about it, about the employees and the schools," Barbara said. "I think he wants them to be the best they can be, and he wants to influence that. I'm very proud of him and how he's run his professional life. I guess I do feel that there should be more of a balance in his life. I feel somewhat, I guess, disappointed in that part of his life."

All three of the Ectons' children had returned home in recent months, which intensified the pressure on Gayle to spend more time with the family. After completing a stint with the U.S. Army's Judge Advocacy General Corps in Seattle, Washington, Scott Ecton moved back to Kentucky with his wife and three children. Scott found a job with a law firm in Ashland, about six hours east of Henderson. Stacy Ecton also had moved back to Kentucky from Florida to take a job teaching high school math in Nelson County, near Louisville. Susan Ecton, the youngest, taught English at a high school in Daviess County, near Henderson.

On top of the emotional issues with his family and career, Gayle Ecton suffered intense physical pain from a bone chip in his left foot. He sought various medical treatments, but none brought him relief. The bone chip made it difficult to walk or exercise, compounding his stress. He was gaining weight and feeling glum.

"There's times I'm so damn weary all I want to do is sit down and say, 'The heck with this,'" Ecton said one afternoon as the rain-swollen sky seemed to glower back at him through the office window. "And then other days I feel excited. I really feel like we're going in the right direction. This has been such an up-and-down crazy year. The more I read about change, I think it's really predictable. This had to occur." He laughed uneasily and shook his head, trying to find some levity in the pain. "Knowing that," he said, "doesn't make it any easier or fun."

A major part of any superintendent's job is inspiring confidence in the community's schools. In the age of education reform, the growing uncertainty about the structure and purpose of teaching made that assignment even more challenging. Ecton knew people were fed up with high dropout rates, low test scores, and the aimlessness of many adolescents. But some of the public's anger was misdirected, he thought. American society moved in its own state of flux, and schools had inherited the same problems that seemed unsolvable outside the classroom. Ecton willingly shared the responsibility for improving schools, but the remedies he and others prescribed angered people as much as the problems they sought to correct. There was no easy way out.

'There's this mentality that we have to go in and get it right the first time," he said. "Where else does that happen? Businesses, how much do they spend in research and development? But in education, we're supposed to have it down pat without any practice.

We honest to God didn't know what to do for most of my career in education. We just kept trying to get better at the same old things that didn't work. Now I think we have a handle on what we need to do and why. But we're still in the infancy stage."

The dilemma for Ecton and other leaders who advocated a new direction for schools was this: in trying to persuade people that the old teaching methods needed massive repairs, they risked eroding the community's confidence further. At the same time, unless they made a strong case for change, schools would continue misfiring with many students—and the public would blame educators for the results.

The pressures certainly weren't unique to Henderson County. In Paducah, Kentucky, for instance, opponents of KERA gathered eleven thousand names on a statewide petition to rescind the education reform law. Apparently, complaining was easier than changing. By attacking Kentucky's school reform plan, the antagonists offered nothing to replace it with except for the same methods that kept the state at the bottom of the nation's academic ladder for more than one hundred years.

Nevertheless, Ecton knew it was foolish to minimize or ignore the public's concerns. The Henderson County district already had lost about $600,000 in state revenue because of the unexpectedly high number of students who chose private schools over public ones. Ecton didn't want to take any more financial hits. "We need to find out why," he told his staff. "In some cases, if you've done all you can do and they still choose to leave, then that's their prerogative."

"I don't want to give the impression that we shouldn't be concerned," responded Howard Crittenden, principal of Henderson County High School. "But we need accurate data to know if it's something we're doing wrong or if it's out of our control."

In Henderson County, student attrition during the 1994–1995 school year left psychological as well as financial scars. Families had to explain in writing why their children—most of them in junior and senior high school—left. The reasons they gave varied considerably. Some parents did not want to be "hassled" by the district anymore because of their children's behavior problems in school. Some knew that if their wayward children stayed in public schools they would not qualify for a driver's license under Kentucky's new "No Pass/No Drive" law. Some wanted to expose their children to more religious instruction at home. And some simply became disenchanted with the public schools.

But in a community where private school enrollment had always been sparse, news about rising public school withdrawals spread about as quickly as an infectious-disease report. Through local media and word of mouth, the community learned that Holy Name, a K through 8 parochial school, was stretched to capacity, adding eighty new students in the past two years, a high percentage of them non-Catholic; an increasing number of Henderson students made the trip across the Ohio River bridge to private schools in Evansville; and, perhaps most significant, a new school, Henderson County Christian School, opened at the end of the summer.

A group of parents unhappy with Kentucky's education reforms started the exodus from the public schools. Anne Manley, a grandmother and Sunday school teacher, was an early opponent. In 1989, before the reform law was passed, Manley kept up with the developments in the courts and legislature and started corresponding with other religious conservatives around the country. In 1992, she and two friends attended a council meeting at Henderson County High School. Manley said they were "appalled" when one of the teachers reportedly said, "I can't wait until they get rid of the rest of the damn school books." Manley considered the statement an admission of contempt for the traditional educational values she revered. And the comment seemed particularly offensive when she considered the teenagers in her Sunday school class who could barely read.

Soon after, Manley organized a meeting that attracted about 150 like-minded folks to the Henderson County courthouse. The group agreed to form an organization, Taking Education And Children Higher (TEACH), that would work to repeal KERA.

Paul and Ann Wilson started attending the group's meetings at the invitation of one of Paul's co-workers. Paul said he initially doubted the complaints that the state interfered with parents' rights; that children had to answer invasive questions about their private lives; that teachers no longer cared about spelling, punctuation, and mathematical computations; and that students had to accept homosexual lifestyles.

"We didn't want to be people who couldn't embrace change," he said. At the time, the Wilsons' daughter, Jennifer, attended a primary school classroom at Seventh Street Elementary in Henderson. When they discussed with Jennifer's teacher some of the issues the opponents raised, the Wilsons said the teacher told them their child was "far beyond where she should be, thanks to KERA."

"I felt really good about it," Paul said. But as the Wilsons continued listening to the TEACH advocates and reading their literature, they recalled Jennifer's inadequate homework assignments and the papers she brought home from school with misspellings that had not been corrected by her teacher. In the second semester of the 1993-1994 school year, the Wilsons moved Jennifer to a Christian school in Evansville where they discovered she was far behind other students in her age group. For months the Wilsons tutored Jennifer in the evenings, trying to help her catch up.

"We were all stressed out," Ann Wilson said. It was a painful period for Ann, a Henderson police officer. Her older daughter from a previous marriage had attended Seventh Street Elementary through the sixth grade, and Ann had been a regular volunteer at the school. "We were really involved in that school," she said. "A lot of people were angry when we left. It was a hard decision."

When asked about the Wilsons's complaints, Mike Freels, Seventh Street's principal, grew defensive and said he didn't want to reveal personal information or engage in a public dispute with parents. He did mention that another family who left Seventh Street at the same time as the Wilsons returned from Holy Name School the following year.

Freels acknowledged that he and his teachers needed to work out some kinks in the early years of school reform, which might have caused some parents to feel anxious about their children's education. Staff members became so busy with new responsibilities that they didn't always communicate clearly with parents. But Freels, who considered himself an authoritarian, traditional teacher before he became a principal in the first year of KERA, firmly believed the reform laws changes were better for students than the old ways.

"The public thinks that everybody needs to be on the same page [on the same day]. That just doesn't work," Freels said. "If those people who leave because of this [reform] can get a guarantee from private schools that at the end of the year—taking *all* the kids we have to deal with—all of them would end up on the same page, they'd have a perfect school. People have assumed that we've had all kids up to the third grade level at the same time. That never, ever happened. If we'd say, 'Okay, you win, we'll go back to straight rows and textbooks,' they'd heave a sigh of relief. But the kids won't all learn their multiplication tables at the same time just because of that."

Nevertheless, Anne Manley and her followers grew impatient with the school district's response to their concerns. In early 1994, they approached Reverend Leslie M. Huff, Jr., executive director of missions for the Green Valley Baptist Association, and asked for his help in organizing a Christian elementary school. The group members said they no longer fit in the Henderson public schools. Huff agreed to help, but he refused to accept any parents who wanted the new school solely because they were disenchanted with Kentucky's education reforms. He believed that if the new school formed on the basis of a knee-jerk reaction to change, instead of a firm commitment to Christian education, it would fail. Indeed, in interviews, he took pains not to criticize the public schools. "I don't think there's a real harsh public reaction to the school system," he said. Any initial antagonism had been channeled into choice, he said. "You do your program and we'll do ours."

Huff found a church, Watson Lane Baptist, that agreed to provide space for the new Christian school. When it opened in August 1994, the school had thirty-seven students, four certified teachers (including one who also served as principal) and an annual tuition of $1,925. Huff selected the teachers from among fifty applicants, searching for those who had experience with traditional instruction and a track record of service to their respective churches. He bought eighty-two old school desks from Holy Name for one dollar apiece and found a local automotive repair shop that agreed to sand and paint them for free.

Henderson County Christian School grouped children according to their ages, but each classroom contained several grades (either kindergarten, 1 through 3, 4 through 5, or 6 through 8 because of the small number of students at each level. The school's only first-grader spent half of the day with the kindergarten class because the principal said the child completed a public school kindergarten without learning the alphabet.) The Christian school emphasized phonics, spelling tests, and strict discipline. Huff also admonished teachers not to let students use computers or calculators until the sixth grade; he wanted them to concentrate on learning basic skills by hand.

The Christian school differed from a typical Henderson County public school in several ways. In the Christian school, students sat in straight rows of desks, not at tables or at desks placed in varied arrangements. Students wore uniforms, read Bible verses, and learned nothing about evolution in the science curriculum. In the half-day kindergarten program, teacher Darla Brooks (who also served as principal) used flash cards and phonetic pronunciations to help the twelve students in her class learn the alphabet. All the students worked at their own pace, and Brooks adjusted the difficulty of the assignment when needed. Later, while some students completed worksheets on colors and shapes, Brooks asked a smaller group of students to join her on the rug where she read them a book about Jesus and talked about proper table manners.

Although many families enrolled their children in Henderson's two private schools to get away from KERA, teachers and principals there said they personally supported and used some of the reform law's recommendations. Brooks, for example, had taught three years at East Heights Elementary School in Henderson. She then moved out of town and decided to stay home to raise her children. Now, she lived in Henderson again and taught full-time. Brooks acknowledged trying some of KERA's instructional techniques, including linking lessons from different subjects, letting students work with older children when they needed more academic challenge, and encouraging teachers to deviate occasionally from the textbook.

"Children do not always learn best with a book in front of them," Brooks said. "Not everything in KERA is wrong. There are things I agree with, such as moving children up or down as needed. I do like the way they use journals and a lot of creative writing. I think that's a good concept. Many of our children were going through school never writing and being creative. But you still need to teach them spelling and punctuation along the way."

Kentucky's education reform opened her eyes to some useful practices, Brooks said. The problem was that KERA moved too far too fast. "At times they took things to extremes and made parents uncomfortable," she said. "They took away textbooks and letter grades and parents had nothing that was the same when they went to school. I think if they had moved more slowly they would have been more successful. As a private school, we can take the best of what we find and apply it and be flexible to change."

At Holy Name, principal Jim Landry expressed similar appreciation for some of the reform law's practices. But like Brooks, he didn't want to buy the whole package. "I think KERA has been good for private schools. The new concepts are challenging us to look at what we do, and why," Landry said. "Even though we are not making dramatic changes, we are changing, and that's good. We're more aware of what's out there."

Holy Name still required teachers to teach a certain number of minutes per subject per day, following the old Kentucky Department of Education guidelines. Teachers still grouped children by age. Holy Name's students wore uniforms, studied religion, used textbooks, and completed a set amount of homework every day. But as part of the changes the school adopted in the wake of education reform, Holy Name's students also compiled writing portfolios, worked together cooperatively in groups, and occasionally tutored younger students. "That's one of our advantages," Landry said. "We don't have to adopt all of KERA. We can pick and choose."

The irony was that while families willingly let private schools experiment with the academic options available to them, they rebuffed the public schools' attempts. Perhaps parents would have accepted more of the public school changes on a slower schedule. Parents wanted choices, but not at the expense of consistency.

To public school educators, however, this message was a paradox and made it difficult to plan. For years, people had grumbled about the terrible condition of Kentucky's public schools. So, state leaders finally responded, which provoked new concerns that Kentucky's classrooms no longer looked the same. State reform leaders could be excused for feeling like hairdressers whose customers beg for dramatic, new hairstyles then recoil in horror when they see their images in the mirror.

Around the country, the drama played out in a similar fashion. Education reform advocates endured the wrath of people who thought public schools should worry less about helping students develop higher-order thinking skills and worry more about teaching them basic skills, such as the ability to write grammatical sentences. Parents insisted that public schools often overlooked the fundamentals of learning. In a series of studies about education reform during the 1990s, for example, the non-partisan Public Agenda Foundation of New York tuned in to an increasingly irritated and alienated population that disliked the outcomes of school change across the country.

"I think we're in a very precarious situation because [support for public education] is very tenuous," said Deborah Wadsworth, the foundation's executive director. "We are discovering a sense among the public that if they had the money, they would turn to private education."

Wadsworth thought Kentucky's reform leaders demonstrated some "sensible responsiveness" by adjusting various components of the reform law after the first few years. But whether KERA had enough staying power to outlast mounting opposition was questionable, she said.

"Four years after passage, the Kentucky Education Reform Act (KERA), aimed at raising standards in Kentucky schools, is neither widely understood nor accepted," concluded Public Agenda's 1994 report, *First Things First: What Americans Expect From Public Schools.* "KERA has attracted opposition from teachers and local school officials and from grassroots organizations such as America Awaken, Families United for Morals in Education, Parents and Professionals Involved in Education, and larger groups such as the Eagle Forum. The Kentucky legislature approved increased funding for KERA in 1994, but only after a highly publicized, bruising battle."

In theory, at least, KERA provided the perfect framework for supplying basic academic skills and supporting different ways of teaching them. The law gave teachers more independence and choices than ever before. It presented some recommended practices, then let schools fill in the details. But in the effort to maximize opportunities for excellence, state education leaders did a poor job of communicating the acceptable minimums. Consequently, a lot of people who claimed to be "doing KERA" had almost nothing in common but the acronym. A great deal of instruction—good and bad—was tossed into the same bag. Teachers often blamed or praised reform for activities that had nothing to do with the law's intent. It was as if the entire population had awakened one morning and discovered that every other person spoke a different language. In the ensuing babble, parents grew increasingly irritated with the public schools. What *is* school reform, they asked? The answers were too disparate to make sense.

In October 1993, the Kentucky Department of Education began the formal process of clarifying KERA's academic standards because teachers wanted specific guidance about the subject content they needed to cover. If the state's curriculum guidelines said fourth-graders should study patterns and systems in science, for example, teachers wanted to know whether they should emphasize electrical or skeletal systems, or something else entirely. It was not until the summer of 1996, however, that the department finished revising multiple drafts of the content guidelines, which circulated among more than 250 different state groups—from teachers and school board members to parents and anti-reform activists—for comment. This ambitious project tried to increase the consensus for school reform over the long term. In time, the process probably would produce more consistent classroom practices. But during the 1994-1995 school year, there was still considerable disagreement about what students should learn. And as the public debated the standards, teachers and administrators reluctantly assumed the role of KERA interpreters. It made many of them hesitant, defensive, and confused.

Rachel Jones, a new health and physical education teacher at South Junior High School in Henderson, recalled attending a birthday party for one of her daughter's playmates and being grilled for two hours by a group of parents who wanted to ask questions and complain about education reform. Jones felt torn. She loved creating lessons that showed students how to make connections to life outside the classroom. She thought the concepts took a lot of the mystery out of learning. But she also understood the concerns of some parents. As the mother of two children in elementary school and another child who was a few years away from school, Jones herself questioned some of the changes in the early grades. "When my daughter went into the primary program, I got absolutely nothing to tell me what to expect," Jones said. "Even as a teacher I didn't know what was going on."

Although her daughter, Brittany, learned to read at age four in a Christian preschool, she was not performing well in the primary program at Hebbardsville Elementary School. When Jones tried to get her daughter to write from left to right instead of all over the page, she said Brittany's teacher asked her to stop. Brittany should learn that skill by reading and by watching other students, the teacher told her. The teacher also reported that Brittany "flutters around the classroom like a butterfly" and became easily distracted. Jones thought she just needed more structured learning. "I don't feel I have a clear idea of how she's performing," Jones said, adding that she would send her children to Holy Name if she could afford the tuition.

At Seventh Street Elementary, veteran teacher Kathy Crawford had heard similar concerns about instruction in the early grades. But as a parent, she saw much more positive results from school reform. Crawford said her daughter had blossomed because of the expansive lessons teachers developed outside the conformity of textbooks. An academically gifted student, Crawford's daughter received both pre-KERA and post-KERA instruction at Seventh Street, and she clearly preferred the latter. A sixth-grader in a combined fifth- and sixth-grade class, Crawford's daughter studied algebra while others in her class attempted much less difficult mathematical problems.

"Several parents have come up to me and said, 'I need that grade [to know how my child is doing],'" Crawford said. "I told them, 'Talk to your children. That shows you much more than a grade.'"

Steve Edmonson, a father of four who had served on the governing councils at two different Henderson County schools, believed there was a lot of "quiet support for KERA," but he acknowledged opponents were more vocal and persuasive. "There's a lot of love-hate," he said. "If you love it, you don't say much. If you hate it, you say a lot."

Edmonson, a tire store manager, objected to parts of the reform law. He didn't have much faith in the testing system, for example, and he thought the state's deadlines for implementing various initiatives were so unrealistic they seemed mean-spirited. Yet, Edmonson had witnessed so many other positive changes from education reform that he considered it critical to stay the course. "I believe in KERA," he said. "If nothing else, it has empowered teachers and administrators to make changes in their schools."

The group most sympathetic to KERA included parents who never measured up academically—consequently, they were much more willing to take chances on new instruction for their children. While others decried the passing of an era in education that served them well, these parents believed change might represent the only hope for children traditionally overlooked in school. Their input was critical to the reform law's success. If KERA could increase the capacity of struggling students to achieve, it would give their families the confidence to challenge those who until now had dictated the terms of the school debate.

Donald Haralson, Sr., was among those who suffered under the old educational system. To compare his experiences to education in the post-reform era, Haralson offered his son as an example. He considered it progress that Donald, Jr. left for Seventh Street Elementary School every morning smiling. The first thing young Donald wanted to do when he finished his after-school snack was start on his homework. Haralson said he never remembered feeling so excited about school. Although he graduated from Henderson County High School, he still read at a fourth-grade level. Now an unemployed father of two, Haralson had been forced to turn down several high-paying truck driver jobs because he couldn't pass the written test to obtain his commercial driver's license.

Young Donald's education had a much better chance to succeed. When their son was in kindergarten at South Heights Elementary, Haralson and his wife, Tanya, attended a "Homework Without Tears" workshop that taught them how to reinforce Donald's school lessons at home. The experience gave them the confidence to approach Donald's teachers with questions or concerns. Now that his son attended Seventh Street, Haralson regularly consulted teachers about his son's progress in school. "The teachers really work with us," he said. "It's a two-way deal. He's not going to go through what I did."

As superintendent of schools, Gayle Ecton was responsible for meeting the needs of all these constituent groups in Henderson County. Private schools could turn away families who didn't agree with their philosophical approaches to learning. Public schools had to find a place for everyone.

Ecton accepted his duty to set the course for the Henderson County Public Schools. But the state's timeline for implementing various KERA initiatives took much of the decision-making out of his hands. Like many other Kentucky educators, he spent a great deal of time following orders. As 1995 dawned, Ecton became so preoccupied with meeting deadlines and keeping the troops in line that he temporarily lost sight of his goals. Expediency got in the way of community. The ensuing controversy not only diverted attention from the school district's pressing problems with education reform, it also caused Ecton to lose vital support for his agenda.

The situation started with a discussion about old school buildings. For several years, Henderson County school officials studied the district's long-term need for space. They produced cost estimates, consulted with architects and contractors, met with community representatives, and listened to recommendations from the Kentucky Department of Education. By state law, the district had to develop a five-year spending plan and rank projects by priority. High on Henderson's list was the need to relieve the district's single, overcrowded high school. In addition, Ecton wanted to consolidate several small, inefficient elementary schools, move sixth-graders from elementary schools to the junior high schools, and move ninth-graders to high school so the junior highs could become middle schools serving grades six through eight.

However, when a committee of school district and community representatives (an advisory group whose participation in the process was required by the state) recommended $36.5 million worth of construction expenses in the fall of 1994, Ecton and the school board balked. The committee's plan, however worthy, was just too costly. Because the school district expected to receive just $5.5 million from the state over the next five years to pay for its unmet construction needs, any additional funds would require a local tax increase. Board members didn't think Henderson County voters would approve one. Few citizens attended the three public hearings about the construction plan, which called into question the potential level of support. So, despite an impending state deadline, the board asked the committee to supply additional information and reconsider its suggestions.

Meanwhile, school officials privately discussed the future of Smith Mills Elementary, an old school on the outskirts of Henderson they had considered closing for at least a decade. With an enrollment of 130 students, Smith Mills was the smallest public school in the county. At a January administrative staff meeting, Nathaniel Green, principal at Smith Mills, announced that he planned to retire at the end of the semester. After inquiring about Green's future plans, the other administrators turned to Ecton. Would Green be replaced as principal, they asked, or would the district finally shut down the forty-eight-year-old school building?

In the brief discussion that followed, the superintendent sought opinions from the group. He was particularly interested in comments from administrators who lived near the school. When the meeting ended, Ecton decided to recommend to the school board that it close Smith Mills. The school's costs per-pupil were about $1,000 more than the district average. The roof needed major repairs. And Chandler Elementary was nearby, a new school with plenty of room. It seemed like an easy call. As Ecton discovered, however, even the most ordinary actions by a school district can take on monstrous proportions when people are uneasy about the future and overwhelmed by change.

Soon after discussing the school's closure with his administrative team and informing the school board, Ecton approached the faculty and PTA at Smith Mills. About one hundred people attended a meeting where the superintendent laid out the facts. Few were hostile, but several expressed sorrow at the news. "If the school board's going to do this, kill us quickly and get it over with," Smith Mills resident Kathy Satterfield said. "I've cried every time it's come up," said Judy Powell, a Smith Mills teacher. "I'm prepared to cry again" (Wright 1995a).

After that initial meeting, opposition to the closure intensified. At the February 20 school board meeting, about two dozen Smith Mills parents showed up and demanded another public hearing. Others took the battle to the media. Editorial writers at the local newspaper urged board members to act decisively to close Smith Mills, but readers had different ideas. "I realize the school needs repairs that are quite costly because they needed them when I was there," Samantha Hoggard wrote to *The Gleaner* in March. "But what's a new roof and other repairs compared to the disruption it will cause if the school is closed? The school is the heart of the town. If it closes the town might as well close too."

Steven Jackson wrote, too, asking "where is the discussion of issues that really impact the education of our children? Let's hear about lower student-to-teacher ratios, an environment easier to maintain discipline and order, and more opportunities for parent and student involvement."

On March 2, two hundred "small-school preservationists" squeezed into the tiny Smith Mills gymnasium for a public hearing on the closure. According to *The Gleaner's* account, the audience jeered and clapped its approval as several speakers accused school officials of delaying making needed repairs to Smith Mills, manipulating cost per pupil figures, and spending public money on luxury hotels at out-of-town conferences instead of on programs for students. Some hecklers questioned Ecton's $90,118 annual salary, implying that he should take a pay cut to spread the financial sacrifice around.

In the weeks that followed, opponents of other school district initiatives stepped up the attack, blaming the Smith Mills closure on excessive spending practices by administrators. Critics of KERA viewed the situation as another example of the lack of respect school leaders have for community concerns about education.

Four months into the battle, Ecton raised the white flag. Public pressure was one of the unfortunate and expected side effects of being a superintendent. He knew the score. But this controversy felt different, and Ecton wasn't sure why. Confused and indecisive, he tried to sort out his thoughts about Smith Mills. One evening he sat before his computer and typed out a four-page memo to school board members.

"The first thing I've tried to keep in the forefront is that this is *not* about winning and losing," he wrote. "It's about making the right decision." The reasons for closing Smith Mills seemed clear, he said. The school district could immediately save $140,000 and send the staff and students from Smith Mills to Chandler.

"We agreed that if something was going to be done, it needed to happen right away to allow for an orderly transition," he wrote. "So, I discussed it with you and told you that [it] looked like the time to seriously look at closing the school was here—even though this meant singling out Smith Mills before the facility plan was completed.

"Looking back, it still seems like the logical thing to do—certainly, to at least take a hard look at it. Which is where we are now—taking a hard look and trying to decide what to do. Is there any doubt? Frankly, I now have a few. (Okay! Okay! I know! I'm the one who brought you to this dance and now you're wondering if I'm going to leave you to find your own way home!) Let me explain."

He said he never had minded making unpopular decisions when he knew the facts were on his side. But somehow, the plan to close Smith Mills just didn't feel right. Two other small elementary schools, Robards and Hebbardsville, were about as inefficient to operate as Smith Mills. Although questions remained about whether the school district had enough space in other schools to absorb the students at Robards and Hebbardsville, Smith Mills seemed to have been treated differently.

"Two things bothered me about that," Ecton wrote to the board members. "First, I pride myself more than anything else in trying to be fair. It really bothers me when I realize I haven't been fair or even if people's perception is that I haven't been fair. Second, and just as important, I also always try to focus on the big picture in making decisions. I believe that if you do this and you can just get people to see the big picture then it is easier to make the right decisions and have support for those decisions. I do feel like we have had the big picture in mind as we have been looking at the whole facilities issue. However, I now feel like the focus at Smith Mills for this immediate issue has not been on the big picture. At least, the big picture has not been communicated. Instead, we focused our discussion on reasons to close Smith Mills which dealt basically, for the most part, with just Smith Mills. I framed the argument wrong! This was my fault for getting in a rush."

By telling people the school was too expensive and needed repairs, Ecton said, he set up a false expectation that more money would fix the problem. So now, supporters of Smith Mills were trying to raise money to keep the school open and were looking for other savings within the school system. Instead, the point Ecton should have made was that Henderson County had too many schools. To get the most efficient use out of its buildings and staff the school district needed to get elementary school enrollments in the four hundred to five hundred student range.

"How do we convince the people of this county about the funding problems we face?" he wrote. "How do we convince people that we cannot afford the number of schools we have? How do we convince people that the operational costs of adding another high school and middle school is a lot more than we can handle without a major tax increase? How do we convince people that we have serious operational funding problems now, such as teacher salaries? How do we convince people that there are very real equity issues which need to be addressed? Maybe we do need an independent financial study. Maybe we need this study before closing any schools. Have I confused you? I hope so because I want some company! This is a tough issue. I want us to be sure we have thought through this very carefully before making a final decision. I will certainly support what you think we need to do."

The Smith Mills controversy exposed some organizational and communication deficiencies in the Henderson County school district. Ecton realized that he needed to get an independent analysis of the district's finances and develop a long-term projection of its financial needs. Utility costs were increasing at double the rate of revenues, which meant recent plans to expand technology in schools might have to be shelved.

Although the public believed the school system had a lot of money and was hoarding it, Henderson County ranked 128th out of 176 state school districts in per-pupil spending for education. Teacher salaries ranked about average at 94th.

"This is really a pretty good effort considering our revenue ranking," Ecton wrote to the school board in March. "However, it looms as a major problem for the future if we are to attract and retain the best teachers."

In mid-April, the Henderson Board of Education, with Ecton's support, decided to give Smith Mills a reprieve. Although some staff members encouraged him "to make the decision and move on," Ecton realized that he couldn't proceed with a process that he thought was rushed and undemocratic. Eventually, the community would have to decide whether it could afford to keep all of its schools, he said, but not now. People needed more information. They needed more time.

"The more I got into this, the more I didn't have a good feeling about what I was doing," Ecton said. "The bottom line is we had jumped out and made a piecemeal decision just because we could. We were doing this at the time we were trying to develop a facilities plan that we were going to involve the public in. But then, in effect, we said, 'Oh, but you can't decide about Smith Mills because we've already made that decision for you.' It seemed incongruous. We decided this was not the way we wanted to do things."

As they had with education reform in general, school leaders in Henderson failed to make their case in terms the public could understand and support. Furthermore, the Smith Mills controversy taught Ecton an important lesson about democracy: once you start sharing power with people, you take it back at political peril.

"Over the years, I became more a part of the bureaucracy than I thought," he said. "We tend to think this is the only way to go because we've always done it this way. I try to put myself in their shoes. Am I really hearing them? If our argument is so good for closing schools, why aren't they buying it? If they want kids in smaller schools and closer to home, maybe we can find a way to do that."

Instead of rebuffing his critics, Ecton listened to them. He tried to reflect and respond. He represented what Jane W. Urschel, director of governmental relations for the Colorado Association of School Boards, calls "the essence of democracy...civility, and persuasion."

"We seek the public's opinion through surveys and polls that never really let the public finish its sentence," Urschel wrote in a 1996 letter to *Education Week*. "The experts relentlessly question: Why do we have to ask permission to do what we know is right? The public counters with: Why can't you ask first? Rarely do policymakers involve the public in deliberation of alternative choices argued with equal authority and persuasiveness. There may be no public education to reform if we do not first create opportunities for serious talk with the public about serious issues."

Through the Smith Mills controversy, Ecton learned rather painfully that true communication with the public must entail a conversation between two parties, not a soliloquy from a sage to the masses. Just as he resented it when state leaders dictated the terms and time frame of education reform in Kentucky, the Henderson community resisted the superintendent's assumptions about what was right for Smith Mills.

As he analyzed the situation, Ecton started to understand how easy it is, how human, to backslide when you are trying so hard to change. "We lost our way," he said sheepishly, "and I was leading the parade."

Chapter Seven

How I Spent My Summer Vacation

Eight months after she returned empty-handed from the Kentucky Teacher of the Year competition, Irmgard Williams drove to the state capital triumphant. Her husband, Dewey, was by her side. South Heights Principal Debbie Key and Henderson County Superintendent Gayle Ecton joined her later. Joel Williams surprised his mother by hitching a ride with friends and traveling fifteen hours from New York to Kentucky to share in her success.

This time Williams basked in the acclaim of winning a "best educator" award. At a luncheon ceremony on May 8, 1995, she was named one of the top ten outstanding teachers in Kentucky by Ashland Oil, Inc., whose annual education competition attracts about nine thousand applicants from four states. (Two years before, Williams had received a Golden Apple Achiever Award, an honorable mention certificate given to the top 15 percent of applicants.) In winning the highly prized Ashland Teacher of Achievement Award, Williams earned a check for $2,500, an engraved crystal apple, and the professional recognition she craved. She was thrilled by all the attention, but privately decided that the event planners "needed a woman's touch" to make the ceremony more intimate.

When a reporter asked her what she planned to do with the cash award, Williams said she might buy a laptop computer because she liked to write. "I don't need this money to be a good teacher," she told him, "but I think this award is important because teachers need some affirmation."

Back in her Henderson County classroom, Williams's students cheered as substitute teacher Dorothy Meador turned on a radio so they could hear an announcement of the award on a local station. The next day, when Williams returned to South Heights, teachers and current and former students streamed into her classroom before the start of classes, bearing gifts, sharing copies of the front-page newspaper article about her award, and smothering her with hugs. Key hung a congratulatory banner across the school foyer, and she and a committee of teachers started planning a surprise party for Williams that would take place the following week.

As soon as the morning bell rang, however, Williams returned to business as usual. Her students took a practice spelling test, working from a list that included several words related to a two-week unit about islands—*Atlantic*, *Gulf Stream*, *loggerhead*, *jellyfish*, *flipper*, and *waves*. Williams's grade report showed that during the school year her younger students had consistently exceeded the six- to eight-word spelling requirement she set, and most of the older students learned about fifteen new words each week. Nearly all of the seven- and eight-year-olds in her class also knew their multiplication tables. "It's amazing what they can do when they're challenged," Williams said.

After studying spelling, the children took turns reading aloud from their journals, with Williams encouraging more reflection through questioning. The classroom was a model of decorum. Even the most fidgety students sat still for short intervals and raised their hands before speaking. Two of the children wore new eyeglasses. Several had grown so tall that their clothes strained to cover them. A seven-year-old with autism who came into Williams's class the previous August unable to make eye contact with adults, smiled, laughed, and participated like one of the gang.

"She has some of the slowest children in the school," said Meador, who knows most of the students at South Heights because of her substitute teaching stints. "They always come out a winner in her class."

As the day wore on, the students read books about sea turtles, searched encyclopedia references for information about the turtle's habitat, and worked together in groups to write short stories based on their discoveries. During one lesson, Williams donned her apron. She pulled rubber fish and plastic plants from one pocket to demonstrate the live food turtles like to eat, then used the other pocket to show what pollution forces them to swallow—bottle caps, paper, and plastic. Working again in groups, the children designed and decorated appropriate turtle grub, then taped their drawings to a huge sea-colored sheet that Williams stretched across the blackboard. Next, the children gave oral presentations about their research to the class. With a few minutes remaining before the closing bell, two students asked Williams if they could dramatize a conversation they had written in Spanish. She nodded her approval, then stood back and watched them, amazed at their initiative and skill.

It had been a good day, she thought, the kind that sent hope coursing through a teacher's veins. She felt certain that her students would finish the term flush with accomplishment. They had learned basic skills, to be sure, but so much more. She had ignited their imaginations, and their growing confidence had carried them to greater and greater heights. The younger students would stay with her another year, graduating to new leadership roles in the class. The older students would move on to another teacher on the team.

But the good feelings about the school year evaporated as soon as Williams turned her thoughts to home. Her husband's heart disease had progressed rapidly, making him more dependent on Irmgard than ever. Dewey Williams had survived a series of angioplasty and heart bypass surgeries in the past few years. His chest pain kept him up most of the night, and Irmgard lost sleep, too.

"Psychologically, I've prepared for widowhood," she said and shuddered. "His health is so bad." As Dewey's heart deteriorated, so did his ability to work, and Irmgard assumed more responsibility for managing the family flower shop. The business continued to lose money many months; Irmgard worried that she would not be able to pay the bills on her $38,710 teaching salary.

Meador was one of the few people Williams confided in about her personal struggles. On rare occasions, she admitted feeling despondent. Yet even as Willliams's closest friend, Meador had learned to watch for signs of trouble. If a few days went by without a phone call from Williams, Meador knew she was probably besieged and needed support. She would never ask for help directly.

Ironically, Meador said, school reform brought Williams some of her greatest comfort. Although many teachers complained that KERA caused their stress, to Williams the challenges of school change took her mind off the greater tensions in her personal life.

Williams felt increasingly positive about the way her colleagues at South Heights had grown in the past few months. They still lost their focus in team meetings, endlessly discussing issues such as the impact of the school's high transiency rate and other "things we can't change." But on the whole, her colleagues seemed to concentrate more on improving instruction. When some teachers complained that selected students couldn't learn, she told them they must teach and reteach concepts to children who needed more help. But this time Williams didn't worry as much about whether they heeded her advice. Perhaps she was being pragmatic, but she realized some things strayed beyond her control. Just as some children developed at slower rates than their classmates, other teachers might need extra time to learn skills that came more easily to her.

"Sometimes we're more patient with our students than with our peers," Williams said. "Maybe the change has come in me. I've learned to delegate more. Those who don't plan as well, I give them specific tasks to do. They're very capable people. I have to trust them. Before, the principal used to do so much of this. Now, I have to learn to lead."

But leadership brought its own challenges—including being willing to confront injustices, intransigence, and incompetence instead of avoiding the potential conflicts by looking the other way. This was the part of school management Williams resisted most, driven by her fear of retaliation and her belief that she had no right to insist other people do things her way. She had spent her whole life trying to get along. She could read people's moods like a barometer reacts to changes in air pressure. It just didn't seem worth it, this late in her career and this close to an impending personal crisis, to gamble her good fortune at school, possibly alienating the very people she counted on for support.

Key urged Williams to take more risks with her team but recognized how difficult it was to take a stand. "She is still very cautious to say, 'Try this,'" Key said.

Williams's ambivalence about how far to extend her influence and how much to stretch her personal comfort zone by meddling in the classrooms of her colleagues will sound familiar to anyone who has observed the organization of schools in this country. Because the American educational system rewards longevity instead of talent, good teachers have little incentive to perform well in their jobs beyond their concern for students, much less challenge their colleagues to strive for greater quality. Often, good teachers give up or give in in order to keep the peace with their peers.

Besides risking antagonism from their peers, many exemplary teachers also resist standing in front of the crowd because they don't think of themselves as leaders. Despite the proliferation of new models of shared authority in schools, such as elected school councils and parent-teacher advisory groups, the lingering perception is that educators become leaders only when they receive a promotion into administration. Neither the public nor the profession takes teachers' views as seriously as managers' opinions. Witness the small proportion of teachers asked to serve on state and national panels charged with recommending changes in schools.

In contrast, Japanese teachers have many opportunities to lead by demonstrating, observing, and reflecting on best practices. Japanese teachers consider it part of the job to bring other colleagues along. "Beginners as well as seasoned teachers are required to perfect their teaching skills through interaction with other teachers," H. Stevenson and J. Stigler write in *The Learning Gap*. "A whole meeting might be devoted to the most effective way to phrase questions about a topic or the most absorbing ways of capturing children's interest in a lesson. In Japanese and Chinese schools, a large room in each school is designed as a teachers' room, and each teacher is assigned a desk in this room. Here they spend their time away from the classroom preparing lessons, correcting students' papers, and discussing teaching techniques. American teachers, isolated in their own classrooms, find it much harder to discuss their work with colleagues. Their desks and teaching materials are in their own classrooms, and the only common space available to teachers is usually a cramped room that often houses supplies and the school's duplicating facilities, along with a few chairs and a coffee machine" (Stevenson and Stigler 1992, 159–161).

The Kentucky Education Reform Act heralded a new era for teachers, one that would encourage professionalism and honor skill. The law gave teachers an incentive (some called it a threat) to work together to change schools by tying rewards and sanctions to their ability to improve student learning. In essence, Kentucky wanted teachers to collectively take control of their destinies.

In reality, KERA did not offer any specific suggestions for removing the barriers—including personal attitudes and union contracts—to changing teacher practice. Ultimately, individual teachers had to be willing to encourage, goad, or force others to move ahead. "The bedrock of accountability will be the extent to which the teaching profession itself takes responsibility for the quality of the workforce," Judith Renyi, executive director of the National Foundation for the Improvement of Education, explained in a 1996 article in *Education Week*. "To this end, peer assistance and review are as fundamental to improving public schools as the time needed to build learning into the teaching job . . . so that good teachers will continuously improve and those who . . . cannot meet professional standards of practice can be counseled out of the profession."

Key was so impressed with the way Williams ran team meetings during the school year—including her detailed agendas and personal recognitions—that she intended to use her approach as a model for other teams the following term. But she also decided that it was time to train some new leaders. Key wanted to rotate team leader positions each year so every teacher on the staff would have a chance to direct. Next year Laura Courtney would take her turn at the helm of the STARS team. Key hoped the leadership stints would broaden the staff's understanding about education reform. She reasoned that if Williams and Sharon Stull, the other veteran primary team leader, continued carrying the heaviest load of planning and decision-making for the primary grades, other teachers would continue to coast. Key wanted the more reluctant staff members to learn by doing, in keeping with the hands-on approach to instruction recommended for Kentucky's primary classrooms.

Key was very concerned about the school's test scores. South Heights had fallen short of its two-year accountability goal, posting a score of 34.0, which was just below the target of 34.7. Because the school was considered to be improving—it had exceeded its goal in the second year of the biennium, but the first-year scores had pulled down the average—the staff would not be sanctioned. But Key knew she had to make some changes to help teachers clear the next hurdle.

Recognizing that the fourth-grade assessments seemed mysterious to teachers outside that grade level, Key and the team leaders decided to base most of the staff's training for the next school year on the test requirements. A school committee's analysis showed that teachers in the primary grades had not focused enough on helping students learn the various techniques and forms of writing, such as appealing to an audience, adopting a narrative voice, and using a variety of sentence structures; some teachers just let their students write whatever they wanted. Primary teachers also focused on basic computation skills, but required only limited math applications. So,

Key and other members of the school council devised a strategy to bring everyone to a higher level. The staff training included six hours of instruction based on "a day in the life of a fourth-grader." This included three hours of focusing on effective problem-solving strategies in math, three hours preparing open-ended questions, and three additional hours learning how to demonstrate open-ended questions in the classroom. Key also intended to take the primary teachers away for a professional retreat.

In addition, South Heights recently received a grant to help boost parent involvement in school activities. The plan included opening the school's computer lab and library some evenings and teaching parents to keep daily writing journals, just as their children did in class.

"I wish the end of school would come so I can finally pull everything together," Key said, as a telephone call from a parent interrupted her train of thought for the umpteenth time that day. "There's never any 'down' time."

Because South Heights' enrollment had declined during the year, the school would lose one staff position for the following term, which probably could be accomplished through attrition. However, Key seized the opportunity to shift some teachers around in the intermediate grades, moving two stressed-out fourth-grade teachers up and two experienced sixth-grade teachers down. She allowed the teachers on the fifth- and sixth-grade team to discontinue their mixed-age classrooms and return to the traditional setup, which sorted students chronologically by age. She also switched some teachers in the primary and intermediate grades, hoping the move would give faculty a better understanding of students throughout elementary school.

Williams watched these changes with interest. But when Key purchased sets of workbooks that focused on grammar, punctuation, and basic math skills, Williams became alarmed. She sensed that some of Key's year-end decisions represented a retreat from the goals of education reform, and she feared the principal had acquiesced to the demands of staff members seeking quick fixes to boost the school's low test scores. Williams had listened as some colleagues pleaded for a return to required textbooks, but she had not been persuaded.

"I won't go back," Williams said with uncharacteristic sharpness. "I will use some things as guides, but I will not go back."

From time to time, usually at the peak of frustration, she thought about how different things would be if she were in charge. Like the little boy in Dr. Seuss's classic book, *If I Ran The Zoo*, she daydreamed about transforming a beloved institution. In his case, the city zoo. In her case, the school. Instead of finding exotic animals like the Elephant-Cat to replace the zoo's humdrum hippopotamuses, Williams dreamed of throwing out outdated teaching methods that dulled a student's senses. She would empty each cage, clean out the waste, and fill the building instead with excited teachers who always would have rich and challenging assignments up their sleeves.

Two weeks before school ended, Williams got her wish. A committee of administrators chose her to be the new director of the district's elementary summer school program. The program brought 266 students to South Heights from all over the county for six weeks of remedial instruction. Williams applied for the job because she taught summer school for several years and considered the program disorganized and lax. She questioned the inconsistent discipline policies and the practice of spending school district money for non-academic field trips, such as the previous year's visits to a movie theater and a commercially run indoor playground. Students who were struggling academically needed targeted tutoring, smaller classes, and exposure to the skills of excellent teachers. They did not need to spend their time in summer school goofing off.

Williams wanted to make the summer session more challenging and stimulating for children. She grew more determined to make a difference when she asked for the previous director's administrative records and was told they didn't exist. It was hard for someone as organized and efficient as Williams to understand that kind of inattention to detail. But her irritation turned to outrage when she thought of the children who were most affected by the apparent pattern of neglect. How could you improve a program if you didn't know where you had started? It boggled her mind to think that there were no records, no evaluations, no policies, and no procedures. Children came to summer school because they needed extra academic help. How could teachers provide that assistance if they did not have knowledge of each student's educational gaps? If the school system failed to turn these youngsters on to learning in the early grades, she feared their futures would be lost.

Henderson County's summer school program had a checkered past. For years teachers considered it a dumping ground for the worst students in the school system. Kathy Crawford, a Seventh Street Elementary School teacher who had spent 24 years in the district, recalled how instructors used to threaten children, saying, "If you don't shape up, you'll be sent to summer school." Summer school had a reputation as a punitive place, Crawford said, instead of one that provided children another opportunity to learn.

Consequently, many teachers didn't want to work in the summer school program. Over the years, the school district had raised teacher pay to $20 an hour to encourage more of them to take jobs. The unintended result was that some teachers just did it for the money. By the time Williams took over, the summer school teaching slots had become highly coveted because they coupled hefty paychecks with limited demands. Some teachers who worked in the program for years used their seniority rights to lock out younger colleagues.

The summer school hiring process had always been vague. This year, administrators asked interested teachers to write short letters expressing their desire to work in the program. The administrators did not interview anyone, or seek recommendations or formal applications. Williams wasn't hired as summer school director in time to participate in the selection process, so she could not choose the staff. But she vowed to set a higher professional standard for the people she would supervise.

"The word is that it's easy in summer school, that you just plug in a video and go," she said. "I'm not going in as a dictator, and I want them to like me, but that's just wrong. That's got to change." She was determined to make the summer school program a model of Kentucky's education reforms. Packing about one hundred hours of planning time into the few weeks before the summer term began, Williams organized her staff of thirty teachers and aides into primary and intermediate teams. She prepared a schoolwide interdisciplinary focus using a circus theme, "Under the Big T.O.P.," an acronym for Time of Progress. She placed a full-sized parachute in the school foyer and got everyone in the building—from the librarian to the cooks—focused on circus-related lessons. She lined up visits from professional clowns, as well as naturalists and storytellers.

Before the summer school session started, Williams held an orientation session for the staff. This was a first for the district. She passed out bags of circus peanuts along with a list of her expectations. Williams's manner seemed so upbeat that some teachers who didn't know her well wondered if it was an act. But Williams didn't substitute enthusiasm for substance. She was dead serious about the coming summer. She and her supervisors told the teachers they would be expected to dress properly—no shorts and cutoffs as in years past. And after seething for years about what she considered the slow-moving pace of the summer school program, Williams stressed that classes would start and end promptly, just as they did during the regular school year. By the second week of summer school, she trimmed the time it took to get students ready for dismissal from an average of thirty minutes to eight. "We don't waste time," she said.

Williams spent seventy-five dollars for books, toys, and supplies that she used as daily and weekly incentives for children. She recognized good attendance, achievement, and behavior. The nominated "performer of the day" and the "class of the day" received special tributes over the school intercom. Although some teachers considered the incentive project hokey and the candy and prizes puny rewards, the students loved the positive attention. Some parents reported that it was the first time their children had ever been recognized publicly for performing well in school.

In the computer lab, Williams set up a performance assessment center to help students and teachers understand and prepare for the new state test. She opened a reading lab full of high-quality children's books to entice reluctant readers. She also developed detailed procedures for the summer school program, typed them up, and placed them in folders so the central office supervisors and next year's director would not have to start from scratch. The summer school budget provided money for a secretary to help her in the office, and the previous director had employed two assistants. Williams considered both positions excessive. She wrote in her program evaluation notes that she would have preferred using the money to hire another instructional assistant.

As principal, Williams spent as much time out of the office as possible, visiting classrooms, observing teachers, and offering suggestions. The summer school instructors came from all the elementary schools in the district, so she hoped to gain some insight about the pace of education reform in other Henderson County classrooms. The evidence was not encouraging.

Some teachers referred discipline problems to the office without trying alternative approaches in their classrooms. One teacher threw a tantrum when she couldn't get more time in the computer lab, and she threatened to call a team meeting to interrupt the day's schedule. Several teachers placed desks in straight rows and handed out stacks of worksheets. Williams was furious when she discovered that one teacher had reproduced a fifty-page workbook for each of her students on the copy machine. "I didn't confront her," Williams said later, deeply regretting her decision. "I should have. I should have."

Williams did observe creative, challenging instruction on some classroom visits. And she was pleased to see that a woman who taught with her during the previous summer session had become much more adept with the primary school methods, including interdisciplinary lessons and group problem-solving exercises. "But that wasn't evident in many classes," Williams said with regret.

Some teachers told Williams they wanted to kick children out of summer school because they couldn't behave. "I thought, 'If you'd change your teaching methods, they wouldn't be a problem,'" she said. "They're bored. That's why they get in trouble."

But Williams didn't say that directly, just as she failed to speak up over the years when some of her colleagues at South Heights blamed students for not responding to uninspiring instruction. She continued to bite her tongue. As summer school principal, she simply told the complaining teachers they should be able to handle their own discipline issues. She was too timid to make demands or issue ultimatums. As much as she cared about helping students, as much as she supported the goals of education reform, Williams still was not willing to risk the alienation of her peers. She could tolerate almost anything but being disliked.

Bridget Townsend, a third-year teacher from Seventh Street Elementary working in her first summer school program, kept wishing Williams would say more. Townsend served as a substitute teacher at every school in Henderson County before she got the full-time job at Seventh Street, and she understood how intransigent some of the staff members could be about education reform. She felt fortunate to have landed at Seventh Street where teachers "focused on what's best for children." She believed Williams had the same high standards.

Although Townsend thought some veteran teachers in the summer school program might have resented the intrusions, she loved it when Williams occasionally popped into her classroom. Children flitted around Williams like hummingbirds seeking nectar. Their mutual affection was palpable. As a young teacher, Townsend looked up to Williams, who was held in such high esteem by educators in Henderson and around the state. "I know how busy she was," Townsend said, "but I would have loved for her to tell me something I could do better or improve. I would have loved for her to have offered some suggestions."

Williams had a hard time giving such guidance, even though she longed for it herself. Caught in the transition from classroom instructor to school leader, she could not see how much other educators admired her and needed her help. The organizational duties of a manager fit her like a glove. She could keep all the troops moving as efficiently as a general. But giving orders, or sometimes even advice, felt awkward. She didn't like making decisions for other people. It wasn't that she lacked confidence in her beliefs about what was best for young students. She just never thought she had the right to tell others what to do.

Nevertheless, Williams managed to "ruffle a few feathers" during the summer, said Jackita Snelling, Henderson County's elementary instructional coordinator and one of Williams's supervisors. "She had really high expectations and held them to it."

As the summer school session ended, Williams decided she wanted some feedback about the changes she had made. She knew she couldn't continue to improve the program without understanding what had worked and what had not. Besides, school reform promised higher standards and accountability. If Williams truly believed that, then she must accept the consequences of her choices.

She used a simple survey, and received seventy-five signed evaluation forms from parents. Williams asked them to rate the summer school program in the categories of discipline, staff friendliness, valued learning, food, and bus service. About 90 percent of the respondents checked "excellent" or "good" when rating the categories; the food and bus service drew the largest number of fair and poor marks.

Williams also asked parents to include additional comments and suggestions for improvement. Several parents said the office staff needed to be friendlier. One parent asked for longer school hours. Some parents pointed out problems with bus transportation. One mother said her daughter had gotten spoiled milk and a moldy hot dog bun from the cafeteria; when the girl complained, the cooks refused to replace it.

Most of the comments were positive. One parent said, "In many ways we were more impressed with summer school than school." Another said, "it help [sic] my child very much." Several parents said their children had looked forward to coming to school each morning. As one mother said, "I am very pleased with what both of my children [sic] learning because my daughter really needed help learning to follow directions."

The evaluation form Williams distributed to teachers was much more detailed than the one she sent to parents. The four-page staff survey asked for ratings and comments about the organization of the summer school program, office efficiency, teamwork, discipline, instruction, food service, and the academic incentives.

The comments were mostly positive. However, several teachers thought Williams had been too miserly with the office staff; these teachers thought the summer school program needed more staff assistance. A few teachers reiterated their beliefs that children sent repeatedly to the office for discipline referrals should not be allowed to stay in summer school. "Discipline problems should not be here!" one teacher wrote.

"About staffing," another teacher said. "I feel that people who have taught [summer school] before should have first priority."

Several teachers singled out Williams for special praise:

"I was impressed with all the work Mrs. Williams had done for summer school."

"Dear Mrs. Williams: You were a wonderful leader!"

When it was all over, Williams was able to absorb some of the good feelings and reflect on the criticisms. She worked hard to make a positive difference in the summer school program, and the evaluations told her she had mostly succeeded. But she laughed when she recalled her naive assumptions about how much one person in authority could accomplish. Management certainly looked a lot different from the inside out. Her respect for Debbie Key, for Gayle Ecton, and for other school administrators had grown in direct proportion to her own experience trying to lead a group of people through change. It wasn't enough to will improvements to happen. Even optimism has its limits.

"I should have done some things differently," Williams said one day as she analyzed her tenure as chief. "I saw a lot of things I didn't really like to see in some classrooms. But it's hard to deal with that. Probably that's why Debbie lets some things slide. We all have room to grow. My impatience is not with people who are trying to change. It's with people who refuse, and those who make it hard for others to grow."

Education reform in Kentucky had thrust teachers like Irmgard Williams into a series of unfamiliar roles, but none was more perilous than leadership. It both terrified and excited them. As team players, as team leaders, teachers suddenly became responsible not only for the children in their care, but for the adults in their midst as well. Certainly there were risks in confrontation—hurt feelings, bruised egos, retaliation. But the alternative was much more grim:

every time professional incompetence went unchallenged, the probability increased that another one of Kentucky's children would be lost to the trash pile of school failure.

As much as she feared the specter of a neglected child, Williams dreaded the alienation and anger from her colleagues even more. So while she recognized that some teachers needed to quit before they did any more damage, Williams kept silent. Her spinelessness shamed her, but still she did not act.

For Williams, the caring, crusading teacher who had devoted so many years and so much love to the state's public school students, one question would continue to nag her:

"Did I take the easy way out?"

The answer is yes.

Chapter Eight

Letting Go

Not a speck of shade cooled the concrete slab outside the Chandler school cafeteria where a gaggle of middle-aged men wielded spatulas over barbecue grills. Fat juices from the beef patties splattered the coals and sweat streamed down the face of the chief hamburger flipper, Johnny Duckworth. As usual, he was right in the middle of the heat. He kept up a casual conversation with the guys, but his thoughts drifted with the smoke. Duckworth traced the hours he spent in the Henderson County courthouse the week before, trying to get help for a troubled student. He remembered a dozen details that he had to check off this night in preparation for the Chandler family cookout that soon would be underway. He raced ahead to the last two weeks of the school year, reminded that some of his best teachers would be leaving.

Absentmindedly, he swatted a fly that kept diving at the crown of his coarse, salt-and-pepper-colored hair. Duckworth was distracted, edgy. He thought about how good a beer would taste right now, then quickly banished the idea. He flipped a row of burgers before passing his apron and spatula to another volunteer. Then he pasted on his principal's smile and went inside to greet his guests.

On this second Monday in May, Chandler Elementary was like an orchestra at rehearsal. At 5:30 P.M., the building pulsated with noise and activity, but all the players seemed to know their places. Teachers, school cooks, and parents harmonized in the kitchen, preparing food for a crowd of about eighty people who would soon swarm into the cafeteria. In the library, two dozen parents watched a video about the school's primary program. In the gym, students and teachers practiced a show-stopping number to be performed later in the evening, the culmination of Chandler's "Family Night." Members of the school council also were on hand to explain their activities and encourage parents to vote in the upcoming elections. Duckworth stood off to the side, shaking hands and greeting people with a phrase straight off the old family farm: "Howdy, Howyou?" His words poured out in that syrupy twang so common among Southerners, in which all the syllables rarely survive pronunciation.

Duckworth held a symbolic baton throughout the festivities, but his direction was never overt. Though his natural inclination was to handle everything himself, he fought the urge to take over. He no longer was the only one in charge. Being an effective principal in the age of education reform meant being out in front but not always being in control. It meant collaborating, coaching, and consorting with committees. It meant leading other people through transitions that you didn't always understand yourself.

For Duckworth, accustomed to knocking down obstacles like a running back streaking toward the goal line, the most difficult lesson of school reform involved restraint. No longer could he manipulate other people to suit his aims. He still could be the guy to go to in a pinch. But if he wanted to keep Chandler's staff on the path to change, Duckworth had to be willing to stand back and let people walk on their own two feet. His job was to coordinate, not intimidate.

"One of the most important lessons in education is letting go," he said. "I know I have a lot of work to do."

As the 1994–1995 school year drew to a close, Duckworth continued wrestling with his own worst tendencies. His transformation from duck-tator to diplomat was not yet complete. Some days Duckworth confused letting go with giving up. He was preoccupied with his personal and professional losses. The first involved the recognition that three of his top teachers were leaving at the end of the term to become principals, promotions that made him proud but sad. Because Chandler had a policy of promoting from within—the school hired certified teachers as instructional aides, then later moved them into teaching jobs if they proved capable—several solid replacements waited in the wings. But Duckworth knew it would take time for the newcomers to assume leadership roles and attain the skills of the departing teachers.

Joyce Hamilton and Sharon Mattingly, two of the teachers who had accepted principalships, currently served on the school council. Duckworth would have to recruit and train two new teachers to take their places. Mattingly took the principal's job at the beleaguered

Smith Mills Elementary in Henderson; Hamilton planned to move to Holland Elementary School in Holland, Indiana, about an hour northeast of Henderson.

Ever since she had started at Chandler six years before, Hamilton had been preparing for a principal's job. She became a teacher later in life after raising her children, and she was eager to move into administration. Duckworth encouraged her to teach a different grade level each year so later on she would be able to advise her staff with the power of personal experience. Although she was ready to take charge in Holland, Hamilton was counting on Duckworth for continued support. In Holland, the faculty wanted to use techniques recommended by KERA, so Duckworth agreed to let the Chandler teachers lead some training sessions as long as Hamilton's new school paid for substitutes. Hamilton also planned to use technology to develop individual education plans for students—an idea she borrowed from Duckworth.

However, she didn't plan to push her staff as hard as Duckworth had prodded her and her colleagues at Chandler. A confident, forthright woman who always seemed on the verge of a smile, Hamilton was uneasy about Duckworth's more aggressive approach to leading people through change. At the same time, she acknowledged that while his methods produced grinding stress, they quickly forced people to work together toward common goals. "In the long run," she said, Duckworth's strategy "was very successful."

Mattingly's departure was more emotional for Duckworth. Although her appointment meant he would gain an ally at Henderson's administrative meetings, he would lose a colleague in the school building who embodied the educational principles he held dear. To Duckworth, Mattingly was a kindred spirit, someone who let nothing stand in the way of helping a student succeed.

Fourteen years before, when he became principal of the old Corydon Elementary School, Duckworth received word from other administrators that Mattingly was a "terrible" teacher and it was best to avoid her. Tall as a good-sized man, extremely overweight, and famously effusive, Mattingly was a physically intimidating woman with a reputation for fighting policies and practices that put her mostly disadvantaged students in jeopardy. Within his first two weeks on the job, Duckworth discovered that only part of the assessment fit. Mattingly was an inspiring teacher with a wealth of compassion and energy. If she was assertive and confrontational with supervisors, Duckworth thought, more power to her. She did it for the kids. But over the years, the criticisms from supervisors had wounded Mattingly, and she began to doubt her abilities. It was the job of the new principal (a man she initially distrusted) to rebuild her confidence.

Eleven years later, at the dedication of the new Chandler Elementary, Duckworth paid special tribute to Mattingly and the role she had played in turning Corydon around. "I wish every child could have a Miss Mattingly in their lives at some time," he told the staff then. "Someone as caring, demanding, and loving. She is not only a master teacher but a master humanitarian. We have to keep stray puppies out of her sight or she takes them home."

Mattingly, a twenty-year veteran of the Henderson district, completed the requirements for principal certification in 1987, but she repeatedly lost her bid for leadership positions. Whether burdened by her previous reputation as a rabble-rouser or by the assumption she was Duckworth's heir apparent, Mattingly's new appointment suggested relations between some of Henderson's education reform advocates and antagonists might be starting to thaw. Because Smith Mills was so small, Mattingly would be expected to teach part-time in addition to serving as the school's principal, a situation that suited her just fine.

"I had no aspirations to be a principal until I worked for Johnny; he taught me so much," she said. "I was free to make mistakes. He never reprimanded me. It was a learning process. In the first meeting I ever had with him, he said, 'There are two things you need to get along here. You've got to love kids, and you've got to be willing to work hard.' I didn't have a problem with either one."

At the same time Duckworth tried to figure out how to do without some of his strongest teachers at Chandler, he struggled to improve his relationship with his son. These were not gentle times between father and son. When Johnny visited Lance, he inevitably ended up shouting at him in frustration. Both of them were bullheaded and proud, but Lance had learned to emulate his mother's calm composure when confronted with Johnny's outbursts. In private, Lance acknowledged being angry at his father because he would not offer to pay for his college education. Lance already worked three jobs—at the funeral home, at an insurance agency that he started himself, and at his grandfather's farm. In addition, he attended classes part-time at Henderson Community College. Lance wanted to pursue a bachelor's degree in mortuary science at Xavier University in Cincinnati and get the chance to live away from home for the first time in his life. He didn't understand why his father, someone who valued education and earned $52,904 a year as a principal, wouldn't help him out. "When I was growing up, Daddy always said, 'I'll put you through school wherever you want,'" Lance said. "Then the drinking got heavy, and the farm went bankrupt, and the money wasn't there. But Daddy makes good money now."

For his part, Johnny said he would gladly contribute to his son's educational expenses, but he wanted Lance to ask him for assistance, not expect it to be given. And so the two men continued sparring, month after painful month. Each of them desired something from the other, but the gifts carried a heavy price. Johnny wanted a relationship with his son. Lance thought he hadn't done enough to earn it. Lance wanted financial help from his father. Johnny wouldn't budge until he showed more respect. Both men held their feelings hostage to principle, setting up a trade-off that could work only by controlling the other's actions. The situation virtually guaranteed that both would lose.

On the sidelines, Cindy Lockeridge, Lance's mother and Johnny's ex-wife, felt like a referee in a boxing match. Remarried and resolute after years of counseling, Cindy's loyalties remained solidly with her son. But she acknowledged Johnny would "always have a place" in her heart. Although Cindy said Johnny had apologized to her for his past behavior, she remained skeptical of his recovery and his sincerity. When he told her he wanted to re-establish his relationship with Lance, a child he did not bother to see during the first week of his life, Cindy responded bluntly, but not without compassion. "I said, 'Johnny, you can establish a new one, but you can't re-establish what wasn't there,'" she recalled. "Johnny missed some very precious years. He was never accountable in his personal life. Johnny is very good in his professional life. It's all he had for a number of years."

Sometimes Johnny Duckworth considered the Chandler staff more of a family than his own. He always felt more at ease at school than at home. During the past few years, he and the staff had grown closer by sharing intimate details of their lives at a series of weekly "Diet and Dialogue" sessions at lunch. Almost any topic of conversation was fair game. They talked about their childhoods, their beliefs, their regrets. They talked about the difficulties they had adjusting to change. They read self-help books together, studied educational research, and watched motivational films. And as they developed a deeper understanding and appreciation of one another, Duckworth and the staff also learned how to work together. They knew what to do when one of their colleagues needed help.

Duckworth's professional family had been quicker to understand and to forgive his many foibles. Perhaps this was because, as his ex-wife suggested, he had been more available to his staff over the years. And yet, it was not unusual for the Chandler faculty to use some tough love techniques with Duckworth, too. Whenever he tried to derail spending requests from teachers during meeting discussions, he was immediately called on the carpet. The teachers reminded him that while the principal might have been able to make those kind of decisions alone in the past, now the school council managed the school's money. The principal was only one member of the council. Duckworth acknowledged the lapse into his old authoritarian ways and vowed to do better.

Sometimes he issued group apologies for his behavior. During one staff training session, Duckworth showed the faculty a film, "The Art of Setting Limits," that discussed methods for dealing with defiance. Although the film emphasized student-teacher relationships, Duckworth turned it into a confession.

"Twenty-five years ago, I had some of you in school," he said to his staff. "Some of those things I did to you all then, the attitudes I had..." He stopped speaking in mid-sentence and rolled his eyes. His face turned red from embarrassment. "I didn't know any better," he said in a voice that seemed to be pleading for forgiveness. "Those things were done to me. But you all are going to be better educators."

Ray Roth, the school psychologist, quickly filled the ensuing silence and reminded his colleagues that people who try to control behavior instead of understand it usually end up making enemies, not progress.

"Guilty as charged," Duckworth said in agreement, and gave examples of his many failings, including his recent altercations with his son. "You cannot dictate how people treat you. You can only dictate how you respond."

It was difficult for a man whose life had revolved around power struggles to treat other people as equals. He was used to being the boss. Some people thought he had undergone an amazing transformation in the past few years. Others thought he had not changed at all.

His relationships with members of the school council brought many issues to the surface. The state law required all schools to have councils by 1996 (except for schools that exceeded their test score goals and chose to adopt other management structures) and Chandler signed on the first year with majority approval by the faculty. The council consisted of the principal, three teachers elected by the staff, and two parents elected by those who had children in the school. The Chandler council decided to set up twelve subcommittees to focus on the school's major responsibilities to KERA—covering everything from finance to instruction. The subcommittees then made recommendations to the full council. Because the school was so small, managing by committee imposed a burden on all the adults who worked in the building. Teachers, parents, the school secretary, the chief custodian—all of them held committee leadership positions under this setup.

It was especially tough trying to recruit parents to serve. Helen Posey had been a member of Chandler's council since it started in 1991. The other parent representative, Gary Hillyard, had served almost as long. Both Hillyard and Posey actively sought parents to serve on school committees, but with limited success. Posey attributed their reluctance to a realization that each position required an enormous amount of work. Hillyard thought parents stayed away because of Duckworth.

If Hillyard could have found someone to replace him on the council, he gladly would have stepped down. Although he recognized the importance of representing the views of parents in school discussions, he grew weary of the responsibilities. Yet, when he asked other parents to consider serving, Hillyard said most people refused to participate as long as Duckworth remained in charge. Hillyard understood their concerns. At thirty-seven, with three children of his own and a demanding job as a manufacturing engineer, he still trembled before Duckworth, remembering the former teacher who terrified him in junior high school.

Hillyard recalled sitting in Duckworth's seventh- and eighth-grade science classes where the teacher regularly belittled and intimidated his students. Duckworth's assignments were challenging, Hillyard said, yet the students were more afraid than interested in class because they never knew when Duckworth would explode. But it was on the football field that Hillyard endured the worst of Duckworth's wrath. He could still remember what it felt like when the coach, wearing metal cleats, stood on his stomach while Hillyard strained to keep his legs six inches off the ground. Whenever a football player failed this test, he had to run laps and endure hazing from teammates. The exercise was supposed to build strong stomach muscles. In Hillyard, it built a deep well of hate for a man who relied on force to control a gangly group of adolescents.

Hillyard eventually left Henderson for several years. When he returned to his hometown, he was shocked to discover that Duckworth was the principal of the elementary school his children attended. "I never understood how someone with his lack of character could be a principal," Hillyard said. "I questioned it then, and I have some questions still."

Although Duckworth reputedly had become more mellow in the past few years, Hillyard did not see evidence of the change. He thought the principal was abrasive with students, and he believed he still controlled the teaching staff through intimidation. Duckworth had not been rude or vindictive to him as a parent, but Hillyard wondered if he got special treatment because he served on the school council. Duckworth could be charming or irascible, depending on the audience. There were reports that the principal regularly assisted families in need, and Hillyard remembered hearing about students in his junior high school classes whom Duckworth quietly helped on the side. To Hillyard, these examples pointed to a "selective compassion" that should not be considered a badge of honor for a man who was supposed to be looking out for everyone's children. "A lot of people talk about wishing he were out of the [school] system, but they won't stand up and say anything," Hillyard said. "I think he needs to step down from the position. His aggressive attitude might be fine in a business environment. But it's not good for kids."

Hillyard recalled the time when his son, Jeremy, then a sixth-grader at Chandler, came home from school and reported that Duckworth had wrongly accused him of mischief on the school bus. When Jeremy repeatedly professed his innocence, the principal told him to be ready to confess the following morning or suffer serious consequences. Hillyard was disturbed by the description. Not only did it remind him of his junior high school dealings with Duckworth, but he believed his son was telling the truth. The next morning, he went to talk to Duckworth. "He was in a cheerful and happy mood," Hillyard said. "He said, 'Oh, there's nothing wrong. It was all a misunderstanding.'"

Hillyard viewed it as another example of Duckworth's tendency to turn his anger on and off to suit his needs. Yet, he was still so nervous around the man that he never confronted him directly about his concerns. He maintained a polite, but distant, relationship with the principal.

Posey, forty-two, had a different perception of Duckworth. She did not have the same history with him that Hillyard did. She spent her childhood in Newark, New Jersey, and moved to Henderson when she was eleven. She passed through junior high school several years before Duckworth joined the faculty. After graduating from Louisiana State University and working in business for several years, Posey joined her husband, Richard, on the farm his family had owned for two hundred years.

Posey was supportive of Kentucky's school reforms from the beginning because she believed the state must do something to raise academic standards. As a parent and council member, however, she saw plenty of imperfect attempts to implement the state's goals. She ran for a position on the school council when the new school building was under construction and the students still attended Corydon Elementary. She heard a rumor that Duckworth wanted to cut funding for the new school library "to bare bones if he could get away with it." Posey was appalled. She thought the library resources already were inadequate. It turned out the rumors were exaggerated, but Posey became a quick study on financial issues to prevent any future power plays from the principal.

"When my first [child] went to Corydon, I was told [Duckworth] was a tyrant," she said. "He never came across that way to me."

Posey said that over the years, whenever she asked people why they disliked Duckworth, some of their reasons seemed almost silly. For example, he apparently made some parents mad nearly a decade before because of his practice of turning the light out in the cafeteria to silence students before they left for their classrooms. As soon as the children quieted down, he flipped the switch back on, but some parents thought his action bordered on cruelty. They had held a grudge ever since.

Posey acknowledged having her own "rounds with him" from time to time. But she was a person who liked to confront problems directly. She didn't believe in stewing about disputes. Duckworth treated her courteously, she said, even when they disagreed. "I go to him and tell it straight," she said. "Other people, they'll complain about something and you tell them to write a letter and take it to the council. 'Oh no,' they say. 'I won't go public.' They're afraid of retaliation against their child. The same philosophy has always held true. It was true before KERA. It hasn't changed. "I think anyone who's insecure is insecure around Johnny. He knows where he's coming from on most issues."

Although he was extremely confident of his abilities as an education leader, Duckworth no longer assumed every question from a parent or a teacher represented a challenge to his authority. Parents said he seemed much more at ease when they were in the building than in years past. He still tried to push his weight around from time to time, but he rarely got away with it.

During one school council meeting, for example, members objected to Duckworth's plan for spending state technology funds. Duckworth, the council's chairman, wanted to add more computer memory to the office machines because he had been unable to store all the KERA documentation required by the state. But other council members wanted to buy a new computer for the school library to speed automation of the card catalogue. The principal assumed the other council members would automatically approve his recommendation. "We wanted to discuss some options," Posey said. "Johnny, at first I think he was shocked that we brought it up."

Eventually, council members agreed to seek more information before making a final decision. Duckworth encouraged everyone to put together a computer wish list that could be used to set priorities for future spending.

"Johnny was pretty quick about getting over it. He thinks fast," Posey said. "I think the old Johnny would have gotten defensive."

In recent months, however, Posey began questioning how seriously Duckworth considered other people's opinions before pushing for a decision. One issue involved the hiring of three new teachers to fill the upcoming vacancies. Since 1991, Posey and Hillyard had participated fully in school hiring decisions, and they expected to be involved again. But this year, Duckworth scheduled three consecutive days of interviews for the candidates, several hours at a stretch. Neither Posey nor Hillyard could afford taking that much time off from work. By not adjusting the interview schedule to accommodate parents, Duckworth seemed to discount the importance of their role on the council.

Duckworth placed a lot of emphasis on the interviews that preceded hirings. He and the teachers had written a series of questions designed to flush out the inner feelings of the candidates. The staff members who served on the evaluation panel were not interested solely in resumes and good grade-point averages. They wanted to assess how well the prospective teachers would fit in with the Chandler culture.

"It's kind of like at recess where you're choosing players," Duckworth said. "We as a team choose who's going to work with us. You'd better, because in times of school sanctions, you're only as strong as your weakest link."

Hillyard and Posey agreed that it was important to hire people who believed in Chandler's mission. After all, they had helped refine the school's goals as members of the council. But they disagreed that a candidate's performance during the interview process should take priority over experience and recommendations. When the two parents announced they could not attend the interviews, Duckworth sent them a package that included each candidate's application. The parents recognized some of the candidates from previous interviews. Using all the data available to them, Posey and Hillyard ranked the candidates and sent their lists back to Duckworth. A short time later, they heard that the candidates who made the bottom of their lists had risen to the top of the lists created by Duckworth and the teachers.

"We were not happy," Posey said. "We flat out told him." Yet, Posey and Hillyard recognized that with only two votes out of six on the Chandler school council, the objections from parents carried little weight. "All we can do is give them the voice of the general public," Hillyard said. "Other than that, I don't think we have much to offer."

Hillyard was not interested in running Chandler on a day-to-day basis. He recognized that professional educators had the knowledge and experience to do their jobs without a lot of second-guessing from outsiders. But he also thought parents brought a reality check to schools—they helped broaden the often insular views of teachers and administrators, and reminded them that they had a responsibility to prepare students for life outside the classroom. For his part, Hillyard tried to keep an open mind during school council discussions. He studied education research and asked plenty of questions for clarification. But he often thought the deck was stacked against full participation by parents. Even the language educators used, full of jargon that assumed an insider's knowledge, tended to exclude parents like him from having meaningful conversations about school reform.

Administrators in the school district's central office were not much help either, Hillyard said. Only twice in four years had a representative from the superintendent's office bothered to attend Chandler's council meetings, and both times the administrators came prepared with "some cart and pony show, not to sit down and listen to what was going on."

Hillyard reasoned that the central office staff might have stayed away out of deference to the council's independent status, but he wished more people, from administrators to the general public, would try to learn what it takes to manage a school. At Chandler, no more than one or two parents showed up at the monthly council meetings. Usually, it was because they wanted to complain about something, not learn about the issues.

In many ways, the experiences of Hillyard and Posey were not unique to Chandler. Other parents also struggled to define their roles as members of Kentucky's school councils. Nearly every group suffered growing pains. At the start of the 1994–1995 school year, 1,500 parents statewide were involved with school councils, up from zero four years before. However, 45 percent of the state's schools continued to exclude parents from management decisions—teachers at those schools had not voted yet to form councils, although they would be required to do so by 1996. Even at schools that had formed councils, voter turnout in elections was small.

State law charged councils with managing school operations, including hiring staff, selecting textbooks and classroom materials, and setting school discipline policies. Every year since 1990, the state had authorized councils to control an increasing share of the school budgets for instruction, staff training, and building maintenance. Councils were not supposed to evaluate or fire staff, set salaries, raise taxes, assign students to schools, or assume any of the broader responsibilities that fell within the power of elected school boards. Nevertheless, disputes arose between councils and school boards from time to time over which group had the authority to make certain decisions. The boundaries sometimes blurred.

The performance of councils also varied considerably from school to school. In an examination of Kentucky's school councils, researchers at the Appalachia Educational Laboratory noted in 1995 that only one of the seven schools studied had achieved the equal participation rates the framers of KERA envisioned (Appalachia Educational Laboratory 1995a). In another study of school councils, researcher Jane David found that either the principal or all the educators together tended to dominate the discussions and decisions and, sometimes, ignore the council's wishes (David 1993b).

David's 1994 follow-up study of school councils found that even the best groups focused primarily on student discipline, extracurricular activities, and building and grounds. Rarely did they concentrate on student learning. "Like teachers accustomed to autonomy and isolation, parents are learning how to play new collaborative schoolwide roles," David observed in the study. "The transition is not easy, especially when all parties bring histories of conflict and defensiveness."

In Henderson, most of the school councils operated from the moment they were authorized by the state. Superintendent Ecton, who had encouraged the schools to form councils quickly, now wondered if he had been too hasty. He believed strongly in participatory management, but thought the state had given councils too much responsibility too soon. Council members could not complete training sessions fast enough to handle all the tasks the state required them to complete. At the same time, state officials did not fully consider how much the decisions of each school council would affect the district as a whole. "They've got autonomy," Ecton said. "But if everybody makes decisions independent of each other, then it's a problem."

Ecton initially supervised the training of Henderson's school council members, then he backed off to give them room to grow. When he returned to take a leading role, he fretted that, in his absence, the councils had gotten "sixteen different translations" instead of the same message.

A case in point concerned financial responsibilities. During the 1994–1995 school year, the Henderson County Public Schools overspent its maintenance budget by $100,000. If a school requested new bookshelves, for example, it got them without too much argument from the central office. But all those individual requests began adding up, and by the time the central office shut down the pipeline, the damage was done. Then jealousy set in. Schools that did not receive new equipment, paint, or furnishings before the austerity push started complaining about those that had. Principals told their staffs that the central office would not let them fix anything in the schools that broke.

"That's not what we said," Ecton responded in frustration. He worried that the parochial interests of each council would tear the fabric of the school system apart. To keep the district in the black, he recommended cutting administrative travel, delaying some equipment purchases, trimming the allotment per-pupil to each school, and reorganizing staff training to reduce the amount of time teachers spent outside the district. Meanwhile, he agonized about how he could help school councils understand the district's financial needs and get each member involved in establishing budget priorities for the future.

At Chandler, Duckworth tried to base the council meetings on academic issues, keeping in mind the goals Ecton and the Henderson Board of Education set for the whole district. He focused the agendas on major topics, such as a discussion of the different ways students learn or what the KERA test data revealed about instruction. "The chairperson's job is to keep the focus on academic improvement," Duckwoth said. "The council is not about what color the cheerleaders' uniforms are."

But as with almost anything involving schools, reality often interfered with strategy. At Chandler, one case in particular sidetracked the council members for months. And as it played out, Duckworth was reminded over and over again how much the principal's job had changed in the wake of education reform.

A Chandler student, a fourth-grader, moved from Hamilton's class to Mattingly's room during the first semester. The boy had severe behavior problems, and Hamilton's patience had worn thin. Mattingly agreed to take a turn. She eventually recommended that the boy be tested for attention-deficit hyperactivity disorder, a malady diagnosed with increasing frequency in recent years for children who have severe problems concentrating in class.

The boy's behavior was extremely erratic, Mattingly said. He could be gentle and sweet one moment, then in the next instance act as if possessed by demons. One day he pulled down his pants and exposed himself to other children. Another day, after the class designed costumes for a special project, he dumped his outfit in a fish tank. He rarely completed assignments.

For a while, Mattingly didn't keep records of the boy's outburts. She tried working with his father, hoping to find some support for her efforts. She wanted to keep the boy in school rather than suspend him because she feared he would fall behind academically. She created a behavior plan, which the boy and his father signed; it included both rewards and punishments. But when those strategies failed to make a difference in the boy's behavior, Mattingly started documenting each infraction according to the school's discipline policy. The policy outlined a series of steps teachers should take in response to explicitly defined misbehavior. Swifter punishments were recommended for multiple violations.

Soon after, a doctor agreed that the boy did indeed suffer from attention-deficit hyperactivity disorder and prescribed the drug Ritalin. But the boy's father would not make his son take the medicine. The boy continued acting out in class. Eventually, at Mattingly's request, Duckworth set up a meeting with the father. The man blamed his son's outburts on children whom he accused of goading the boy. He wanted to know if teachers had punished the other children. Duckworth told him he could not discuss other children because of legal restrictions about student privacy. The father then claimed the pets in Mattingly's room distracted his son from his lessons. He also accused Mattingly of picking on the boy.

In mid-November, the father threatened Duckworth in the principal's office. Later that afternoon, with his son in the car, the man drove through the parking lot at high speed and nearly hit a school bus. Duckworth filed charges against the father for terroristic threatening and reckless driving and asked the police to physically remove him from school property.

In January, the father called the superintendent to complain about the school's treatment of his son, and Ecton referred him to the Chandler school council as the next stop for appeals. The father then petitioned the council to speak at an upcoming meeting. When he arrived at the meeting with his son, Mattingly and Duckworth excused themselves from the discussion because of a conflict of interest. Hamilton, who no longer taught the boy, took over the meeting.

Posey and Hillyard were especially courteous and solicitous, mindful of their roles as the father's elected representatives. They gave him extra time to speak and to explain his problem, forgoing the usual five-minute limit for people who addressed the council. The father repeated his complaint that his son had been suspended while other students had not. The council members responded the same way Duckworth had: Legally they could not discuss the treatment of other children. Then they showed the father the behavior contract he had signed and agreed to support, reminding him that he had not kept up his part of the bargain. The council found that Mattingly and Duckworth had followed the correct procedures and acted in the best interest of the child.

The next month, the father addressed the council again. Duckworth and Mattingly excused themselves once more, and the four remaining members listened as he ranted for most of the meeting. Afterward, they told him that if he was still dissatisfied with their response, he could appeal by filing a grievance with the central office, which he did. "It was a little disappointing," Hillyard said, not only because the father didn't get the answers he wanted, but because "we couldn't seem to help him. I don't think he understood the role of the council. He avoided any answer as to how to resolve the issue. He went right for the jugular. I never felt like we got to first base."

A school district hearing officer listened to the father's complaints, and he concurred that the school had followed procedures. The father appealed the decision to Ecton who met with him in late February. Although Ecton agreed that the Chandler staff had done just about everything possible, he urged the school council to try once more to help the father understand how the boy could succeed in school. Council members talked to him again. Then the school guidance counselor came up with a daily behavior modification list for the father to use with his son.

By March, the boy had been suspended for a total of nine days. His behavior was no better. Rather than suspend him for new infractions, however, Mattingly and Duckworth elected to keep him in school, working in isolation from other children. But later that month, the boy brought some plastic bags full of powder to school, told other students that the bags contained hallucinogenic acid, then tried to sell the "drug" for $1 a bag. When Duckworth found out about it, he called the state police who confiscated the powder and took the boy to juvenile court. Duckworth sat through a series of meetings with the boy's father, the school psychologist, and a district court hearing officer. The process strained everyone's nerves.

It also interfered with other children's learning. For the Chandler staff, the situation raised deep concerns about how far a school should be expected to go to meet the educational needs of each student if one individual could throw an entire group into turmoil. "He was part of the group that was taking the state assessment" for fourth-graders, Mattingly said. "It affected every other student."

Duckworth eventually filed criminal charges against the boy for trying to sell look-alike drugs in school. At his arraignment in April, the boy pleaded not guilty and the judge assigned a hearing date in early May. The hearing lasted four hours. The father acted as his son's attorney and brought in the child's classmates to testify. At the conclusion of the hearing, the judge determined that the boy was out of control, and he ordered the father to make his son take the prescribed medicine. The judge also ordered a social worker to meet with the boy's teachers and counselor at school.

By this time, Mattingly was preparing to leave for Smith Mills, and the Chandler staff began to shift its focus to the following school year. Duckworth, the counselor, and the school psychologist agreed to ascertain if the boy's behavioral problems could be caused by a condition covered under federal special education services. If so, they might be able to get additional help. The boy still had two more years to go at Chandler. Something must be done.

As the school year drew to a close, members of the Chandler council looked back on the episode with the boy and his father as a defining moment for their group. Against great odds, they found unity in conflict. One child nearly exhausted the many adults entrusted with his care, yet he could not pull them apart. It would have been easy to splinter their responses during tense meetings, to find fault with each other, and to lose sight of their goals. They could have focused on personalities and chosen sides, or directed their frustration and anger at the boy. Instead, they stuck together. They continued seeking the best treatment for the child.

"It was one of those issues that you knew could tear everything apart that we had worked toward," said Posey, whose daughter was in the boy's class in school. "We had to make sure we did everything to be as fair as possible. Obviously, in the old days, there would have been nobody else involved."

If the school council had not been part of the process, Duckworth would have determined the course alone. Before education reform, parents could appeal a principal's decision to the superintendent and to the school board, but Duckworth would have fought to keep the upper hand. He didn't like it when people, even his supervisors, suggested through alternative strategies that his methods were wrong.

Although it took him several years to figure this out, Duckworth realized that school councils had reduced the burden on Kentucky principals. By giving up absolute power at Chandler, he had accumulated all the headaches and inefficiencies of group management. At the same time, he had gained a supporting cast of players who agreed to share the responsibility for making tough decisions. Letting go did not have to count as a loss.

"Every time I get into trouble it's when I've tried to be efficient, not effective," he said. Shared management is "a very laborious thing, but it's in the best interests of the children. Rather than trying to be a barrier, you've got to let go and follow the process. If you haven't got good relationships, the principalship is hell on earth."

Duckworth believed that education reform built in more safeguards for families. There were more opportunities to challenge decisions and more people to offer help. Although he occasionally dreamed of returning to the simplicity of his previous dictatorship, he no longer considered it the best way to lead a school. Involving teachers and parents in school management was not quick or easy or smooth, he said. But it was right.

Chapter Nine

The Long Goodbye

In the spring of 1995, Gayle Ecton hired a Louisville public relations firm to evaluate how well the citizens of Henderson County understood and accepted both education reform and the school district's ability to implement it. The firm interviewed groups of students, parents, educators, and members of the general public. Their comments revealed a strong current of anxiety within the community. The controversy over the proposal to close Smith Mills Elementary had taught Ecton that he had to do a better job of listening before formulating and then communicating his plans. His circle of influence was only as wide as the number of people who understood what he was doing—and why he was doing it. The ensuing conversations strongly suggested that he still had a great deal of work to do.

In general, the focus groups signalled a lack of consensus about the quality of Henderson's public schools. For every story about parents who had pulled their children out of the public schools, there was another story about parents who believed their children were flourishing in them. For the educators, the further away they got from the magnifying glass in Henderson the more excited they felt about the reforms. One administrator talked about spending an hour on the telephone with the president of a New York State teacher's union who was seeking information about Kentucky's education reforms. "He was absolutely amazed. He said, 'I hope you all are successful because you're leading the way for the rest of the country.'"

The discussions also revealed how little the public knew about the details of KERA and how often they blamed the reform law for problems that were unrelated to it, such as racial tensions at the high school. Most of the participants were not openly hostile to school change, but they were confused and uncertain about the future. They feared waking up one day and finding out they had been duped, victims of a smooth sales pitch. Some of them doubted that their children would get a solid education in Kentucky's public schools. "I struggle with this every day," a parent said during one focus group discussion. "My husband is Catholic, and he would prefer that our daughter go to Holy Name [School]. He thinks the education is better, and I try to prove to him every day that it's not."

Another parent, a financial adviser who formerly taught at a local junior high, said he was no longer confident the public school system was the best choice for his children. "To be quite frank, I would not be surprised that Holy Name does provide a superior education," he said. "If I had to do it all over again, I might consider it, although it's expensive, and I don't earn a whole lot of money."

Another parent complained that he was confused about what was happening in the public schools. "I frankly am hard-pressed to say what all KERA entails."

In other focus group sessions, teachers, principals, and central office administrators said they supported the changes introduced through KERA. Almost no one wanted to return to the pre-reform practices, but they expressed feelings of frustration and fatigue at the never-ending push to do more. They complained that the school district seemed to favor ideas over results. And they feared they could not live up to even higher expectations. "We're at the point now that we've got to step back and reflect on what we can do to relieve some of the pressure," one principal said, "or we're going to lose a lot of good people real quick."

On the whole, school employees were much more positive about reform than either parents or students. "It's hard to step back and reflect on what's been accomplished in Kentucky in the last four years," one administrator said. "When you look at the writing and the math increases and the learning going on, there are a lot of good things happening. Things are really better for kids, I think."

"We have so many good things going on in this district right now," another administrator said. "We are so far ahead, not only of the state, but even the nation in so many initiatives that we have going. You've got to go outside to appreciate what we have inside."

Inside is where Gayle Ecton sat, however. And from his vantage point, outside praise was having little impact on his effort to build confidence in the Henderson County public schools. The school district was by no means in a crisis situation. Ecton continued to see progress. Yet, it was difficult to build a new model of education when so many people continued chipping away at the foundation. Too many educators still accepted mediocrity. And large numbers of the public did not believe the plan to invigorate Kentucky's public schools was either valid or effective.

Although the school district's test scores had improved, the district's dropout rate had worsened. In the 1989–1990 school year, 74 percent of the Henderson County students who started high school finished, a figure that was better than the statewide rate of 67 percent. By the 1994–1995 school year, the results had flip-flopped. Kentucky's graduation rate improved to 70 percent—the highest level in its history—but Henderson County's graduation rate slipped to 68 percent.

However, at the same time, Henderson County steadily boosted its average scores on national college-entrance examinations. The gains occurred despite the growing number of students taking the tests, which usually deflates the scores because of participation by those previously not considered "college material." More than two-thirds of Henderson County's students took the ACT and 14 percent took the SAT in the 1995–1996 school year, up from 55 percent and 8 percent, respectively, during the year before KERA was implemented. From 1989–1990 to 1995–1996, the district's average ACT composite score rose from 18.8 to 20.9, continuing to surpass the state averages of 17.8 and 20.1, respectively. Over the same period, Henderson County's average verbal scores on the SAT jumped from 480 to 575 and the average math score from 534 to 582 on an 800-point scale. The state averages on the SAT remained essentially flat during the period, nearly 100 points lower than Henderson County's average verbal scores and 60 points lower in math.

Although Henderson County officials sent this test information to community members in an annual report distributed with the local newspaper, the public remained skeptical about the school district's academic progress. During the focus group discussions, a newspaper editor who also was a public school parent acknowledged that the district had been a leader in Kentucky's effort to restructure its schools. But he also believed Henderson County's educators talked about the game better than they played it. "I don't know if the objective data would put this district among the elite in Kentucky," he said. "I think Henderson County is about average. I think a lot of people would be unhappy with me for having said that."

There was a time in Henderson when people held the public school system in the highest regard. A decade after the Civil War ended, the state superintendent of public instruction observed that "this city is probably the wealthiest, in proportion to population, of any municipality in the United States. It contains a people remarkable for their refinement. Yet the Public School has swallowed up all private institutions, and is the pride of the wealth and intellect of the city" (Arnett 1976, 84).

Henderson was a boom town during America's Reconstruction era. Called the "Dark Tobacco Capital of the World," the city profited from its easy access to river traffic, its moderate climate for agriculture, and its abundance of coal reserves. Henderson was home to the nation's second millionaire, and merchants, coal barons, and plantation owners built boulevards lined with stately Victorian homes for their families. Tobacco money helped pay for the city's first modern hotel, a grand, six-story structure built in 1890 that occupied most of a city block and was famous for placing private hitching posts along the street in front of the building (Henderson County Genealogical and Historical Society 1980, 136).

Henderson's first public high school for white students opened in 1869. City leaders started a two-room elementary school for black students in 1872, but did not build a high school for blacks until 1905. In 1870, the Center Street School opened with all twelve grades in one building, and other elementary schools soon followed to handle the overflow of students. The city's public schools became hugely popular with the gentry, who saw no reason to continue subsidizing the small private academies and seminaries that had flourished up to that time. Citizens gave much of the credit for the success of the public schools to the city's first superintendent, Maurice Kirby, an inspiring teacher who held high standards for his students and "never allowed unreasoning ignorance to dictate his policy" (Arnett 1976, 84).

The educational picture wasn't nearly as bright outside the Henderson city limits. The unincorporated areas of Henderson County supported a smattering of one-room, log cabin schools that stayed open only three to five months of the year, employed teachers of hugely varied skills, and possessed few resources. At the Sugar Creek School, also known as "Hell's Half Acre," the teacher used "whatever textbooks the pupils might own," according to *The History of Henderson County Kentucky, 1888–1978*. Few of the county schools were accredited, and county students who wished to attend the city's high school had to pass stiff entrance exams to prove they were up to the challenge.

In 1976, the city and county school systems merged into one of the largest districts in the state. But by this time the public no longer considered the city schools the jewels in the crown. Many affluent and middle-income families had moved to new housing developments that ringed Henderson, and they placed their typically higher-achieving children in the suburban public schools. Schools within the city limits became responsible for an increasing number of children whose parents were poor and had had little formal education. In their attempts to control these new first-generation students, teachers abandoned many of the unstructured lessons that became popular during the 1960s and reverted to more conservative practices such as drills, workbooks, and strict discipline. "Minimal competency," not high standards, became the goal. As former Henderson County Superintendent Bill Rideout noted in 1976, schools locally and throughout the state were emphasizing vocational training to give students "a sellable skill. There will be fewer people going to college in the '80s," he predicted, "since a lot of people have found that a degree doesn't mean a job."

Teachers and parents accustomed to students receiving more challenging, stimulating assignments became increasingly fearful about the academic standards in the Henderson County public schools. Some believed the larger number of disadvantaged students had diluted the quality of the school system. Classrooms no longer seemed predictable or safe.

The community's confidence eroded further in the mid-1980s with the revelation that transferred corporate executives from some new plants that had opened in recent years bought homes in southern Indiana so their children would not have to attend Henderson's public schools. It wasn't clear whether these out-of-towners reacted to the bad reputation of Kentucky's school system in general or Henderson's classrooms in particular. But their actions implied that Henderson's public schools did not satisfy people who could afford to choose. The snub wounded Henderson's pride, and a decade later people still talked about it.

This is the situation that Gayle Ecton encountered when he took over as Henderson County's superintendent in the summer of 1986. And to a great extent, he was still responding to the public's insecurities nine years later. Ecton had seized the chance to push through some needed changes in the school district, a campaign enhanced a few years later by the state's own effort to raise academic standards. But in exposing the school system's problems, Ecton and others made their case almost too well to a wary public. The all-out effort to improve instruction in Henderson's schools must mean that the current methods were deficient. That scared parents, and it angered teachers.

All over the country public schools were dealing with a much tougher group of students, emotionally and academically, than in years past. Weaker economic and social supports for families had reduced the ability of many parents to be involved in their children's education. "We're a reflection of society. All these things undermine public education," Ecton said. "The more visible we are about handling it, the more we suffer from a negative image. If we weren't dealing with anything else besides changing the way we teach kids, it would be monumental enough. But you put all that other stuff in the mix and it's staggering."

In a twenty-six page report about the focus group sessions and related research on the school district, the Louisville public relations consultant recommended that the Henderson County schools develop a plan to speak "with a unified voice" about education reform and stop framing everything around the acronym KERA because of its negative connotations.

"The communications challenge for Henderson County Schools is to assure/convince its publics, both internal and external, that it is delivering a solid, yet innovative, education to the children of the community," the report said. "Successfully communicating reform will require delivering the message that [the school system] is both honoring the past and preparing for the future."

Ecton reviewed the report's action plan, which included seventeen major recommendations—from setting up a student speaker's bureau and hiring a full-time public relations specialist to appointing a task force that would study the district's declining enrollment. The consultant also suggested that the district spread the word about successful schools and teachers. In a sense, the firm urged Ecton to use a controlled megaphone to spread his message. Nevertheless, he recognized that such a plan would require the staff to accept even more responsibility. However worthy the suggestions, Ecton knew the staff could not handle any additional projects. "People are worn out," he said, speaking as much for himself as for the staff. "I think it's time to let them draw a breath."

So Ecton put the consultant's report on a shelf and started streamlining. In May, he told the principals he was cancelling their twice-monthly meetings until the new school term started in August. He also rescinded a requirement that each administrator submit a collection of memos, letters, and other materials written during the school year along with a written self-evaluation. Ecton made the assignment initially because he wanted the staff to understand the state's similar process for evaluating students. He had forced himself to meet the same standard the previous year. It was a good idea, he thought, but it still created another task for principals to complete and for him to review. Administrators rejoiced at Ecton's change of heart. "Have I told you lately how wonderful you are?" Tom Hurt, principal of Spottsville Elementary School, wrote to Ecton in a computer e-mail message.

Ecton appreciated the sentiment, but it didn't do much to brighten his mood. He knew that letting go of a few deadlines and demands would help him as much as anyone, but his decision seemed more like an effort to placate, not to lead. Ecton strived to be a statesman, a leader who inspired others to reach for the same high standards he set for himself. He was frustrated that things had not gone as well as he had hoped. He had failed to persuade people to accept his vision for the Henderson County schools.

The last year had been particularly tense. Colleagues such as assistant superintendent Sue Williams knew Ecton was occasionally dispirited, but Ecton had not shared his feelings with many others. He had few close friends, partly because he spent so much time at the office. But he also had ethical concerns about mixing business with pleasure. As the superintendent in a small town, where the school district was a major employer, he did not feel comfortable establishing personal relationships with people he supervised or with those who did business with the school system.

Because of the long hours he spent at work, Ecton didn't develop many outside interests. He liked to read—mostly books about education. He listened to country music and jazz. He had tried to learn how to play the hammer dulcimer. But his mind was almost always focused on his job.

He had started to understand why other supporters of school reform, teachers in particular, often expressed ambivalence about their jobs. Like Ecton, they could not shake the sense that they had lost more than they had gained by having "no life" outside of school.

It would have been a good time to turn to his family for support. But Ecton made so few personal investments over the years that there was little accumulated interest to tap. His wife was busy with her own career now, his children focused on their jobs and families. They weren't disinterested, just distant. Essentially, he had disconnected them from the most meaningful part of his life. From time to time Gayle still talked to Barbara about his struggles at work, but he wasn't sure it was worth the energy anymore to try to bring her up to speed on the important issues in his field. To a degree, he was responding like a soldier returning from war. He found it difficult to reveal the depth of his emotions to those who hadn't spent time beside him on the firing line. The more he experienced the trials and tribulations of school reform, the more he gravitated toward people who did not need an explanation.

Although education reform increased his stress, Ecton had been consumed by his work for years. He rarely took a vacation. The previous summer he traveled for three weeks to the western United States with his wife and daughters—a peace offering of sorts. He usually let his unused vacation days lapse at the end of each year. "There have been times when we felt that family should have taken precedence," Barbara Ecton said, "and it didn't. Gayle and I may have different ideas about why."

Scott Ecton said he had known since childhood that his father was a "workaholic." He was not neglectful, his son said. He attended school plays and games when his children were growing up. He kept up with their studies in school. But he was frequently absent from the family, spending many nights and weekends at work instead.

Scott followed his father's career with interest over the years. Although he found it hard to accept his father's life-long devotion to work, Scott knew his father was good at his job. Public schools needed leaders like him, but they also burned them out. The demands on a superintendent's time were staggering, especially in the era of education reform. But Scott also believed some of the stress was self-imposed. His father thrived on tension like a seed sought water. The challenges made him feel alive. "I don't think he's happy unless he's stressed," Scott said. "I think he likes pressure to a certain extent because he's such a driven person."

Now that he was raising his own three children, Scott said he was much more involved in their lives than his father had been with him and his two sisters. He accepted the emotional and financial demands of being the main provider for his wife and children, but not at the expense of spending less time with them. In Scott's view, it was more important to be a hero at home than at work.

Whatever bargains Ecton made with his career over the years, whatever opportunities he sacrificed with his family, he had passed the point of no return long before the 1994–1995 school year. His heart was with the superintendency. Ironically, he was about to lose that, too.

As the school year drew to a close, Ecton realized he would be eligible to retire on his next birthday. He would be fifty-five with twenty-seven years of experience in Kentucky's public schools. Although he didn't want to leave his job, he started analyzing his options. He had three years left on his contract with the Henderson County Public Schools, and no one had suggested that he step down prematurely. But because of the incentives provided through the Kentucky Teacher Retirement System, it would be foolish to stay to the end.

His pension would be based on a percentage of his average salary from the last five years. Because of his length of service and his position as head of one of the state's largest school districts, Ecton was among the highest paid superintendents in Kentucky. Consequently, his salary was unlikely to grow substantially in the years ahead. Additional years of service would not count for much. The regulations almost encouraged Kentucky educators to retire in the prime of their careers. If he left Henderson County soon, Ecton still would be young enough to start over in another school district and could look forward to an additional, supplemental pension.

But he would have to move to another state. He could not retire from one Kentucky school district and go work in another if he wanted to continue investing in his state pension. He also could not take a teaching or administrative job at most of the state's public universities because their employees were covered by the very same pension plan. The situation infuriated Ecton. Some of his options seemed to be closing off before he had been given a fair chance to examine them.

Although he wasn't ready to leave Henderson just then, he also didn't want to base his decision solely on what was financially prudent. But was it worthwhile to stay in Henderson, in a job he loved, if it meant his pension would decline in value? He had worked in Henderson for a decade, longer than anywhere else in his career and longer than the average length of service for superintendents in America. He had invested so much time learning the intricacies of the school system and the state's education reform law. Meanwhile, the Henderson County Board of Education probably would have to find his replacement outside Kentucky because of a shortage of qualified administrators inside the state. "We're losing too much

Kentucky talent," Ecton said, "and importing people who have no ownership in the state. Just like I would do in another state, they would plan to come here to work a few more years and then go back to their home states and retire."

Statewide there had been an unprecedented turnover among superintendents—110 of the 176 positions had changed hands since 1990. Kentucky school districts were having a tough time finding replacements who understood how to meet the challenges of school change. Nevertheless, Wayne Young, executive director of the Kentucky Association of School Administrators, was not ready to blame education reform or the early retirement option. Statewide surveys showed that, on the whole, superintendents were more supportive of KERA than any other group of educators. Young also did not believe the high turnover among superintendents was necessarily bad. He thought some people who had quit probably needed to retire because they did not have enough energy or enthusiasm left. And because of the huge number of openings, more women and veteran administrators from other states had been hired in Kentucky districts. "I don't want to be critical of those who left," Young said, "but we've attracted a number of impressive people." In addition, the Kentucky Board of Education had removed several state superintendents because of corruption and misconduct, a process that almost never happened before the reform law.

If Ecton had been certain that he wanted to stay in Henderson County after he retired, he might not have made such a fuss about the pension law. It would not be worth the trouble to uproot just to retire more comfortably. But the truth was that he was ambivalent about the future. He often thought about teaching at a university, helping to train future principals and superintendents. Without a sizeable pension to balance the salary of a beginning professor, however, his income would have to be halved. And what if he really wanted to keep working as a superintendent but thought it was time to leave Henderson? In that case, it seemed ridiculous that the pension law would prevent him from taking a similar position in Kentucky.

Frustrated, Ecton looked for another solution. Perhaps he could get the retirement system changed. Over several months, he talked casually with some of his colleagues on the Commissioner's Advisory Council, a group of forty superintendents whom Kentucky Education Commissioner Thomas Boysen had selected to bring concerns about education reform to his attention. Ecton found an ally in Jack Rose, superintendent of the nearby Calloway County Public Schools.

Rose agreed to support Ecton's plan to amend the law so veteran teachers and administrators could stay in Kentucky after they reached retirement age. The two men talked to some state legislators and enlisted the help of Kenneth Shadowen, superintendent of the nearby Marshall County Public Schools, who served on the board of the Kentucky Teacher Retirement System. Shadowen took Ecton's three-page proposal to a committee that reviewed legislative recommendations.

After the committee received a report from an actuary, however, the proposal began losing steam. Only one other state, Kansas, offered the option that Ecton sought, and officials there claimed that the open retirement policy had created numerous problems. Teachers and administrators moved around so much that it had become difficult to keep up with the personnel changes. Some educators had established three separate retirement accounts with the state.

Kentucky officials also feared the increasing costs that the state might incur if educators became eligible to retire in one state school district and start over in another. Pat Miller, executive secretary of the Kentucky Teacher Retirement System, said the state legislature's 1988 decision to lower retirement eligibility from thirty years experience to twenty-seven years had cost the state $300 million more than the original estimates because so many people took advantage of the option. Ecton's proposal had the potential to be just as expensive, he said.

"Any time a person retires sooner than expected, we'll be paying more over time," Miller said. "We couldn't control or predict the flow. We wouldn't know if we'd have three superintendents take advantage of it or fifty."

In the end, Ecton's proposal did not make it out of the legislative committee or come up for a vote at the Kentucky Teacher Retirement System board meeting. There would be no exceptions to the rule.

Rose, the Calloway County superintendent, considered it "almost a crime" that Kentucky might lose Ecton's talents as a superintendent. Although he understood the politics, perhaps even the practicality, of the state's decision to prohibit retired Kentucky educators from drawing a second pension in the state, Rose lamented its impact on Ecton. His admiration of his colleague had grown over the years, even when they disagreed. Ecton was a person of integrity who did not stoop to manipulation or backbiting to accomplish his aims.

"If someone said to me, 'Give me the names of five people who epitomize the characteristics of an effective superintendent,' Gayle, if he wasn't at the top of the list, he'd be in the top five," Rose said. "And frankly, I can't think of anyone to put ahead of him."

At the end of the 1994–1995 school year, Ecton decided to retire. "I really have mixed feelings" about leaving, he said. "There's a lot I want to see finished here." But he also believed it was time to make a break. He thought the school system might benefit from new leadership. By continuing to push through Kentucky's education reforms, a new superintendent could persuade people that the cause was bigger than one man's dream.

"After a while you just get burned out on certain problems," he said. "If I'd stayed ten more years I'd probably still be working on those same problems."

Although he didn't plan to leave until the summer of 1996, Ecton gave the school board almost a year's notice of his impending departure. He wanted the board to have enough time to find his replacement, and he wanted enough time to plan his future. He thought he could enjoy the familiarity of his current position while looking for another one. Ecton considered becoming an educational consultant who could advise school administrators around the country. But that would involve a lot of travel. More than anything, he just wanted some time to think. "It's been more than a job" for me, he said. "It's been my life."

Finding something as challenging and as satisfying as the Henderson County superintendency would be difficult. Ecton knew that. He had enjoyed unusually smooth relations with a supportive and progressive school board. He had built an administrative team that included many hard-working professionals. He cared deeply about his adopted community and had earned its respect. So it was an emotional evening at the August 9th school board meeting when Ecton made his plans public.

"Nine years ago, the school board here gave me the greatest opportunity of my career when I was employed as the Superintendent of Henderson County Schools," he said in a letter that he read at the meeting. "I love Henderson—the city and the county—and I love our school system. This is really a great community, and I have enjoyed living and working here more than any place I have ever lived."

Ecton said he would retire the following June. To help smooth the transition, he recommended that the school board work with community representatives and the Center for Leadership in School Reform, a Louisville consulting firm, to identify goals for the district and decide what kind of person should lead it. He stressed that education reform could endure after his departure. If the ship sank after he left, it would mean that he had not been a very good captain. "I wanted to tell you now to allow time for an orderly transition," he told the board members. "I certainly owe you that."

School board president David McKechnie fought back tears several times as he accepted Ecton's resignation. "I know the Henderson community schools have been blessed to have you here," McKechnie said.

Two days later, an editorial in *The Gleaner* praised Ecton for demonstrating the "class" and "loyalty" that had become the hallmarks of his administration. "Even those who have crossed swords with the superintendent over such inherently emotional issues as proposed school closings have never had good reason to question either his ability as an educator or, more important, his commitment to the school community as a whole," the newspaper said.

"The next superintendent will inherit leadership responsibilities for a school district that has stayed the course in its mission to make learning—and life—better for our students. In that important test, Ecton has scored high marks."

Chapter Ten

Reconsidering the Revolution

The Kentucky Education Reform Act passed one of its toughest tests during the 1994–1995 school year: It survived. That was no small achievement, given the increasing attacks on school reform initiatives both inside and outside the state. After five years of hovering over Kentucky's public schools, the specter of KERA no longer seemed fleeting. It had changed shape but it had not gone away.

And yet change still had not penetrated deeply into the state's psyche. Education reform was tolerated, not beloved. After five years, fewer people ignored the directives but more complained about them. People demanded impressive results from KERA. They just didn't want to work hard for those gains.

In reality, broad-scale school change in Kentucky was not so much a revolution as an ultimatum. The state Supreme Court issued a mandate to fix the state's schools, but the population did not agree on the remedies. Without a consensus about education reform, there was little likelihood that people would make the serious and lasting changes needed to move the state from the bottom of national education rankings. Some of the state's classrooms undoubtedly were better than before, perhaps most of them were in one way or another. Certainly, more teachers and students had learned to appreciate the importance of reaching higher academic standards. But too many hearts still hardened against the promise of progress, and too many attitudes stayed stuck in reverse.

People continued to complain that KERA involved too many changes and not enough time. Yet, because the state court had declared Kentucky's school system unconstitutional and imposed tight deadlines for making it more fair, state education leaders had to make heavy demands on schools.

"Nevertheless, in some schools and districts acceptance of the reform effort remains mixed, and there is still confusion about how specific elements of the reform program are supposed to work together to produce change," observed a 1996 report by The Partnership for School Reform, a coalition of leaders from business, government, agriculture, and labor dedicated to the successful implementation of KERA.

"There are, as well, those who either remain skeptical about the reform philosophy or are uncommitted to reform and their own participation in it. On recent surveys, for example, only about half of principals and a third of teachers registered agreement with such basic KERA beliefs as: 1) all children can learn at a relatively high level; 2) we should set high standards for all children; and 3) demonstrating mere knowledge of facts is not enough; children should be able to demonstrate that they can apply what they know.

"Success in education restructuring remains uneven, and there is lingering reluctance on the part of some to adopt the spirit of reform," the report continued. "On the part of some teachers and schools, there has been a lack of initiative in taking advantage of the resources available to help them put reforms in place locally. In short, many teachers and schools have yet to take full responsibility for their roles in reform."

Some of KERA's problems resulted from poor decisions inside Kentucky. Consider, for example, the initial reluctance of Henderson County High School teachers to give students more thoughtful and timely writing assignments to improve their scores on the state test. But such mistakes also seem to be an inherent product of institutional reform. One of the common conflicts is the tension between revolutionary and evolutionary change. Radical change, which requires people to throw out the past and start over, often appeals in the short term but withers when the intensity for something different cools. Deliberate change has the opposite effect—it moves too slowly to address the most pressing needs. Similarly, top-down mandates rarely work because the authorities don't have enough commanders to keep everyone in line. But people toiling in the trenches can't produce coherent change in the overall system.

Was there a better choice for Kentucky? There is no question that KERA's framers created an inspiring model of school change. They demonstrated courage and foresight by introducing a radical restructuring plan in a state that had built no foundation for excellence in education. But the boldness of the creators led to some serious miscalculations. Many people in Kentucky wanted to catch up to the rest of the country by taking baby steps, not by leaping ahead. They favored moderation over revolution. It is true that a state so backward in its beliefs about education needed a transfusion of new ideas. It is true that nothing short of a sweeping transformation could produce the dramatic results that were necessary to give Kentucky's students a chance to compete with the best. Yet it was also abundantly clear that many people refused to take the medicine prescribed for them. Kentucky's history of low expectations continued to haunt the current generation of teachers and students.

"Only a few of the KERA innovations are well-integrated into school culture," researchers from the Appalachia Educational Laboratory observed in a 1996 report, "Five Years of Education Reform in Rural Kentucky."

The irony in all of this is that education is supposed to be about change and growth. It ought to be constantly evolving. And yet people are so fearful of breaking from the past that they have become paralyzed in the present. Nowhere else do people try to block the flow of progress more aggressively than in education.

If history has shown us anything, it is that change in education involves a series of individual adaptations. All progress in the classroom begins and ends with a teacher and his or her students. The farther you go from the center of instruction, the less control you have over the outcome. By focusing on school reform in its broadest outline, state officials neglected the importance of teaching's traditions and practices.

One of KERA's lessons to the nation is that school reform will not advance without constant training and reassurance of the people most directly involved in change. Studies have shown that people usually need several years of regular practice to successfully make major shifts in their ordinary work habits. In Kentucky, teachers, principals, and students were expected to perfect about a dozen new practices simultaneously. Is it any wonder they fell short of the mark in the early years of school reform?

Teachers also need to recognize that times have changed in education. They cannot hold up their own instruction as the model for the future any more than doctors can practice modern medicine by recalling episodes of *Dr. Kildare*. Teachers must understand that ongoing learning is a basic requirement of the job.

"What teachers know and do is the most important influence on what students learn," the twenty-five member National Commission on Teaching & America's Future observed in its 1996 report on teacher training. "A recent study of more than one thousand school districts concluded that every additional dollar spent on more highly qualified teachers netted greater improvements in student achievement than did any other use of school resources. School reform cannot succeed unless it focuses on creating the conditions in which teachers can teach, and teach well."

The designers of KERA worked from the premise that children learn in different ways and deserve instruction that accommodates their needs. But there was no recognition of the different strengths and weaknesses of individual teachers. Although some teachers were strong candidates to keep the same students for several years during the primary grades, for instance, other teachers had no business being in the classroom at all. Their skills, temperaments, and professional training varied greatly. The failure to recognize those gaps, and to adjust the training of teachers accordingly, did more to derail the progress of school restructuring in Kentucky than any other factor.

Teachers need models of excellence, they need regular exposure to new practices, and they need guidance and support while they're trying out new techniques. They also need smaller class sizes. Asking teachers to give individualized instruction to large groups of students is a recipe for failure. Even the most talented and dedicated teachers will suffer under the strain.

Nearly every major study of KERA has recommended that state and local school districts improve staff training. Some have suggested the state's education reform plan is doomed without it. Early prophets, such as the leaders of the Council on School Performance Standards, urged state officials to spend more time and money helping teachers adopt new strategies. In the formative years, however, those who had the major responsibility for retraining the state's public school teachers didn't pay enough attention to quality and consistency. Professionals in the Kentucky Department of Education contended their various programs and reference books were adequate, but their customers disagreed.

"We've had a great deficiency in training from the state department," one teacher said during a 1995 focus group interview with researchers from the Appalachia Educational Laboratory. "We had Transformations training sometime back, but there has really been no training in how to use these [curriculum guidelines]."

Another teacher told the researchers, "I think one of the things that really irritates me as an educator is when the state comes in and shows us these handy-dandy films. They would lose a classroom in five minutes. I just wish in their training they [would] model what they expect us to do in the classroom. All I have seen is a videotape of someone sitting in a chair telling me in lecture form, holding up an overhead."

However, for all the legitimate complaints teachers have about receiving inadequate and inappropriate training, they also must shoulder the blame for ignoring some of the truly useful lessons KERA tried to teach them. Kentucky's reform law was predicated on the assumption that teachers would respond to its promise of professional growth with tremendous cooperation and energy. When many of them did not accept the offer, the law offered no recourse. KERA provided a mechanism for the staffs at poor performing schools to gain assistance from distinguished educators, but the law did not address the broader reality of teacher indifference and the systemic resistance to excellence. Despite the state's grand expectation that all Kentucky classrooms would become incubators for intellectual growth and achievement, too many public schools continued offering safe havens to apthetic and ill-suited teachers. Without an effective way to fire them, given the protections of tenure and union contracts, KERA would never reach the academic heights it so desperately sought to scale.

Kentucky's reform contractors also misjudged the entrenchment of the educational bureaucracy at both state and local levels. Although KERA dismantled the Kentucky Department of Education and made all employees reapply for their jobs, most of the old guard stayed put. Bright newcomers joined the ranks of state department outreach specialists, and some thoughtful educators emerged as leaders in local school districts. But on the whole, the state's support staff still acted more like cops than counselors.

The task of persuading Kentucky teachers to buy into education reform was daunting from the start. It is far easier to take potshots at state education leaders than to acknowledge the challenge of their assignment. Nevertheless, many education leaders showed the same limitations as many teachers: the inability to change under pressure.

The same could be said of public school parents who often sat back and let educators accept full responsibility for teaching their children without offering any outside support. Parents complained but rarely participated. Some of the apathy could be attributed to the historical animosity between educators and the public, a division engendered by teachers and administrators who did not want anyone telling them how to do their jobs. Parents traditionally haven't been welcome in many public schools. And yet when Kentucky's education reforms opened the school doors to parents in new ways, particularly in the important governance work of school councils, few parents bothered to get involved. They, too, share the blame.

The Partnership for Kentucky School Reform lamented in its 1996 report, "From Dilemma to Opportunity," that "the success of school-based decision making remains somewhat uneven, the pace of adoption of councils is behind expectations, and low parent participation is disappointing . . . a residue of vagueness hangs over the role school councils are supposed to play in achieving reform goals at the local level. Even among those councils that have been active, few have learned how to use the power they have in ways that are most effective for enhancing the quality of what goes on in classrooms."

At its essence, KERA is all about the distribution of power. The school reform model recognizes that all students have the power to learn, in different ways. It honors the power of parents to advocate for their children's education. It respects the power of teachers to design appropriate lessons and interpret the goals of reform to fit the needs of students. And it acknowledges the power of principals to assimilate all of these interests.

But public schools have almost no experience operating in such a democratic fashion. Power struggles are much more common than power sharing. Establishing true equality in Kentucky's public schools will require all the players to accept responsibility for carrying the load, recognizing that everyone loses unless everyone wins.

It is impossible to judge fairly the impact of KERA in its first five years because so few people got it right. Miscommunication and false starts were far more common than successful application. Evaluations showed that in classrooms where teachers took the recommended changes seriously, instruction and learning advanced considerably. Those same conclusions could not be made on a larger scale, however. Mistakes should have been expected, of course. Anything new takes time. If good intentions were coupled with supervised practice, more people could move ahead. But patience never has been among the public's most practiced virtues, in Kentucky or anywhere else.

In a 1995 statewide poll conducted by *The Courier-Journal*, about half of Kentuckians who said they had heard about KERA disapproved of the reforms, up from one third of the people who were surveyed two years before. In November, Republican Larry Forgy, who made the governor's race a referendum on KERA, came within two percentage points of defeating Democrat Paul Patton in a state that had not elected a Republican governor in nearly 30 years. Six months later, a member of the Kentucky Board of Education claimed that "the whole reform movement is about to slide over the cliff." Tom Gish, a newspaper publisher from Letcher County in eastern Kentucky, accused his colleagues of acting like an "amen chorus" instead of asking tough questions about school reform. The following November, voters in the northern Kentucky city of Covington ousted Democratic state Senator Joe Meyer, the chairman of the Senate Education Committee, and voters in the central Kentucky region near Shelbyville nearly toppled veteran Democratic Representative Marshall Long. Both men were early and strong supporters of KERA. In another central Kentucky race, anti-KERA candidate Ricky L. Cox beat Representative Michael Stephens. In each case, the Republican candidates received help and endorsements from individuals and groups that had been highly critical of Kentucky's education reforms.

"I ran a grassroots campaign. And education was one of those issues that just kept coming up," Jack Westwood, the Republican who beat Meyer, told the *Lexington Herald-Leader*.

"This, I think, is a major, major development because Joe (Meyer) is seen as one of the twin pillars of support for KERA in the senate," Martin Cothran, a policy analyst for the conservative Family Foundation in Lexington and one of the leaders of the anti-KERA forces, told *The Courier-Journal*. "With one of the pillars gone, I think the KERA structure is a whole lot weaker."

Despite such projections, legislative leaders responded that the General Assembly was more inclined over the next few years to reinforce, not eviscerate, Kentucky's education reforms. However, when rebel Democrats and Republicans took control of the Kentucky Senate in the second week of 1997, that long-term assessment suddenly seemed as reliable as a coin toss. On the first day of his appointment, Larry Saunders, the new Senate President from Louisville, pledged to appoint an equal number of Republicans and Democrats to the Senate Education Committee, giving much greater visibility to members who opposed Kentucky's school reforms. Previously the Democratic majority had rebuffed Republican attempts to change the law.

While legislative leaders kept Kentucky's school reforms suspended by whim, public attitudes toward KERA continued shifting back and forth. By late 1996, Preston Osborne Research, a Lexington firm, found that positive ratings from a representative sample of the state's registered voters rose 10 percent—to 46 percent—from the same period a year before when the gubernatorial candidates publicly attacked school reform. Nearly 50 percent of the respondents in 1996 could not cite a weakness in KERA.

"The overarching point in the survey is that people are still uncomfortable with change, even though our survey indicates a slight improvement in attitudes toward education reform," said Phil Osborne, president of Preston Osborne Research. As critics become more vocal about education reform, "the . . . uneasiness that's just beneath the surface with most Kentuckians rises."

In an article reprinted in several Kentucky newspapers in the summer of 1995, Robert Sexton of the Prichard Committee for Academic Excellence, a pro-KERA group, pointed out that substantial improvements had occurred since 1990, including a state education bureaucracy that was 28 percent leaner, a 47 percent gain in education spending, a 51 percent reduction in the spending gap between the poorest and wealthiest school districts, and higher achievement in 95 percent of the state's schools.

"By any fair measure," he wrote, "it's indisputable that thousands of Kentucky educators have been trying and succeeding at what people in the school business think is an almost impossible challenge: implementing the nation's most rigorous and demanding educational reform program. We're halfway home, with a long way to go in the climb out of the nation's educational cellar."

Indeed, evaluations of state test scores showed that KERA had come close to fulfilling one of its major promises—closing the financial gaps between rich and poor schools. Because the reform law provided more money for schools in the poorest districts, funding had become more equalized since 1990. The difference in the amount the poorest and wealthiest school districts spent on each student had narrowed from $1,199 to $588 in five years. The extra resources had a direct impact on student achievement. According to an analysis by the *Lexington Herald-Leader*, 73 percent of the state's poorest schools, determined by the percentage of students who qualified for free and reduced-priced lunches, met or surpassed their state test goals during the 1994–1996 scoring cycle. In some cases, students in the poorest schools made up so much ground that they matched or exceeded the skills of students from the state's most well-supported schools.

These indicators gave state leaders the confidence to push for additional improvements in Kentucky's public schools. In December 1996, for example, the state Board of Education gave initial approval to the tougher high school graduation requirements recommended by Wilmer Cody, Kentucky's new Commissioner of Education. Although some local school districts already had implemented similar standards, the state moved to require all high schools to increase science, social studies, and art credits, and to require more advanced courses in mathematics, including algebra and geometry, instead of lower-level survey courses. The changes were not enough to put Kentucky students in the company of giants, but they signalled the state's increasing reluctance to accept their status as intellectual midgets.

Meanwhile, outsiders continued to shower praise on KERA. For example, Walt Disney Company reported that it was adopting many features of Kentucky's educational model—including the ungraded primary program and the family resource centers—in the new school system it would create in Celebration, Florida, the company's planned community. And in October 1997, the Ford Foundation and Harvard University's Kennedy School of Government named Kentucky Education Reform Act one of the ten most innovative government programs in the nation. The two groups gave their prestigious Innovations in American Government Award to the Kentucky Department of Education. The department received a $100,000 grant and the recognition that it had set a national standard of excellence. It seemed that Kentucky's education reform plan was destined to be recognized as a success by more people outside the state than in it.

KERA is still a work in progress. As its weaknesses have been exposed, its detractors have multiplied. Its future now rests in the hands of a group of people who represent the population's best and worst characteristics—courage and peevishness, diligence and despair. Public school educators, and those who support them, live a fragile existence that vacillates between our need for heroes and our acceptance of scapegoats. They are as good and as bad as we allow them to be.

Irmgard Williams, Johnny Duckworth, and Gayle Ecton demonstrate poignantly how much we expect from public school educators in this country, how irregularly we support them, and how little faith we have in their ability to succeed. The three of them believed in the possibility of progress. They refuse to accept the widespread belief that Kentucky could do no better for the least of its citizens and should not bother raising the stakes for its most able scholars. Each of these educators spent the twilight of his or her career trying to set a new course for Kentucky's public schools. Each ignored the catcalls of those who were more afraid of change than failure.

Were the results worth the struggle? As a society, we have to ask ourselves if comprehensive school reform is realistic when some of the best educators in the land struggle to make gains against such staggering odds. Do we really deserve better schools?

Chapter Eleven

Endings and Beginnings

Irmgard Williams ran out of patience with her colleagues at the start of the 1995–1996 school year. She no longer believed most of them would adjust to Kentucky's education reforms over time. If anything, she found increasing evidence they were backsliding, teaching the way they always had. Some no longer bothered to go through the motions of trying new techniques.

Now that Laura Courtney had assumed the team leader's role, Williams could not organize meetings and exert the same influence with her colleagues as before. Some weeks, team meetings didn't take place at all. Principal Debbie Key feared the South Heights staff was dangerously close to losing whatever momentum it had gained in the previous five years. But she honestly didn't know how else to inspire the teachers. "I worry that . . . it'll all go back to where it was before—writing spelling words ten times each and using textbooks as the basis of everything," she said.

Like Williams, Key took it personally when teachers did not draw out the best from students. At this point in the implementation of KERA, she felt weighed down by the collective mistakes made at South Heights, in the Henderson County district, and around the state. "We've had so much to do and learn," she said as she supervised the school lunchroom one day. "Maybe we let some things slip by."

The possibility of so many unknown failures suddenly moved Key to tears. She had worked so hard to make KERA successful, but it seemed she could never do enough. She turned her head and wept quietly, trying to hide her anguish from the students and teachers who passed by.

The 1995–1996 school year brought some simmering problems to a boil, including the staff's growing dissatisfaction with the primary program. The critics included some of KERA's earliest supporters, such as Carolin Abbott, who previously praised the state's plan to restructure elementary grades. Now she had serious misgivings.

Abbott's concerns had more to do with the structure than the strategies of primary school. She strongly supported efforts to help children learn by completing projects and demonstrations instead of memorizing lists. She also liked trying different methods for teaching students to read, write, and think. But she believed there was a limit to how well she could reach any child when confronted with such a broad range of ages and abilities in a single classroom. "There's no way you can effectively teach first-, second-, and third-graders all in one room in six hours," she said, defying the research and ignoring the practice of teachers who had found a way.

Abbott said she could balance the needs of two age groups in the classroom, but she preferred teaching students who were mostly the same, making adjustments for the few children who were behind or ahead of the rest of the class. During the 1995–1996 school year, for example, her class included twenty first-graders and four students who should have been in the second grade according to their ages. One of the second-graders was extremely bright but emotionally immature. She gave him more challenging assignments but knew he wasn't ready to move on to the next level. The other three older students lagged behind grade level and would have been retained if the state had permitted failures before fourth grade. Instead, the older students stayed with the younger students and repeated the previous year's work. They had little motivation to do better, however, a situation Abbott and other teachers blamed on the elimination of letter grades in the primary program at South Heights. They argued that in their zeal to remove the stigma of failure from elementary school, state leaders forgot that children still needed terse reminders of their progress.

"So I got a sad face on my paper," Abbott said. "Big, hairy deal. The kids can take it. Why can't we have A, B, C, or Excellent, Above Average, Average, and Progressing? Now everybody is on the same keel. Everybody is mediocre. I think that primary school could be saved and do a good job if they would let teachers honestly evaluate students. They need grades. They need consequences."

Traditional evaluations in early elementary grades were not prohibited in Kentucky, just discouraged. Some schools and school districts still used a variation of letter grades, in addition to detailed comments from teachers. In the Jefferson County [Louisville] Public Schools, for example, report cards in the primary grades included written comments from teachers but also carried subject grades—the symbols of RP, SP, PH, and LP, which stood for Rapid Progress, Steady Progress, Progressing with Help, and Little Progress, respectively. Other districts used "SUN" marks—Satisfactory, Unsatisfactory, and Needs Improvement. However, most elementary schools in Henderson County used a strictly narrative report card called KELP (Kentucky Early Learning Profile) that the Kentucky Department of Education designed. Instead of giving parents merely an accounting of where their children stood in relation to the rest of the class, as indicated by ABC grades, the narrative report card aimed to show how far the children had progressed in learning certain academic and social skills. Yet, many teachers and parents considered the new report card unwieldy and confusing.

Abbott's other major complaint—that teachers should not be forced to work with older and younger children in the same classroom—found support around the state. In a 1995 survey by Wilkerson & Associates of Louisville, 90 percent of Kentucky school administrators, teachers, and parents said that if the state law did not require schools to mix students by age, they would want students assigned to classes according to their chronological ages. The General Assembly responded to the dissatisfaction with the grouping practices by amending the law during the 1996 legislative session.

Harry Moberly, Jr., the Democratic representative from Richmond who sponsored the bill, said that focusing so much attention on the combination of students in the classroom distracted teachers from the more important goals of using "developmentally appropriate practices" and "continuous progress." He believed that if teachers tailored instruction to students and regularly evaluated their progress, they would automatically group children of different ages together to meet their various needs—and they didn't need a state law to tell them how and when to do so.

Multiple studies of Kentucky's primary program contradicted that assessment, however. In one evaluation of teachers considered among the best in their field, University of Louisville researcher Ellen McIntyre found that the "multi-age mandate 'forced' them to re-examine the children's development" and create appropriate lessons to challenge each student. "Because they faced children of such varied ages, experiences, interests, learning styles, and personalities, the teachers had to rethink many of their accepted and often-practiced activities," McIntyre wrote. In other studies, researchers found that teachers who had done the least to implement the primary program rarely used flexible grouping with students. Thus, observers raised concerns that if teachers were not required to mix students by age and ability, many would ignore the recommended primary practices altogether. As one teacher said in a 1995 interview conducted as part of a broader study by Connie Bridge for the University of Kentucky's Institute for Education Research, "I might discontinue multi-age, but I fear that would probably lead to traditional ways of teaching, and I would not be in favor of that."

The debate about how to best teach primary school carried over to Irmgard Williams's classroom during the fall 1995 semester. The incident showed that even though Kentucky had its hands full trying to retrain veteran teachers, the state also needed to pay attention to the training of teachers just entering the profession.

Williams agreed to supervise a teaching intern from Western Kentucky University for twelve weeks, allowing the young woman to both practice and observe in her South Heights classroom. In just a few weeks, Williams could see that the woman genuinely cared about young children, but she had developed few effective classroom management skills. Before Williams could suggest some improvements, however, the intern turned the tables. She criticized Williams for not allowing students to spend time each day in learning centers—separate stations of exploratory activities that help children study thematic units through art, technology, writing, and so on. The intern said her college instructors told her that learning centers should be the heart of the primary program. "This school is more un-KERA-like than any I've seen," she said.

The comment stunned Williams. She reviewed the state guidebooks and consulted her colleagues, discovering to her relief there was no requirement for daily learning centers in primary school classrooms. She explained to the intern that she used learning centers when she thought they would boost students' understanding of key concepts, but she didn't believe the centers were appropriate every day. She encouraged the intern to visit several classrooms to study the practices of other teachers. Williams thought she used a good mix of methods, but perhaps she was wrong. "I have room for improvement, I'm sure," she said.

Williams acknowledged that she might be overly sensitive, but the intern's criticism hurt her pride. A few weeks later, toward the end of the semester, she was able to put the experience in a different perspective. The education professor who was the intern's college supervisor visited Williams's classroom one day to observe the young teacher in action. After watching the demonstration lesson, the professor, who had not taught in elementary school for thirteen years, gushed about the intern's performance and her apparent affection for students. She told Williams she planned to give the young teacher an A for the semester, then confided that she "would feel terrible" giving any intern a lower grade.

Williams was appalled. She had given the student teacher just an average review. She strongly disagreed with the professor's policy of inflating grades just to make college students feel better. That kind of treatment only reinforced the public's notion that anyone could teach. The internship was one of the last opportunities to weed out ineffective instructors or to motivate them to change. Prospective teachers would never appreciate the high level of skills the job demanded if entry-level standards were so low. "She was sweet and warm and did some things well," Williams said about the intern, "but she was really just an average teacher. As hard as jobs are to get in Henderson County, they're looking for the best."

The episode confirmed Williams's suspicions that many teachers paid more attention to the process of the primary school program than to the substance of their lessons. Good teaching involved so much more than following steps as you would when reading a recipe. Good teaching required training seasoned with instinct and flexibility. New ideas often improved instruction, but experience counted, too. It seemed ironic that Kentucky was working so hard to change the bad habits of older teachers when some of the newer teachers needed just as much help.

The following spring, Williams got a chance to do something besides fret about the quality of teaching in Henderson County. She learned that the school district had hired her again to run the elementary summer school program. The selection process was much more rigorous this time, not a last-minute decision made by an administrator who was a few weeks away from retirement. Mike Freels, the former principal of Seventh Street Elementary School, had moved into the school district's central office. He served as the overall coordinator of the summer school programs at the elementary, middle, and high school level. After he hired Williams, Freels supported her suggestion to open the hiring process for teachers and to expand the pool of candidates—not to automatically allow the previous staff to return. Freels also approved her plan to develop the first formal summer school application, a two-page form that asked elementary teachers and aides a series of questions about practices Williams considered essential. The practices included collaborating with other staff members, accepting extra duties, and involving special education students in the regular classroom.

Williams, Freels, and two other administrators reviewed each candidate's application and, where appropriate, compared it with the candidate's evaluation from the summer before. They hired twenty-four of the forty candidates. Some of the most senior teachers were not asked to return. Every teacher selected was placed on a team so he or she could learn from colleagues. Williams caught plenty of flak because of the changes, but Freels and Jackita Snelling, the school district's instructional coordinator, backed her up. They reminded the staff that they would not accept the lax practices of the past. "I didn't want summer school to be a remedial program that operated like schools did twenty years ago," Freels said. "I wanted the director of summer school to know we're not running a day care. That was no problem for Irmgard. She is very good about documenting how she does things. She kept records of everything—how it was done, who did it, whether it worked."

Williams planned most of the summer school program from the hospital where her husband, Dewey, received a series of emergency heart treatments over several weeks. Throughout the summer, she continued to nurse her husband, keep the family business going, and run summer school.

The strain eventually proved too much. One night in the hospital waiting room, her pent-up fears and frustrations finally spilled over. She wept for a long time—a hard, cleansing cry that helped to clear her mind. She told her son, Joel, how difficult it had been to hold everything together during the past few years, trying to be all things to all people. She had put everyone's needs ahead of her own, and she was exhausted, emotionally spent.

As it had in years past, school became a life raft for Williams. Summer school was another spectacular success. When the six-week session ended, Freels, Snelling, and Ecton all thanked Williams for turning around a beleaguered program and making it a model for the school district. She previously had demonstrated her skills in the classroom, they said; now she also had proved that she was an effective leader. "I think sometimes when you gain confidence and people believe in you, you can do almost anything," Williams said.

"In the pre-KERA days, nobody ever told me I was good. Maybe I'm just a late bloomer."

Snelling encouraged Williams to obtain certification so she would be eligible for future administrative openings beyond summer school. Although she was flattered by the suggestion, Williams quickly dismissed it, even after her children encouraged her to try. She had obtained principal certification years ago in Tennessee but never sought to transfer the license to Kentucky. When her children were young and she was busy serving the church as a pastor's wife, she didn't want the added responsibilities of a principalship. Now that she had more time, she had other excuses for sticking with what she knew: She was too old to go back to college. She needed to stay close to home in case Dewey suffered more trauma to his heart. She could not abandon her mother in the nursing home.

In the end, Williams didn't change course. She decided not to fulfill the requirements to become a full-time administrator in Kentucky. Any positions she accepted would be temporary, like the Henderson County summer school job. Her role would stay small, restricted to the wonderful influence she had each year with the two dozen children in her care.

KERA had taught her a lot in the past few years—including the limits of her ambition. Leadership was a role she enjoyed trying on from time to time, but she did not want to wear it for long. The classroom was her home.

Johnny Duckworth spent the summers of 1995 and 1996 traveling the western United States, scouting possible locations for his next venture in education. He considered retiring from the Henderson County Public Schools at the end of the 1996–1997 school year—after twenty-seven years—and starting over somewhere far from home. He would be fifty years old, young enough to make a difference yet mature enough to make better choices than he had earlier in his career.

Toward the end of 1996, however, Duckworth changed his plans. Under the leadership of new superintendent John W. Vaughan, the former head of the Troy, Alabama public schools, the Henderson County system had resurrected its "strategic planning committee." The group first needed to determine the future use of school buildings and resources. Duckworth served on the committee, and he considered it likely that the members would recommend closing Smith Mills Elementary, the same issue that had dogged Ecton about eighteen months before. In the event that Smith Mills shut down, most of the students would transfer to Chandler. Duckworth thought he could help smooth the transition. "I really want to see that work," he said. "I want those people to feel welcome here and feel a part of decision-making at Chandler."

Duckworth figured he could stay two to three years after he became eligible to retire in Kentucky before he encountered the financial liabilities that prompted Ecton to quit. Meanwhile, he continued putting out feelers about administrative jobs around the country whenever he attended training workshops or met with the education consultants he knew. He quickly discovered that a veteran principal with substantial experience in education reform was highly marketable. School officials in Atlanta, Dallas, and parts of New Mexico and Colorado already had talked to him. "I guess, really and truly, money is not the issue," he said. "It's whether it's a good fit for me."

Ironically, the Henderson County outlaw had discovered that he fit in pretty well in his hometown after all these years. Although some people in the school district still refused to forget his past transgressions, more and more people were warming up to the man. Debbie Key was among those who had given him a second look.

Key had graduated a year behind Duckworth in high school, but they were not friends. She knew him mostly by reputation. Later, she taught his son, Lance, in the sixth grade, and she remembered how much the boy suffered because of his father's indifference. In addition to the impact on his family, Key also believed Duckworth's alcoholism affected his job performance more than he realized. He might not have imbibed at work, but he tended to view everything through a haze of belligerence and rage. Lately, however, Key had noticed true change. Duckworth seemed to be trying much harder to be a team player at administrative meetings. He listened more intensely before announcing his opinions. He often praised her and other administrators in public instead of belittling them as he had in the past. One time Duckworth pointed out that Key frequently put herself down at meetings, and he encouraged her to appreciate, not denigrate, her contributions. Another time he privately expressed his sympathy when he learned she was involved in a painful divorce. Key also appreciated his offer to load onto her computer at school the South Heights transformation plan. Duckworth had done the same thing with Chandler's plan, which made it much easier to refine the state-required document during the year. Unfamiliar with computer technology and too busy to learn, Key considered

Duckworth's gesture magnaminous. "Would he ever have said that before? Would I have wanted him to?" she asked, laughing at the absurdity of two such different and distant principals working together at last. "I respect him more as a colleague than I ever have."

When other district administrators disparaged Duckworth's accomplishments at Chandler, Key found herself sticking up for him. She acknowledged that he had not been a model citizen in the past, but she urged her colleagues to recognize his efforts to change. Some people "still want to see him fail," she said. They would not give him a second chance.

Duckworth tried to be patient. He knew he had not melted the chill completely, but he appreciated the warming trend. "I'd probably be the last to know," he said in response to a question about the changing attitudes of his colleagues. "But I don't see as much jealousy and resentment, especially from about four years ago."

Realistically, Duckworth's colleagues might have been reaching out to him in recognition of his skill with school reform. Like it or not, it became increasingly difficult to ignore the impact of his leadership at Chandler. State test scores showed that the school's staff was doing something remarkably well.

When the latest round of scores were released in October 1996, Chandler was one of 450 schools in the state—about one-third of the total—that earned cash rewards for the second straight biennium. Four other schools in Henderson County earned the same distinction. Overall, nine of the county's sixteen public schools exceeded their state goals in the second two-year cycle, and all but one school had improved, boosting the entire district into the reward category for the first time. The district's honor meant the central office staff, not just the faculties at successful schools, would receive cash bonuses from the state.

Chandler's test scores included both good news and bad. The school's average score for the past two years—47.6 on a 100-point scale—was well above its goal of 44. However, the school's score dropped sharply in the second year of the cycle, from 58.2 to 40.6. Over four years, Chandler's scores had soared. Viewed in terms of long-term progression, Chandler was fifteen points closer to the goal of having every student at the "proficient" level. But the uneven pace of that performance pointed to some inconsistencies in instruction that cried out for attention.

The writing portfolios presented one problem for Chandler. From the beginning, Kentucky allowed teachers to score the student writing samples, believing it would help them understand how well the children stacked up against the state standards. The setup included a built-in bias, however. Teachers tended to boost the scores of students who expended a great deal of effort on their writing, or who traditionally earned good grades, whether or not their entries actually met the objectives.

As usual, the staff at Chandler did things a little differently. Nearly every teacher in the school participated in these portfolio scorings, not just those who taught fourth grade. Duckworth wanted every instructor to understand the state's expectations. Working in groups, the teachers graded the entries without knowing the names of students. (Of course, some teachers were able to recognize the style and voice of individual writers even without the names attached, but the group process tended to minimize individual bias.) The teachers rated the writing samples, and then a second group evaluated the same collection. If the two groups awarded different scores to the same portfolio, all the teachers would read it again and reach a consensus.

From time to time in Kentucky, schools volunteered to have portfolio scores reviewed by independent auditors trained to evaluate the writing samples. In Chandler's case, a 1995 analysis showed that the staff had missed the mark 57 percent of the time, one of the worst rates in the Henderson County school district. About half of Chandler's portfolio scores were considered to be inflated, which might have accounted for the school's huge gains on the state accountability index during the 1994–1995 school year. In response, Duckworth said, the staff graded much more conservatively the next year and probably overcompensated to the point that the school's score fell sharply.

The inconsistency in grading was not unique to Chandler. Beginning in the 1992–1993 school year, state education officials invited schools to submit student writing portfolios for practice audits, hoping to reduce some of the anxiety about scoring. The state selected other schools for review either because their scores varied so much from year to year or because their writing scores were significantly higher than other portions of the state test. Based on that initial audit, the state lowered the scores an average of thirty-five points at 101 of the 105 schools reviewed. By 1996, however, the state made far fewer corrections, which officials attributed to teachers having greater understanding of the academic standards. The original and audited scores now proved consistent 75 percent of the time. (Chandler's writing samples had not been audited *formally* in any of the cycles, so the school's accountability score was never changed as a result of any discrepancies.) Nevertheless, the subjectivity involved in the portfolios scores continued to unnerve many people who challenged the validity of the state's test and the merits of rewarding schools based on their performance.

Duckworth did not waste much time arguing about the merits of the test. He had concerns about it. Most people did. But he supported the basic thrust of the exams and believed he should help his staff understand the rationale behind them instead of joining the chorus of critics who were hoping for their demise.

"One thing we know, without this KERA assessment, we would not have the broad changes we've seen in children," he said. "Without this assessment, we would not have seen the changes in teaching methodologies to focus on the different ways children learn. We'd be doing the same old stuff and getting the same old results. Instead, we're doing different things and seeing different results."

The high-stakes test shook people out of their lethargy, he said. Two years before, when Duckworth attended a state education conference conducted by a national group called Effective Schools, about seventy-five principals showed up. He said a similar conference held in the fall of 1996—right after the state released the latest round of school accountability scores—attracted 1,400 principals. Some administrators had just learned that their schools had fallen into the "crisis" category (only nine schools statewide earned this grade), reflecting the first time since KERA was passed in 1990 that state sanctions could be imposed. Principals, teachers, and parents at those schools received letters from their district offices, informing them that members of the school staff could lose their jobs and that students were eligible to transfer to more successful schools.

The state's practice of assigning distinguished educators to help troubled schools had been hugely successful. All fifty-three schools that received help after the first biennium had improved their scores—thirty-two of them earned cash rewards in the second testing cycle. Yet by 1996, state leaders said they had only enough money to pay for half of the distinguished educators who were needed in schools around the state, demonstrating once again that promising programs still were being held hostage by shifting political priorities.

Chandler's faculty was determined to stay out of trouble with the state. Instead of asking a few teachers to examine the details of the school's performance on the state test (the practice in the first few years of KERA), Duckworth involved the entire Chandler staff in the evaluation process during the fall of 1996. Staff members met for a half hour, two or three days each week, to find the clues that would help them match instruction to the state's academic standards. They found it helpful to have four years' worth of information about the test because it was possible now to identify trends and to make more accurate observations about the strengths and weaknesses of students. "When our scores shoot up, we have to look at why [that is] just as we have to do when our scores go down," Duckworth said. "You need to look at the positive data just as hard. What caused us to be that good that year?"

The earnestness with which Chandler's staff approached the state tests undoubtedly contributed to the school's progress over time. A 1996 study of Kentucky schools that earned cash rewards found that the most consistently successful schools had carefully analyzed their test results "and had made improvement a clear priority." In these schools, staff training was focused on helping teachers match their instruction to what the state expected students to know. "Teachers understood and expressed a strong belief in the focus of the new curriculum and assessment, indicating that they would 'never go back' to their former teaching styles. In other schools, teachers showed much less confidence in the direction of the assessment and in their ability to improve student performance on it" (Kelley and Protsik 1996).

At Chandler, Duckworth considered focused training the key to making sure teachers helped students meet the state standards, especially now that he supervised a less experienced staff. He continued passing on important research and encouraging regular conversations about successful teaching practices. He also revived the staff's weekly "Diet and Dialogue" sessions (lunchtime discussion groups) when he started noticing "some cracks in the shared vision" of the school.

Since 1990, Duckworth's leadership at Chandler had demonstrated the critical role principals play in Kentucky's school transformation. In the process, he was able to leave behind in the dust the old cliche about a principal's job being more about "buses, budgets, and butts." In his own school, Duckworth married the two most important components of KERA implementation. He made the choice to couple intensive, focused staff training and forced collegial dependence, a partnership that kept everyone on staff moving ahead together, a shared commitment that made each person responsible for the success of all. This practice of self-determination made all the difference. Who would have guessed that Johnny Duckworth, a principal who once personified the worst stereotypes of Kentucky education, would grow to become as talented a leader as the superintendent he so admired?

As Duckworth looked back over the last half decade of his life, he felt extremely grateful for the challenges he had faced. He knew that he would always have to fight his bad habits, but he had learned that practice was much more important than perfection. A man born with an array of natural talents could now appreciate the honor in effort. One of Duckworth's biggest strengths as an administrator was getting results. He stayed on track until he accomplished his goals. But in the process, he often neglected the needs of those around him and ignored the issues outside his narrow range of vision. The secret, he realized now, was finding a balance between activism and analysis. "It is easier to be a trailblazer and a pioneer than it is to be a settler," he said.

Duckworth still worked hard to stay sober. As a recovering alcoholic, he probably always would. He found it particularly difficult to refrain from using alcohol and cigarettes when he went out for entertainment. He liked to listen to live music in nightclubs. He enjoyed betting on horse races at Ellis Park in Henderson and Churchill Downs in Louisville. He occasionally tried his luck at Casino Aztar, the new riverboat gambling club in Evansville. At all of his favorite places, it seemed, drinking and smoking were part of the scene. He didn't want to give up every pleasure, but he knew he had to be vigilant.

He recalled a time, about a year into his sobriety, when he attended a meeting at a Henderson hotel. A tray of drinks rested on the table in the hospitality room. During a conversation, Duckworth instinctively reached over, grabbed a glass, and brought the drink to his lips, a reflex as familiar as crossing his legs or adjusting his tie. When the smell of liquor alerted his senses, he quickly set the glass on the table and walked away. A close call. He knew he would have others.

Perhaps Kentucky's new accountability system played a similar role with the state's public schools—it reminded everyone of the hard work still ahead. It was easy to get complacent about some of the initial successes of school reform, much harder to shake the behaviors that could land the state in the gutter again. Duckworth was as unsure about the future of KERA as he was about his own, but he realized that the only way to change was to try. "We have been able to be a beacon to give other people hope," he said. "Think about how much farther ahead we are as a state than we were five years ago. We're not nearly as far as we want to be, but we've started."

Gayle Ecton knew he would have a hard time leaving Henderson County, but he had not counted on the difficulties in staying. By announcing his retirement almost a year before his actual departure, he thought he would give everyone, including himself, time to adjust to a change in administration. It seemed the ethical and the fair thing to do. In hindsight, he realized he had stayed too long. He completed some of his pet projects in the last months of his superintendency, but he also longed for different challenges. He guessed his staff wanted new leadership, too. The extra months gave Ecton too much time to brood. Like a patient with a disabling illness, he started resenting other people for getting on with their own lives when his was placed on hold. "There was a lot of grieving and depression and a certain amount of paranoia for me," he said. "I started thinking, 'Well, some of these people are really glad to see me go.' I had some feelings I didn't think I'd have. It was a little bit like death or a divorce."

Ecton spent so many years trying to keep everyone else focused on the future that he lost his own sense of direction. What was his next move? He really didn't know.

When the Henderson County school board hired a new superintendent the following April, Ecton experienced a few more pangs of regret. Board members selected John W. Vaughan from among forty-seven other applicants from twenty-eight states. With seventeen years experience as a superintendent, Vaughan had retired from Alabama and, now that he had taken a new position in Henderson County, would be eligible to draw a second pension from Kentucky after five years. Ecton had nothing against Vaughan personally, but the appointment fed earlier concerns about the unfairness of the Kentucky Teacher Retirement System. As he predicted, Kentucky made it possible for Vaughan to boost his earnings late in his career while the state effectively barred its home-grown superintendents from taking advantage of the same option.

Vaughan did not start his new job until two weeks after Ecton left, so there was no overlap in their responsibilities. But knowing the transition in leadership was imminent weighed heavily on Ecton. Some days he wondered what it would have been like if he had stayed in Henderson County indefinitely.

Assistant superintendent Sue Williams understood how hard it was for her friend and colleague to step down after ten years. His ambivalence was painful. "I think it started to affect him when we started interviewing superintendent candidates," she said. "He's ready to make that change, but it kind of hit him hard that he's leaving."

Williams was eligible to retire, too, but as a native of Henderson County, she had more ties to the community than Ecton did. With five grandchildren in the school system, she wanted to stick around to make sure the initiatives she had started with Ecton and others would continue. Williams, who had worked for several different superintendents, credited Ecton with keeping her "excited about education" toward the end of her career.

Duckworth was another administrator who was sorry to see Ecton go, but he felt confident the superintendent's crusade for academic excellence and democratic leadership would continue after he left—certainly at Chandler Elementary. "I think Chandler is a legacy to Dr. Ecton, a legacy of what can be," Duckworth said. "I think he created the environment for some of the things that we've done at Chandler. We might have tried some anyway, but he gave us time to nurture it and grow."

During the spring of 1996, Ecton scouted other superintendent jobs in neighboring states. He was a finalist for the top job in an Illinois school district before he withdrew from consideration. The more he thought about it, the less he wanted to start over in another school system. He also wasn't much interested in leaving Kentucky, he discovered. He had spent almost thirty years trying to improve the condition of education in his native state. Abandoning that quest at this point in his career would seem intellectually dishonest, almost cheapening the cause. If he could not serve the state as a superintendent, perhaps there were other ways for him to contribute to education reform.

"I want to feel like I've made some difference beyond what I've done here," he said. "I don't want it to sound like an ego thing, but I think I have much more to give. Some of the stuff has been learned at a painful price. I want to be able to do something with those lessons."

Before he left Henderson County, Ecton had two major goals. One was to involve a broad spectrum of the community in setting future priorities for the school district, a project that the school board endorsed to maintain the momentum of education reform after Ecton departed. His agenda included helping people reach a consensus about the focus of schools and helping them understand their roles in promoting that mission. If they could agree about what was important, they would not have to waste time changing directions when the new superintendent took over.

Initially, Ecton had planned to take about sixty-five people from the community—no more than half of them school employees—on a two-day retreat to Rough River State Park, about two hours southeast of Henderson. He thought the getaway would help people relax and bond. However, after the local newspaper and some members of the public questioned the wisdom of spending tax dollars for such a purpose, Ecton rescheduled the meeting in Henderson.

As a result of the planning session, the participants drafted and pledged to support twelve "Shared Promises" for the Henderson County schools. These included: an agreement to provide a challenging education to all students, a recognition that instruction had to improve to accomplish that aim, and a commitment to continue letting parents, teachers, and principals manage their own schools. KERA was still the law of the land, and by this action representatives of the Henderson County community had publicly endorsed its most important tenets.

Moving the school system into a position to keep those promises was the second major goal Ecton hoped to achieve before stepping down as superintendent. Given the previous difficulites of finding a balance between the rights of the elected school councils and the responsibilities of the school district as a whole, he decided to involve school council members in key discussions about the school system's budget. In February and March of 1996, he and his staff conducted five two-hour seminars where they explained the intricacies of school finance. The meetings were well attended, despite the difficulty of scheduling them around the televised games of the University of Kentucky's men's basketball team, which was on its way to winning the national championship.

In addition to helping the school council members understand how their actions affected the school district, and vice versa, Ecton had an ulterior motive. He had to cut the school district's budget again for several reasons: a continued drop in enrollment, higher expenses related to a state-mandated pay raise for teachers, the district's commitment to providing extra paid days for staff training, and the state's failure to provide money promised for technology purchases. Henderson County administrators had predicted the loss of students to private and home schools would level off. Instead, enrollment continued to decline, falling 3.5 percent in the past two years, a loss of 282 students. Meanwhile, school employment stayed constant. The projected deficit for the current school year was now $574,000. Ecton knew that any cuts he recommended would affect the work of school councils, so he decided to give their members a prominent role in the budget-cutting process.

Although a representative from each school council had served on the district budget committee with other employee and community groups in the past four years, Ecton thought more people needed to understand how the school district distributed its money. How else would the various groups start thinking about their symbiotic relationships and stop making decisions in isolation? "This year it's critical that everybody hear the same message," he said.

He wanted to establish some trust among various schools so people would work together instead of fighting over some elusive pot of gold. As Bob Hall, the school district's finance director, explained during one meeting, schools had to get used to working with less money because of the difficulty of predicting how much the state would provide each year. "This year and last year are two of the most mixed-signal years that I've ever seen," Hall told the group one night, adding that the state's projections of payments to local districts "have changed nine times in the past seven months."

In the end, Ecton believed the budget discussions had helped educate more people about critical issues that the school district faced. Whether they used the information responsibly in the future, however, would be the next superintendent's concern. It was time for him to leave.

By mid-summer, Ecton was working at Midway College, a small private school near Lexington. The college was founded as an all-women's school, and its day program remained that way. But in 1989, Midway responded to its declining enrollment by starting co-ed evening and weekend programs to help older students with families and jobs earn bachelor's degrees. The majority of students in the new degree programs worked during the day. Midway's courses, which enabled the mostly older students to complete a portion of their work through independent study, required fewer hours in the classroom than was typical at other colleges. Midway also offered some courses on site at the huge Toyota plant in nearby Georgetown.

Ecton taught two courses included as part of a business degree in organizational management. His classes (organizational and group behavior and organizational concepts) focused on the leadership skills needed to move through social and management changes and on the importance of developing effective relationships within and among departments. Ecton's responsibilities at Midway also included creating other off-campus degree programs.

By contract, Ecton was obligated to work at Midway 80 percent of the time. The rest of the work week he devoted to the National

Alliance for Restructuring Education, an organization based in Washington, D.C., that hired him to consult about leadership with the Kentucky Department of Education and selected schools. His primary responsibility was designing a training model for principals that would teach them how to help staff and students meet higher academic standards. Sue Williams and Johnny Duckworth were among a small group of Kentucky administrators whom Ecton had, in turn, hired to help him design and test the training program.

At Midway, Ecton discovered that he enjoyed teaching again, but he preferred the part of his job that enabled him to work directly with people intimately involved with school reform. Thus, his position with the National Alliance for Restructuring Education proved to be more satisfying in the last half of 1996 than the management courses he taught. Instead of focusing on general leadership courses, he wanted to help other educators become more effective leaders in their schools and school districts. Educational management, not business management, was his specialty.

His desire for a more customized job reflected recent insights about school reform. A few months away from the daily grind of the superintendency had given him a new perspective on issues that bedeviled him in Henderson County. The opportunity to confer regularly with educators in Kentucky and around the country stimulated him intellectually. He believed that if every administrator in Kentucky had similar time for reflection and study, KERA would be much farther along. He knew from personal experience that in trying to meet the state's deadlines and boost student test scores, Kentucky educators erred more often than they might have in a less frantic environment. "You're trying to survive," he said. "You miss some things that should have been obvious."

For example, he could see now that in trying to follow the letter and spirit of the state reform law, he turned over too much authority to Henderson County's school councils too quickly. Ruie Murphy was right. Ecton made the switch without giving enough direction and training to either the council members or the central office administrators who worked with them. As a result, Ecton said, the councils "got all over the map" instead of making sound decisions that would address their specific problems and complement the goals of the school district. If he had done a better job of helping everyone analyze all the available data—from the trends apparent in the state's test results to national research about the most effective ways of changing human behavior—Ecton believed people in

Henderson County might have reacted more logically than emotionally to the demands of KERA.

"It's not like all of a sudden I've gotten religion, or I've got all the answers now," he said. "I've just seen some ways we might have changed direction to be more effective. It's just amazing how much knowledge is out there that's not getting to the school level. It wasn't that my people weren't working hard. They were working their butts off. But sometimes I think we just worked harder at doing things the old way."

In addition to the professional lessons that he learned during his time away from Henderson County, Ecton engaged in some personal soul-searching as well. Now that he wasn't as consumed by his position, he was more aware of the stress and strain that his job placed on his family over the years. He could acknowledge without resentment the claims that he was "a workaholic" for most of his adult life.

One of Ecton's most startling revelations came during the fall of 1996 during a management class he taught to Toyota employees. As a company, Toyota offered some of the best pay and benefits for manufacturing jobs in Kentucky, but the factory employees paid a heavy price. They were asked to work frequent overtime and to change shifts. Many also endured long commutes from their homes. One class session, when Ecton talked about his new appreciation of managers having "a balance" in their lives—scheduling adequate time for work, family, and self—many of his students grew defensive as they tried to dodge their guilt about their inattention to the two latter sides of the triangle. As they dismissed the impact of their work choices on their families, Ecton heard echoes of his own justifications over the years.

"I rationalized that I was doing this for my family," he explained later, his voice choking with emotion. "I had to make more money. I had to make them proud of me. I had to be better than I was. I didn't spend the time I should have with my family, with my kids. I missed out on some important things. Thank God they were in the same school districts that I worked in where I had more opportunity to be around them. Or frankly, I probably wouldn't have been...because I was so obsessed with working nights and weekends."

Ecton said he was just starting to understand the reasons and the repercussions of his slavish devotion to his work. He did not believe in blaming other people for his troubles because he accepted responsibility for his own actions. And he was too circumspect to reveal specific injuries. But he acknowledged that his behavior had been conditioned by the messages received in childhood that his best wasn't good enough. If he wanted approval, the voices told him, he had to work harder. Like Irmgard Williams and Johnny Duckworth, Gayle Ecton spent most of his life trying to prove himself worthy of other people's praise, striving for the unreachable point of perfection. Where one buried her pain in excessive volunteerism and the other numbed himself with alcohol, Ecton hid his hurt in a compulsive need to excel.

Perhaps Henderson County benefitted from his devotion. Ecton wasn't sure. He considered the possibility that the extra hours spent at work might not have improved his performance as superintendent. For one thing, he said, the relentless pace drained him of the energy to be nimble in heavy traffic, to know when it was more effective to coast than speed ahead. "I had an awareness of this on an intellectual level," he said. "But it's like quicksand, it's hard to get out of unless someone hands you a rope. You can see the problems and not know how to stop."

Relieved of the duties of the superintendency, he took the time to learn. And he discovered that the emotional release from letting go of so many restrictive behaviors could be a powerful catharsis. Increasingly, Ecton was able to give in to impulse instead of treading a path that he felt obligated to follow. Although he occasionally received inquiries from school districts searching for new superintendents, he could decline the offers now without regret. And when the president of a regional university in Kentucky offered him a position as vice president, Ecton turned him down after discovering that the job would demand about eighty hours a week. He no longer wanted to work all the time.

After Ecton explained his predicament with the Kentucky Teacher Retirement System, the university president interceded with state officials to get a special dispensation from the rules. He wasn't aware of the problem until Ecton told him about it, and he became concerned that he would not be able to attract the best educators—from Kentucky or any other state—unless they could resolve the issue of dual pensions. The resulting change enabled the state's public universities to hire educators vested in one retirement system and let them start a second pension plan through the colleges. The upshot of the ruling was that as of January 1997, six months after leaving the superintendency, Ecton was eligible to join the education faculty at any public university in Kentucky.

When the right position opened, he would go. His internal compass seemed to be pointing him toward a place where he could help shape the future of education reform in Kentucky by molding new school leaders. He had many lessons to share. The first and by far the most important one concerned training and nurturing people. Everything else, he knew, would follow.

Bibliography

Appalachia Educational Laboratory. 1995a. *AEL Study of KERA Implementation in Four Rural Kentucky School Districts, 1993–1994 Annual Report.* Charleston, WV: Appalachia Educational Laboratory.

———. 1995b. *From Dilemma to Opportunity.* Frankfort: Kentucky Institute for Education Research.

———. 1995c. *The Needs of Kentucky Teachers for Designing Curricula Based on Academic Expectations.* Frankfort: Kentucky Institute for Education Research.

Appalachia Educational Laboratory. 1996. "Five Years of Education Reform in Rural Kentucky." *Notes From the Field: Education Reform in Rural Kentucky.* Vol. 5, No.1, Febuary 1996, p. 3.

Arnett, M. 1976. *The Annals and Scandals of Henderson County, Kentucky, 1775–1975.* Corydon: Fremar Publishing.

Associated Press. 1962. "New Form of 'First Grade' Tried Out." *The Courier-Journal,* December 28, sec. A, p. 1.

Boysen, T.C. 1994. *Kentucky's 'No-Nonsense' Assessment.* Frankfort: Kentucky Department of Education.

Bradley, A. 1995. "What Price Success?" *Education Week,* November 22:1.

Brammer, J., and K. Wagar. 1989. "Floyd Adults Won't Pay for Their Schools, so Kids Raise Money Door-to-Door." *Lexington Herald-Leader,* November 16, sec. A, p. 1.

Bridge, C.A. 1994. *The Implementation of Kentucky's Primary Program, A Report of Research Conducted by the Institute of Education Reform.* Lexington: University of Kentucky.

———.1995. *The Implementation of Kentucky's Primary Program, A Report of Research Conducted by the Institute of Education Reform.* Lexington: University of Kentucky.

Bridge, C.A., M. Compton-Hall, and S.C. Cantrell. 1996. *Classroom Writing Practices Revisited: The Effects of Statewide Reform on Classroom Writing Practices.* Lexington: University of Kentucky Institute on Education Reform.

Combs, B.T. 1991. "Creative Constitutional Law: The Kentucky School Reform Law." *Harvard Journal of Legislation,* 28:2.

David, J.L. 1993a. *Redesigning an Education System: Early Observations from Kentucky.* Washington, D.C.: National Governors' Association and The Prichard Committee for Academic Excellence.

———. 1993b. *School-Based Decision Making: Progress and Promise: Second-Year Report to the Prichard Committee.* Lexington: The Prichard Committee for Academic Excellence.

———. 1994. *School-Based Decision Making: Linking Decisions to Learning: Third-Year Report to the Prichard Committee for Academic Excellence.* Lexington: The Prichard Committee for Academic Excellence.

Dove, R.G., Jr. 1991. *Acorns in a Mountain Pool: The Role of Litigation, Law and Lawyers in Kentucky Education Reform.* Lexington: The Prichard Committee for Academic Excellence.

Ecton, G.W. 1979. "A History of the Lincoln School, Simpsonville, Kentucky, 1966–1970." Ed.D. diss., University of Kentucky.

———. 1994. Portfolio Evaluation Narrative for Dr. Gayle Ecton, Superintendent, Henderson County Schools, 1993–1994.

Editors of *Education Week.* 1993. *From Risk to Renewal: Charting a Course for Reform.* Washington, D.C.: Editorial Projects in Education.

Ellis, L. 1995. "Teachers Lose 5 Training Days in New Calendar," *The Courier-Journal,* Oldham, May 3, County Neighborhoods section, p. 1.

Estep, B., and J. Brammer. 1989. "Woe to the Educator who is Politically 'Wrong.'" *Lexington Herald-Leader,* November 26, sec. A, p. 1.

Fiske, E. 1990. "Lessons: In Kentucky, Teachers, Not Legislators, Will Be Writing the Lesson Plans." *The New York Times,* April 4, final edition, sec. B, p. 6.

Gerth, J. 1996. "Meyer's Loss Means Democrats Will Have to Close up Their Ranks." *The Courier-Journal,* November 7, sec. A, p. 13.

Hambleton, R., R.M. Jaeger, D. Koretz, J. Millman, and S.E. Phillips. 1995. *Review of the Measurement Quality of the Kentucky Instructional Results Information System, 1991–1994.* Frankfort: Office of Educational Accountability, Kentucky General Assembly.

Hamlett, B. 1914. *History of Education in Kentucky.* Frankfort: Kentucky Department of Education.

Harp, L. 1995. "Kentucky Schools Put on the Line in Bonus Budgeting." *Education Week,* April 26 14:1–9.

Henderson County Geneological and Historical Society. 1980. *History of Henderson County, Kentucky, 1888–1978.* Henderson: Henderson County Geneological and Historical Society.

Holland, H. 1994. "A Passion to Teach." *The Courier Journal,* December 4, sec. C, p.1.

———. 1995. "Change Come to Bluegrass Country." *The American School Board Journal,* April 1995, 4:28.

———. 1995b. "The Truth about KERA." *The Courier-Journal,* October 15, sec. D, p. 1.

———. 1995bc. "In Kentucky, New Money, New Techniques, New Assessments Lift 'Worst State in the Country'." *Catalyst* VII 3:1.

Johnson, J., and J. Immerwahr. 1994. *First Things First: What Americans Expect from the Public Schools.* New York, NY: Public Agenda Foundation.

Kelley, C., and J. Protsik. 1996. "Risk and Reward: Perspectives on the Implementation of Kentucky's School-Based Performance Award Program." *Educational Policy,* May 13, 10:19–20.

Kentucky Department of Education. 1995. *Principals' Survey: 1–3 Years Experience.* Frankfort: Kentucky Department of Education.

Kentucky General Assembly. 1960. *Report of Special Committee to Investigate Education to the House of Representatives of the Kentucky General Assembly.* Frankfort: Legislative Research Commission.

———. 1995. Office of Educational Accountability. *Annual Report.* Frankfort, KY.

The Kentucky Institute for Education Research. 1994. *Statewide Education Reform Survey.* Frankfort: The Kentucky Institute for Education Research.

The Kentucky Institute for Education Research. 1996. *Focus on Kentucky's Education Reforms.* Frankfort: The Kentucky Institute for Education Research.

May, L. 1995. "Poor Schools as Likely as Rich to Hit KERA Goals, Earn Rewards." *Lexington Herald-Leader,* February 9, sec. A, p. 1.

———. 1996a. "Both Rich and Poor Schools Test Well, Analysis Finds." *Lexington Herald-Leader,* November 4, sec. A, p. 1.

———. 1996b "Role of KERA in Legislative Races Disputed." *Lexington Herald-Leader,* November 7, sec. C, p. 1.

McDiarmid, G.W. 1994. *Realizing New Learning for All Students: A Framework for the Professional Development of Kentucky Teachers.* East Lansing, MI: Michigan State University National Center for Research on Teacher Learning.

McKinney, M. 1970. "NEA Teams Get First Look at Kentucky's Schools." *The Courier-Journal,* November 10, sec. A, p. 1.

National Commission on Teaching and America's Future. 1996. *What Matters Most: Teaching for America's Future.* New York, NY: Report of the National Commission on Teaching and America's Future.

National Education Association Commission on Professional Rights and Responsibilities. 1971. *Education in Kentucky: A Legacy of Unkept Promises.* Washington, D.C.: National Education Association Commission on Professional Rights and Responsibilities.

Olson, L. 1995. "The New Breed of Assessments Getting Scrutiny." *Education Week,* March 22, 14: 10.

The Partnership for Kentucky School Reform. 1996. *From Dilemma to Opportunity: A Report on Education Reform in Kentucky Five Years*

After the Kentucky Education Reform Act of 1990. Lexington: The Partnership for Kentucky School Reform.

The Prichard Committee for Academic Excellence. 1990. *The Path to a Larger Life: Creating Kentucky's Educational Future.* Lexington, KY: University of Kentucky Press.

———. 1995. *The Primary Program: Report from the Task Force on Improving Kentucky Schools.* Lexington, KY: The Prichard Committee for Academic Excellence.

Raths, J., L. Katz, and J. Fanning. 1993. "The Status of Primary School Reform in Kentucky and Its Implications." In *Redesigning an Education System: Early Observations from Kentucky.* Washington, D.C.: National Governors' Association and The Prichard Committee for Academic Excellence.

Renyi, J. 1996. "The Longest Reform: When Teachers Take Charge of Their Own Learning." *Education Week*, November 13, 16: 34.

Roberts & Kay, Inc. 1993. *Kentuckians' Expectations of Children's Learning: The Significance for Reform.* Lexington: The Prichard Committee for Academic Excellence and the Partnership for Kentucky School Reform.

Schaver, M. 1994. "KERA Driving Some Teachers into Retirement." *The Courier-Journal*, July 4, sec. A, p. 1.

———. 1995a. "Dividing Rewards May Breed Discord in Schools." *The Courier-Journal*, February 6, final issue, sec. B, p. 1.

———. 1995b. "Overall Support of School Reform Slips, Poll Finds." *The Courier-Journal,* April 16, sec. A, p. 1.

———. 1995c. "School Rewards Causing Friction: Money Disputes Lead to Lawsuits." *The Courier-Journal*, June 13, final issue, sec. A, p. 1.

———. 1996. "Gish Says State Board Ducks Tough School Issues." *The Courier-Journal,* April 6, final, sec. A, p. 5.

Sexton, R.F. 1995. "Keeping the Bargain of School Reform." In *Perspectives.* Lexington, KY: The Prichard Committee for Academic Excellence.

The Shelby Sentinel. 1967. Editorial, October 19.

Squires, S. 1996. "Emphasis on Assessment Puts Schools to the Test." *The Washington Post,* reprinted in *The Courier-Journal*, March 17.

Stevenson H., and J. Stigler. 1992. *The Learning Gap.* New York, NY: Summit Books.

Tisdall, W.J. 1968. "A High School for Disadvantaged Students of High Academic Potential." *The High School Journal*, 51–61.

Tomizawa, T. 1961a. "Rural Blackboard Jungle . . . and a Lesson in Civics." *The Courier-Journal*, March 2 sec. 2, p. 1.

———. 1961b. "Sharply Critical Probers Call for Changes in Kentucky's School." *Louisville Times,* September 2, sec. A, p. 1

Urschel, J. 1996. "Putting the Public Back into Public Education." *Education Week*, 15: 41.

Walker, R. 1990. "Lawmakers in Kentucky Approve Landmark School-Reform Bill." *Education Week* April 4, 9: 1.

Wilkerson, T., and Associates. 1995. *1995 Statewide Education Reform Survey of Teachers, Principals, Parents and General Public.* Frankfort, KY: Kentucky Institute for Education Research.

Wilson, R. 1972. "Kentucky Education: A Progress Report." *The Courier-Journal*, December 24, sec. E, p. 1.

Winograd, P., E. Anderman, and T. Bliss. 1996. *The Relationship Between Kentucky's Reward System and Teachers' Attitudes Towards Teaching, Learning and Reform.* Frankfort, KY: University of Kentucky Institute on Education Reform.

Wright, S. 1995b. "Smith Mills Residents Make Plea for School." *The Gleaner*, March 3, sec. A, p. 1.